THE DISCIPLES
IN NARRATIVE PERSPECTIVE

Society of Biblical Literature

Academia Biblica

Saul M. Olyan,
Old Testament Editor

Mark Allan Powell,
New Testament Editor

Number 9

The Disciples
in Narrative Perspective
*The Portrayal and Function
of the Matthean Disciples*

The Disciples in Narrative Perspective
The Portrayal and Function of the Matthean Disciples

Jeannine K. Brown

Society of Biblical Literature
Atlanta

The Disciples
in Narrative Perspective
The Portrayal and Function
of the Matthean Disciples

Copyright © 2002 by the Society of Biblical Literature

Library of Congress Cataloging-in-Publication Data

Brown, Jeannine K., 1961-
  The Disciples in narrative perspective : the portrayal and function of
the Matthean Disciples / by Jeannine K. Brown.
    p. cm. — (Society of Biblical Literature Academia Biblica ; 9)
Includes bibliographical references and indexes.
  ISBN 1-58983-048-2 (pbk. : alk. paper)
 1. Jesus Christ—Disciples. 2. Bible. N.T. Matthew—Criticism,
interpretation, etc. 3. Apostles. I. Title. II. Series: Academia
Biblica (Series) ; no. 9.
BS2440 .B672 2002
226.2'06—dc21
                          2002014398

07 06 05 04 03 02   5 4 3 2 1

Printed in the United States of America
on acid-free paper

For My Family

They have encouraged me in my writing

and daily have extended grace.

For Tim, Kate, and Libby

TABLE OF CONTENTS

PREFACE

This book is a slightly revised version of a Ph.D. dissertation presented and accepted at Luther Seminary in October of 2001. While studying Matthew 19 and 20 for a doctoral seminar project, I was struck by the interplay between Jesus and the disciples. In my reading, the disciples repeatedly misunderstand Jesus' teaching, an observation quite at odds with redaction-critical readings of Matthew.

This book offers a narrative-critical reading of Matthew focused on the disciples' characterization. I argue that not only do the disciples frequently fail to understand Jesus' mission and teaching; they do not progress toward greater understanding as the story unfolds. Such a conclusion begs the question, "What is the point or effect of the disciples' frequent misunderstanding?" The function of the disciples' portrayal is the final and most pressing issue for this study. By encouraging the reader of Matthew to evaluate the disciples in light of the author's point of view, the disciples' propensity to misunderstand functions as part of the Matthean view of discipleship. The contribution of the last major chapter is to provide a model of the way discipleship is configured in Matthew.

My hope is that this study will invite increased dialogue between literary and historical approaches regarding Matthew's characterization of the disciples and specifically their level of understanding. Having been trained in redaction criticism, I have great respect and affinities for the results of that method. More recently, narrative criticism has contributed quite significantly to the study of characterization in the Gospels. Unfortunately, the methodological move to bracket out historical questions has typically bracketed out interaction with the results of historical-critical approaches as well, including redaction criticism. This has short-changed Matthean studies from a significant and potentially fruitful interaction between historical and literary methods.

Many people deserve acknowledgement for their support of this project. I would first like to express my thanks to Luther Seminary and Arland Hultgren, my dissertation advisor. Dr. Hultgren's guidance and encouragement were unflagging throughout the dissertation process. His insightful suggestions and careful editing were invaluable. I am grateful as well for my dissertation readers. My introduction to rhetorical criticism in a course with James Boyce helped me to understand more clearly the function of the disciples' portrayal in Matthew. Mary Hinkle provided an often-needed historical-critical challenge to my narrative perspective as well as being a personal role model of a woman in biblical studies.

I also want to express my thanks to the faculty and administration of Bethel Seminary who provided teaching opportunities as well as encouragement during my doctoral work. I owe a great debt to Robert Stein who took me on as his teaching assistant during my master's work at Bethel and believed in my gifts even before I recognized them myself. More recently, my colleague, Donald Verseput, has invested time in many conversations with me that have shaped my understanding of Matthew for the better. I have greatly benefited from both his published works and these informal conversations. Finally, I am grateful to Gloria Metz who worked her magic on my manuscript to format it for publication.

Above all, I want to thank my family. My gratitude to my parents, Carolyn and James Holmen, is inexpressible. They fostered in our home an environment of affirmation and modeled an active faith lived in service to others. Without my husband, Tim, I could not have completed this dissertation. He provided opportunities for me to write by taking our toddlers to the park, sending me to the library, and making many personal sacrifices on a daily basis. He has truly been my encouragement on the journey and as he puts it, "my biggest fan." It is to him and to my daughters, Kate and Libby, that this book is dedicated.

LIST OF ABBREVIATIONS

AJBI	*Annual of the Japanese Biblical Institute*
ANTC	Abingdon New Testament Commentaries
AsTJ	*Asbury Theological Journal*
AThR	*Anglican Theological Review*
b. Yebam.	*Babylonian Talmud Yebamot*
BDAG	Bauer, W., F. W. Danker, W. F. Arndt, and F. W. Gingrich. *Greek-English Lexicon of the New Testament and Other Early Christian Literature*. 3d ed. Chicago, 2000
BJRL	*Bulletin of the John Rylands University Library of Manchester*
BSac	*Bibliotheca sacra*
BTB	*Biblical Theology Bulletin*
CBQ	*Catholic Biblical Quarterly*
CBQMS	Catholic Biblical Quarterly Monograph Series
CurBS	*Currents in Research: Biblical Studies*
EKKNT	Evangelisch-katholischer Kommentar zum Neuen Testament
FoiVie	*Foi et vie*
GBS	Guides to Biblical Scholarship
GR	*Greece and Rome*
HTKNT	Herders theologischer Kommentar zum Neuen Testament
ICC	International Critical Commentary
Int	*Interpretation*
JBL	*Journal of Biblical Literature*
JR	*Journal of Religion*
JSNT	*Journal for the Study of the New Testament*
JSNTSup	Journal for the Study of the New Testament: Supplement Series
KJV	King James Version

L&N	*Greek-English Lexicon of the New Testament: Based on Semantic Domains*. Edited by J. P. Louw and E. A. Nida. New York, 1989.
List	*Listening: Journal of Religion and Culture*
Metaph.	Aristotle's *Metaphysics*
NAC	New American Commentary
NASB	New American Standard Bible
NCB	New Century Bible
Neot	*Neotestamentica*
NIBCNT	New International Biblical Commentary on the New Testament
NIV	New International Version
NKJV	New King James Version
NovT	*Novum Testamentum*
NovTSup	Novum Testamentum Supplements
NRSV	New Revised Standard Version
NTS	*New Testament Studies*
OBO	Orbis biblicus et orientalis
QR	*Quarterly Review*
RB	*Revue biblique*
RSV	Revised Standard Version
SBLDS	Society of Biblical Literature Dissertation Series
SBLSP	*Society of Biblical Literature Seminar Papers*
SBLSymS	Society of Biblical Literature Symposium Series
SNTSMS	Society for New Testament Studies Monograph Series
SP	Sacra pagina
TDNT	*Theological Dictionary of the New Testament*. Edited by G. Kittel and G. Friedrich. Translated by G. W. Bromiley. 10 vols. Grand Rapids: Eerdmans, 1964–76.
THKNT	Theologischer Handkommentar zum Neuen Testament
ThTo	*Theology Today*
TJ	*Trinity Journal*
WBC	Word Biblical Commentary
WW	*Word and World*

CHAPTER 1

THE DISCIPLES OF JESUS IN THE GOSPEL OF MATTHEW: A SURVEY OF THE RELEVANT LITERATURE

The role of the disciples in Matthew is an issue that has been discussed and debated within Matthean scholarship of the last fifty years. This discussion has focused on the role of the disciples in two distinct areas, namely, their portrayal and their function. The disciples' role has been investigated primarily using redaction criticism and narrative criticism.

The *portrayal* of the disciples and their *function* for Matthew's community/reader(s) are two quite different, albeit related, issues. For example, Matthew's portrayal of the disciples as those of "little-faith" is a quite different issue than the exact nature of the relationship between the disciples and Matthew's reader(s). Nevertheless, most scholars who focus their attention on the disciples attend to both of these dimensions in some manner. Therefore, in this review, the major scholars who have studied the role of the disciples in Matthew will be summarized by means of these two categories: the disciples' portrayal and their function.

There are two prominent methodologies by which the disciples have been investigated in Matthean scholarship of the last half of the twentieth century. Prior to the 1980s, Matthean research had been dominated by redaction-critical methodology, which relied upon a comparison of Matthew with his sources to determine his theological purposes. This method had sketched a somewhat agreed upon presentation of Matthew's portrayal of the disciples.[1] In the last 15–20 years of the twentieth century, however, a great variety of methodologies

---

[1] For helpful descriptions of redaction criticism, cf. Norman Perrin, *What is Redaction Criticism?* GBS (Philadelphia: Fortress, 1969) and Robert H. Stein, "What is Redaktionsgeschichte?" *JBL* 88 (1969) 45–56.

became increasingly prominent in biblical studies in general and Matthean scholarship in particular, and most of these have continued to have on-going significance. One of the most prominent of these methods in Matthean study has been narrative criticism, which sets aside an examination of source material and focuses on the narrative alone and in its entirety to determine the message of the first Gospel.[2] Application of narrative-critical approaches[3] to the disciples in Matthew has yielded results that tend to diverge from redaction-critical views of the disciples.[4] For this reason, it would be instructive to discuss the major proponents of each of these methods in regard to the issues of the portrayal and function of the disciples in Matthew.

Based on these considerations, this chapter will be sketched as follows. Redaction-critical study of the disciples in Matthew will comprise the first section of the chapter. Major redaction critics who have focused attention upon the disciples in Matthew will be reviewed in relationship to their understanding of (1) Matthew's portrayal of the disciples and (2) the function of the disciples. The second major section of the chapter will focus upon narrative investigations of the disciples in Matthew. Recent narrative approaches which focus attention upon the disciples will be reviewed in a similar fashion by highlighting key scholars' understandings of (1) Matthew's portrayal of the disciples and (2) the function of the disciples. Finally, a third section will discuss the critical issues that emerge from this review for the task, method, and thesis of the remainder of the work.

---

[2] The distinction identified in this paragraph between redaction criticism and narrative criticism will be used to distinguish which scholars fall under which discipline in the following analysis. Thus, all scholars who use source analysis for even part of their method will be identified as redaction critics.

[3] The plural is appropriate, since there is no uniform agreement on the exact nature or application of narrative criticism. Examples of this ambiguity include the emphasis upon *discourse* by some narrative critics and *story* by others as well as the divergent definitions of the implied reader by various narrative critics.

[4] The redaction-critical approach continues to be employed in studies of the disciples in Matthew with a stronger emphasis upon the whole gospel (i.e. what Matthew has retained from his sources as well as what he changes in his sources). This is sometimes referred to as compositional criticism and can be seen in the work of Wilkins and van Aarde on the disciples in Matthew (cf. subsequent discussion).

REDACTION CRITICISM AND ITS APPLICATION TO THE DISCIPLES IN MATTHEW

The Portrayal of the Matthean Disciples in Redaction Criticism

There is no single redaction-critical viewpoint concerning the portrayal of the Matthean disciples. There are, however, specific areas that exhibit quite a bit of agreement by redaction critics (and thereby approach a tentative consensus). In terms of the disciples' portrayal, all redaction critics reviewed in this chapter acknowledge that the disciples exhibit an insufficient level of faith and are described by Jesus as those of "little faith," pointing to the Matthean prominent use of ὀλιγοπιστία or its adjectival cognate to characterize the disciples (at 8:26, 14:31, 16:8, and 17:20; cf. also 6:30). Nevertheless, there is disagreement as to the nature of Matthew's faith-concept, specifically its relationship to understanding.

The "Little Faith" of the Disciples

Gerhard Barth was one of the early Matthean scholars to apply redaction criticism to the first gospel. In "Matthew's Understanding of the Law,"[5] he focuses considerable attention on the portrayal of the disciples by Matthew as compared to Mark. His study is particularly significant because many subsequent scholars make reference to and rely upon his work regarding the portrayal of the Matthean disciples.[6] Barth explores three characteristics of the disciples in Matthew: understanding ("Συνιέναι"), faith ("Πίστις"), and unbelief/sin.[7] In his discussion of the disciples' faith, Barth deals in depth with the usage of ὀλιγοπιστία at Matt 14:31–33 and 16:5–12 and observes that in Matthew the disciples have insufficient faith. Barth concludes that Matthew takes his concept of πίστις primarily from Christian tradition but places a greater emphasis upon the element of trust. For Matthew, πίστις is trust in the fatherly kindness of God and supremely in the authority of Jesus.[8] In addition, it

---

[5] This was Barth's dissertation under Bornkamm and was subsequently published in English in G. Bornkamm, G. Barth, and H. J. Held, *Tradition and Interpretation in Matthew* (Philadelphia: Westminster, 1963) 58–164.

[6] Including Luz, Sheridan, and Wilkins of this review.

[7] Barth's two other headings in this section, "conversion" and "disciples as μικροί," do not deal with disciples as a character group. Rather, they address these particular aspects of discipleship in Matthean theology, focusing on Jesus' teachings concerning discipleship in the Matthean discourse material.

[8] Barth, "Matthew's Understanding," 112.

includes a significant element of willing, denoting obedience and faithfulness to God's demands.[9]

In his definition of the Matthean concept of faith, Barth introduces a distinction that has influenced subsequent scholarship on the disciples' portrayal. He asserts that unique to Matthew's concept of faith is its clear distinction from understanding. In contrast to his Marcan source, Matthew separates faith from understanding.[10] According to Barth, understanding is no longer a part of the πίστις–concept in Matthew. In his analysis of 14:31–33, Barth speaks of the disciples having knowledge yet lacking faith; and in 16:5–12, he asserts that they have decisive understanding but lack faith.[11] Barth concludes, "The intellectual element which is contained in the πίστις–concept of Paul and John and also in the editor of Mark is excluded from the πίστις–concept of Matthew and transferred to συνιέναι."[12] Clarifying the relationship between faith and understanding, Barth speaks of understanding as the *presupposition* of faith in Matthew.[13]

In an important essay, "The Disciples in the Gospel according to Matthew" (originally published in 1971),[14] Ulrich Luz affirms much of Barth's work in the area of the disciples and faith in Matthew. He notes the emphasis on their lack of faith and, following Barth, sees a separation of faith and understanding in Matthew. In fact, Luz favorably cites Barth's conclusions regarding Matthew's removal of the intellectual element from his use of πίστις. He disagrees, however, with Barth's conclusion regarding understanding as the presupposition of faith. "With the one exception of 16:8f., understanding is not the presupposition of faith but is separated from it."[15]

Mark Sheridan, in his article, "Disciples and Discipleship in Matthew and Luke,"[16] paints a portrait of the Matthean disciples that relies heavily upon the work of Barth. Sheridan agrees with Barth's conclusion that Matthew has removed the noetic moment from his concept of faith.[17] Drawing on Barth, he

---

[9] Barth, "Matthew's Understanding," 115.

[10] According to Barth, the relationship between faith and understanding is, for Matthew, one of necessary presupposition: "πιστεύειν in Matthew always has συνιέναι as its presupposition and is impossible without it" ("Matthew's Understanding," 116).

[11] Barth, "Matthew's Understanding," 113–14.

[12] Ibid., 113–14 and reaffirmed on 115.

[13] Ibid., 113.

[14] Ulrich Luz, "The Disciples in the Gospel according to Matthew," in *The Interpretation of Matthew*, ed. Graham Stanton, 2d ed. (Edinburgh: T&T Clark, 1995) 115–48.

[15] Ibid., 121.

[16] Mark Sheridan, "Disciples and Discipleship in Matthew and Luke," *BTB* (1973) 235–55.

[17] Ibid., 247.

sees understanding as a presupposition for faith.[18] Sheridan defines faith as the reliance upon the fatherly goodness of God to care for his creatures (cf. 6:30) and asserts that Matthew omits Marcan references to the disciples' lack of faith because of his concern for the problem of insufficient faith on the part of the Matthean church.[19]

Robert Gundry, in his commentary on Matthew,[20] does not treat the portrayal of the Matthean disciples independently. Nevertheless, he does repeatedly refer to the way Matthew portrays the disciples in contrast to their portrayal in his sources. Gundry points out the characterization of the disciples as those of "little faith." He does not, however, see Matthew separating faith from understanding as Barth, Luz, and Sheridan have done. Rather, Gundry, in his discussion of the story of the Canaanite woman (15:21–28), points to Matthew's heightening of her faith and closely correlates her faith with her understanding of Jesus' identity.[21] Dealing specifically with the disciples' faith in relation to their understanding, Gundry contends that the addition of ὀλιγόπιστοί at 16:8–9 "attributes the disciples' puzzlement to 'little faith,' which is corrected by further instruction."[22] Thus, Gundry diverges from Barth and others who claim that Matthew has removed the cognitive element from his concept of faith.

Andries van Aarde in his article, "The Disciples in Matthew's Story,"[23] affirms that the disciples display a tendency toward ὀλιγοπιστία. The frequent result of this lack of faith is a perspective that is similar to the perspective of Jesus' opponents in Matthew (i.e., a lack of obedience in living and proclaiming the will of God).[24] Although van Aarde does not indicate the exact nature of the relationship between understanding and "little faith" in the disciples, he does observe that Matthew portrays the disciples as exhibiting "little faith" prior to a "peak of insight" in three consecutive sections within Matt 13:53–17:27. He

---

[18] Sheridan, "Disciples," 249.

[19] Ibid., 247.

[20] Robert H. Gundry, *Matthew: A Commentary on His Literary and Theological Art* (Grand Rapids: Eerdmans, 1982). The second edition was published with a new subtitle: *Matthew: A Commentary on His Handbook for a Mixed Church under Persecution*, 2d ed. (Grand Rapids: Eerdmans, 1994). The second edition has been used in this literature review.

[21] "Here that faith is seen particularly in the understanding of Jesus as Lord and Son of David, the Messiah of the Jews but also the Emperor of all" (Gundry, *Matthew*, 319).

[22] Ibid., 326.

[23] Andries G. van Aarde, "The Disciples in Matthew's Story," *Hervormde Teologiese Studies Supplement* 5 (1994) 87–104. The centerpiece of his article is a narratological analysis of the disciples' characterization in 13:53–17:27.

[24] Ibid., 88.

concludes that the characteristics of "little faith" and understanding merge in this section of Matthew.[25]

To summarize, all redaction critics affirm the characterization of the disciples by Matthew as those of "little faith." There is less agreement among them regarding the exact relationship between the concepts of faith and understanding in Matthew. While Barth, Luz, and Sheridan speak of understanding as separated from Matthew's faith-concept, Gundry and van Aarde assert the correlation of the two at a number of points in the gospel. In addition, Barth (and Sheridan along with him) asserts that understanding is the presupposition of faith in Matthew, while Luz argues against this idea.

The Understanding of the Disciples

In addition to a basic consensus regarding the characterization of the disciples as those of "little faith," most redaction critics also speak of the *characteristic understanding* of the disciples in Matthew, although there is a difference of opinion as to the exact nature of their understanding. Prior to discussing redaction critics who have analyzed the understanding of the disciples, it would be helpful to mention briefly William Wrede and his influence upon redaction criticism in this area.

Although predating the rise of redaction criticism by almost fifty years, Wrede anticipated redaction analysis of the Matthean disciples in his *Das Messiageheimnis in den Evangelien* of 1901.[26] After devoting most of his study to the gospel of Mark, Wrede discusses Matthew and Luke in comparison to Mark. He notes that Matthew's attitude toward the disciples differs in essentials from that of Mark, in that for Mark there is a sharp separation between the understanding of the disciples before and after the resurrection.[27] Although Wrede points out that the tendency to cast the disciples in a negative light still remains in Matthew (e.g., 15:16; 8:26; 14:31; 16:9, 23),[28] he affirms that the

---

[25] Cf. van Aarde, "The Disciples," 93.

[26] Here cited in its English translation: William Wrede, *The Messianic Secret*, trans. J. C. G. Greig (Cambridge: James Clarke, 1971) 158–64.

[27] Wrede, *Secret*, 160. The Matthean examples he cites include the comprehension of the disciples at 13:51, the omission of Mark's statement that the disciples do not understand Jesus' passion prediction (Mark 9:31/Matt 17:22–23), and the change of the request for left and right hand seats in the kingdom from the lips of the sons of Zebedee to their mother (20:20).

[28] He attributes this opposite tendency to Matthew's inability to erase all of the weaknesses of the disciples from his Marcan source.

portrayal of the disciples in Matthew is essentially one of understanding.[29] In this way, Wrede set the stage for redaction-critical work on Matthew's disciples.

Barth's view regarding the understanding of the disciples in Matthew (as with his work on their "little faith") has been extremely influential in subsequent redaction-critical assessments of the Matthean disciples of the past thirty years.[30] Barth observes that Matthew has omitted or reinterpreted all the passages from Mark in which the disciples lack understanding.[31] In addition, in Matt 13, understanding is precisely what separates the disciples from the hard-hearted crowd.[32] After examining these passages, Barth concludes that in Matthew, in contrast to Mark, the disciples are given understanding before the resurrection.[33] Even in the special cases in which their understanding is incomplete (specifically, their lack of understanding of parables and enigmatic sayings in 13:36 and 15:15), Matthew emphasizes that Jesus gives them the understanding they need through his teaching. "Thus the disciples generally understand the preaching and teaching of Jesus about the demand of God, about the teaching of the Pharisees, about forerunners, Messianic deeds of power, suffering, and resurrection."[34]

Luz also characterizes the disciples as those who understand. Since the purpose of his essay is to critique Strecker's concept of the idealization of the Matthean disciples, Luz emphasizes that Matthew (following Mark) continues to speak of their lack of faith (e.g., 21:21), doubt (e.g., 14:31), and fear (e.g., 14:30).[35] He concludes that the *only* point at which Matthew improves the image of the disciples taken from Mark is their understanding.[36] This is not due

---

[29] "Thus to be sure some momentary weaknesses in knowledge do remain in the picture to the disciples, but these do not lay too much to their charge" (Wrede, *Secret*, 160).

[30] Less attention has been paid to Barth's conclusions concerning their unbelief and sinfulness.

[31] For example, Matt 13:14–15; 13:19, 23, 51; 14:31–32; 16:9, 12; 17:9, 13, 23.

[32] Barth, "Matthew's Understanding," 106–07.

[33] Barth notes that the emphasis in Matthew is upon understanding as a gift from God (Ibid., 110).

[34] Barth, "Matthew's Understanding," 110. The Matthean texts he cites in proof of this include 13:10–17; the omissions from Mark at 6:52; 8:17; 9:6, 32; and the additions at 17:10–13; 13:51; 16:12.

[35] Strecker's view of the idealization of both Jesus and the disciples was part of his larger argument that Matthew had historicizing, ethicizing, and institutionalizing tendencies (in an essay first published in 1966). See Georg Strecker, "The Concept of History in Matthew," in *The Interpretation of Matthew*, 2d ed, ed. Graham Stanton (Edinburgh: T&T Clark, 1995) 81–100.

[36] Luz, "Disciples," 119.

to a historicizing tendency (as claimed by Strecker). Rather, Matthew eliminates the Marcan motif of the disciples' failure to understand in order to emphasize that the disciples come to understand by means of Jesus' teaching. Jesus' very frequent special instructions for the disciples in Matthew mean "the disciples often fail to understand, but that they come to understand through Jesus' explanation. For Matthew it is important that the disciples do finally— after Jesus' instruction—understand."[37] The difference between Barth and Luz (acknowledged by Luz himself) is the degree of misunderstanding allowed the disciples. While Barth speaks of their incomplete understanding in only special instances (e.g., parables), Luz states that the disciples often fail to understand *before* Jesus' instruction.

According to Sheridan, it is a "striking fact that the disciples in Matthew understand everything Jesus teaches."[38] In addition to their understanding of Jesus' teaching, the disciples also understand who Jesus is (8:25; 14:28–33; 17:4; 20:33). In this regard, Sheridan mentions the frequent use of *Kyrios* as a christological title on the lips of the disciples.[39] Sheridan borrows from the general contours of Barth's understanding of the disciples without reflecting the more nuanced analysis of Barth (or Luz for that matter). While Barth recognizes that the portrayal of the disciples' understanding is not completely uniform (i.e., their understanding is, at times, incomplete), Sheridan speaks of the "categorical assertion" of understanding at 13:51 (they understand everything) and affirms that the disciples understand everything Jesus teaches and is.[40]

Gundry's viewpoint regarding the understanding of the disciples can be seen throughout his commentary. In general, he speaks of a "thoroughgoing program that pervades [Matthew's] gospel" by which Matthew removes the misunderstanding of the disciples from his Marcan source.[41] He points this out in the specific passages in which Matthew omits a Marcan statement about the disciples not understanding something Jesus says (cf. 14:32–33; 17:22–23).[42] In addition, Gundry notes that even when Matthew has retained some language of misunderstanding, the author provides a temporal qualification (e.g., "yet").[43]

---

[37] Luz, "Disciples," 120. Luz describes the disciples as "ear-witnesses" of Jesus, since they have heard and understood all that Jesus taught (122).

[38] Sheridan, "Disciples," 244.

[39] Ibid., 246.

[40] Ibid., 246.

[41] Gundry, *Matthew*, 624.

[42] Ibid., 301, 354.

[43] "Are you still without understanding ['Ακμὴν...ἀσύνετοί ἐστε]?" at 15:16; and "Do you not yet comprehend [οὔπω νοεῖτε]?" at 16:8–9 (Ibid., 326).

For Gundry, Matthew emphasizes that the disciples have some understanding and gain additional comprehension through Jesus' teaching.[44]

In dealing with passages that do not contain the language of understanding and yet improve upon the portrayal of the disciples from Mark, Gundry frequently cites these as evidence of Matthew's desire to portray the disciples as understanding. For example, in dealing with the story of Jesus and the children (19:13–15), Gundry notes that Matthew omits the statement that Jesus was indignant. This omission "dulls the edge of Jesus' words and generalizes them in accord with Matthew's portraying the disciples as understanding."[45] Finally, in dealing with passages that do not contain the language of understanding and yet seem to imply that the disciples do *not* understand, Gundry at times marshals even these texts as evidence of the programmatic portrayal of the disciples. At 16:22 he states that Matthew "turns Peter's rebuke into a confession of Jesus' lordship. The emphasis falls on the side of what Peter does understand about Jesus rather than on what he does not understand."[46] Thus, Gundry asserts that Matthew consistently characterizes the disciples as those who understand, particularly after Jesus teaches them.

Michael Wilkins, in *The Concept of Disciple in Matthew's Gospel*,[47] studies the term μαθητής in ancient Greco-Roman and Jewish literature and usage. In his final chapter, he analyzes Matthew's use of this term using a redaction-critical analysis[48] and affirms that the disciples understand in Matthew (as opposed to Mark). For Wilkins, their understanding underscores Jesus as effective teacher.[49] Wilkins reemphasizes this thought in his 1991 essay, "Named and Unnamed Disciples in Matthew: A Literary-Theological Study."

---

[44] "Thus the disciples appear as those who are deficient but not lacking in understanding" (Gundry, *Matthew*, 326–27).

[45] Ibid., 384; cf. also 401 and 520.

[46] Ibid., 338. Another such example occurs in Gundry's discussion of the disciples' question, "Who is the greatest in the kingdom of heaven?" at 18:1. "This is an innocent question, even a knowing question—just as we should expect, since Matthew stresses understanding as necessary to discipleship" (359). It should be noted that in this regard Gundry rightly attends to Matthew's indirect as well as direct characterization of the disciples, analyzing texts that do not explicitly speak of the disciples' understanding but that nonetheless implicitly address the issue. I simply disagree with his interpretation that the question at 18:1 shows the disciples to understand. I think it demonstrates the opposite. Cf. ch. 3 for my analysis of this verse.

[47] Michael J. Wilkins, *The Concept of Disciple in Matthew's Gospel*, NovTSup 59 (Leiden: E. J. Brill, 1988).

[48] Wilkins speaks of his method as including both redaction criticism and composition criticism (*Concept of Disciple*, 6, 126–27).

[49] Ibid., 166.

In a discussion of the features of the Matthean disciples, Wilkins speaks of "something of a consensus" which has been reached regarding certain characteristics of the disciples in Matthew by means of redaction criticism, literary criticism, and sociological approaches.[50] One of these features is that the disciples understand Jesus' teaching in Matthew. "Typically, Matthew shows how difficult it is to understand all that is transpiring in Jesus' earthly ministry, but after Jesus has finished teaching, the disciples finally understand."[51] In this way, Wilkins' view closely resembles that of Luz.

Van Aarde affirms the redaction-critical observation that the Matthean disciples understand. Van Aarde engages in what he terms a narratological analysis, defined as the analysis of the "narrator's particular portrayal of the disciples in terms of his redactional narrative technique."[52] Using this method, van Aarde analyzes the portrait of the disciples in Matthew. In his initial comments, he speaks of the disciples as a complex type of character, exhibiting both positive and negative characteristics.[53] While observing the tendency of the disciples to disobey their call to be helpers,[54] van Aarde nevertheless affirms that the Matthean disciples do possess understanding. "[T]he disciples in the Gospel of Matthew, unlike in Mark...have full 'insight' into the nature of Jesus' vocation. They apparently also understand the nature of their own vocation."[55]

Following these general introductory comments regarding the portrayal of the Matthean disciples, van Aarde provides a narratological analysis of Matt 13:53–17:27 (which he divides into three parts).[56] Each subsection of 13:53–17:27 ends with redactional material related to Peter as representative of the disciples in general. According to van Aarde, these three sections "often focus on a concluding report about Peter (Matthean redaction), peaking with

---

[50] Michael J. Wilkins, "Named and Unnamed Disciples in Matthew: A Literary/Theological Study," in *1991 SBLSP* (Atlanta: Scholars Press, 1991) 419–20.

[51] Wilkins, "Named and Unnamed Disciples," 422. Wilkins then demonstrates this proposal in a brief discussion of Matt 13.

[52] Cf. van Aarde, "The Disciples," 89. This methodology seems to best fit the category of compositional criticism, which lies closer to redaction than narrative criticism. For this reason, I have included van Aarde under redaction criticism rather than narrative approaches since the latter bracket out the source analysis which van Aarde continues to utilize.

[53] Here, he utilizes narrative terminology for the disciples as character group.

[54] Cf. van Aarde, "The Disciples," 88.

[55] Ibid., 88.

[56] The three sections are 13:53–14:33; 14:34–16:20; 16:21–17:27.

'insight' on the part of the disciples (Peter)."[57] In fact, each unit ends with a higher level of insight by Peter than found in the preceding unit.[58]

Van Aarde concludes that there are two emphases concerning the disciples which prevail in Matthew, namely, their "total insight" and their "ὀλιγοπιστία nature."[59] These two character traits merge in 13:53–17:27 in such a way that the disciples understand the role of Jesus (as the obedient Son of God) and their own role (as sons of God), as well as comprehending the danger "that formalistic exclusivism holds for the Jewish leaders."[60] What the disciples do not understand, according to van Aarde, is the danger that this formalistic perspective holds for the Jewish crowd whom the disciples are called to impact and help. Thus, van Aarde, in spite of his assertion of the disciples' "total insight," seems to provide a more nuanced portrayal of the Matthean disciples in terms of what they do and do not understand as the narrative progresses.

Up to this point, each of the redaction critics reviewed affirms that the Matthean disciples can be generally characterized by understanding (either in a thoroughgoing way or at least after they are taught by Jesus). One redaction critic, however, significantly disagrees with this conclusion. Andrew Trotter, in his dissertation, "Understanding and Stumbling: A Study of the Disciples' Understanding of Jesus and His Teaching in Matthew," speaks of a large majority of scholars who agree "that Matthew has consistently removed Marcan incomprehension and replaced it with a thorough-going comprehension of Jesus and his mission."[61] Nevertheless, he notes that some scholars (e.g., Held) point to Matthew's inconsistency in carrying out this tendency.[62] Thus, Trotter attempts to resolve some of the problems that arise from prevailing redaction-

---

[57] Cf. van Aarde, "The Disciples," 93.

[58] This argument is particularly weak in the final section that van Aarde delineates. There is no language regarding understanding used in 17:24–27, and, more importantly, there is no indication of Peter's "insightful" response. His answer (17:26) to Jesus' question concerning whom earthly kings tax (17:25) can hardly be viewed as insight into the 'son of God' motif, as van Aarde claims (Ibid., 102).

[59] Ibid., 103.

[60] Ibid., 103.

[61] Andrew H. Trotter, "Understanding and Stumbling: A Study of the Disciples' Understanding of Jesus and His Teaching in the Gospel of Matthew" (Ph.D. diss., Cambridge University, 1986) 15.

[62] Although Held does point out the variable portrait of the disciples' understanding, he agrees (with the viewpoint expressed by a number of redaction critics in this review) that the Matthean disciples understand after Jesus instructs them. Cf. H. J. Held, "Matthew as Interpreter of the Miracle Stories," in G. Bornkamm, G. Barth, and H. J. Held, *Tradition and Interpretation in Matthew* (Philadelphia: Westminster, 1963) 291.

critical views.[63] In the two major sections of his dissertation, Trotter studies Matthean narratives which have been used to prove the understanding of the disciples (e.g., passages that use συνιέναι to describe the disciples) as well as narratives in which σκανδαλίζειν is used to describe the disciples.

Trotter concludes that (1) the disciples understand when the object of their understanding is Jesus' teaching on the parables, the danger of the teaching of the Jewish leaders, the relationship of John the Baptist to Elijah and the saying about the blind guides; (2) their portrayal is much more mixed concerning their understanding of Jesus' deity and mission (e.g., their response to the three passion predictions);[64] and (3) the disciples stumble over Jesus and his mission (e.g., 16:21–23). This stumbling involves *misunderstanding* Jesus and his mission.[65]

An extended quotation from Trotter's final chapter helpfully summarizes his view of the understanding of the Matthean disciples.

> We have…seen that the things the disciples do understand in Matthew are often tainted with partial understanding and wrong perceptions; the stumbling block motif brings this out very clearly. They "understand" him to be Son of God (Mt 14:33; 16:16), but later refuse him the right to go to Jerusalem to die (Mt 16:21–23) and, later still, put him on a par with Moses and Elijah, drawing down upon themselves the correction of the voice from heaven (Mt 17:1–8). They supposedly understand the Kingdom parables (Mt 13:51–52) and yet often deny their teachings by their actions in later parts of the Gospel; they have understood the warning against the teachings of the Pharisees and Sadducees (Mt 16:5–12) and yet they need to be warned even more stringently about them later (cf. Mt 23, esp. v. 1) and so on. Virtually everything they "understand" in the Gospel is understood with a grain of salt; Jesus has taught them clearly and well, but their own dullness and especially their over-riding misunderstanding of the nature of his messiahship clouds their understanding until the resurrection.[66]

For Trotter, misunderstanding rather than understanding characterizes the disciples in Matthew until after the resurrection. Nevertheless, because Trotter's dissertation has not been published further, his dissenting voice has had little impact on the issue of the disciples' portrayal within redaction-criticism.

---

[63] Trotter rightly acknowledges that there is not one view but several concerning the issues surrounding Matthew's portrayal of the disciples (and their supposed understanding); "Understanding," 14.

[64] Trotter, "Understanding," 279.

[65] Ibid., 282, 285. Consequently, for Trotter, the nature of understanding in Matthew is more of an occasional, dynamic kind of understanding than a relatively static, ontological type of understanding (283).

[66] Ibid., 284.

The Function of the Matthean Disciples in Redaction Criticism

We have seen that the majority of redaction critics have focused on the portrayal of the Matthean disciples in terms of two primary characteristics: their understanding and "little faith." But there is another aspect to redaction-critical discussion of the disciples, namely, the function of this characterization. All these scholars speak about the purpose (i.e., function) of the disciples' portrayal at some level. Since the category of function is quite broad and discussion of it often lacks clarity, Kari Syreeni's three-tiered model will be utilized to organize the conclusions of scholars regarding the function of the Matthean disciples. Syreeni speaks of three worlds in relationship to a gospel: the textual world, the concrete world, and the symbolic world.[67] These categories correspond quite nicely to the observations made by scholars regarding the function of the Matthean disciples. Redaction critics speak of the function of the disciples' understanding within the story of Matthew (the textual world), the function of the disciples in relation to the Matthean community (the concrete world), and the function of the disciples in relation to Matthew's concept of discipleship (his symbolic world).

Regarding the function of the disciples within the textual world, a number of redaction critics have asserted that the disciples' understanding functions to highlight Jesus as effective teacher. Barth speaks of the incomplete understanding that the disciples exhibit in the special case of Jesus' parables and enigmatic sayings. But he quickly affirms that, even in this special case of incomplete understanding, Jesus gives them understanding.[68] Luz even more strongly asserts that, while the disciples often fail to understand, they come to understanding through the teaching of Jesus. "So Jesus is shown here as a good teacher who successfully gives the disciples full instructions about everything. They do not understand of their own accord. They come to understand through Jesus' instruction."[69] Trotter also speaks of Matthew's motive for redacting the understanding of the disciples as that of showing Jesus as successful teacher.[70]

---

[67] Kari Syreeni, "Separation and Identity: Aspects of the Symbolic World of Matt 6:1–18," *NTS* 40 (1994) 523.

[68] Barth, "Matthew's Understanding," 110.

[69] Luz, "Disciples,"120.

[70] Trotter, "Understanding," 280. It should be noted that Trotter does not view the Matthean disciples as understanding in any comprehensive way but is referring to those points where Matthew has redacted Mark to show that the disciples understand some part of Jesus' teaching. Trotter also offers this idea:… "if Matthew does have an ecclesiological motive…it would seem to be in order to bolster the authority and veracity of the apostles' teaching for his church" (281).

Finally, Wilkins asserts that Matthew portrays the disciples as understanding to accent his Christology, namely, to emphasize Jesus as effective teacher.[71]

The second area in which redaction critics speak of the function of the disciples is in relation to the concrete world of the Matthean community. It is one of the fundamental assumptions of redaction criticism that the individual gospels function to illuminate the first-century communities out of which they arose. Thus, redaction critics of Matthew focus on the third *Sitz im Leben* of the gospel, i.e., the way in which the text provides a window to the historical reality of Matthew's community.

Redaction critics who have done substantial work on the disciples in Matthew consistently affirm that the disciples are 'transparent' for Matthew's church either in part or whole.[72] Barth asserts that the disciples are transparent for the reality of the Matthean community precisely because of their characteristic understanding. "By consistently removing the difference according to Mark between the disciples before the resurrection of Jesus and after it, Matthew again here writes the situation of the Church into the life of the disciples during the earthly activity of Jesus."[73]

Luz also affirms transparency, stating that behind the disciples of Jesus stands the Matthean community:... "[t]he disciples of Jesus are transparent for the present situation."[74] Sheridan speaks of Matthew superimposing the life of the church on the narrative's life of Jesus.[75] Sheridan gives a specific example of this in his discussion of ὀλιγοπιστία. This theme "most likely represents the problem of a church which knows who Jesus is, but has experienced difficulty in maintaining an adequate level of trust as his coming has been delayed."[76]

---

[71] Wilkins, *Concept of Disciple,* 165. "Typically, Matthew shows how difficult it is to understand all that is transpiring in Jesus' earthly ministry, but after Jesus has finished teaching, the disciples finally understand" (Wilkins, "Named and Unnamed Disciples," 422).

[72] The one exception from the scholars reviewed here is Trotter who, although not denying transparency, does not address it in any detail.

[73] Barth, "Matthew's Understanding," 110–11. The concept of the transparency of the disciples for the Matthean church was first prominently expressed in a landmark essay by Günther Bornkamm ("The Stilling of the Storm in Matthew" in *Tradition*, 52–57). "Matthew is...the first to interpret the journey of the disciples with Jesus in the storm and the stilling of the storm with reference to discipleship, and that means with reference to the little ship of the Church" (55).

[74] Luz, "Disciples," 128. As Doyle puts it, "Matthew achieves the involvement of his church members in the Gospel by casting them in the role of disciples of Jesus;" B. Rod Doyle, "Matthew's Intention as Discerned by his Structure," *RB* 95 (1988) 48.

[75] Sheridan, "Disciples," 242.

[76] Ibid., 247.

It is clear that Gundry also understands the disciples to be transparent for a historical reality in Matthew's church. This can be noted at many points in his commentary, even by a quick perusal of his headings (e.g., "Obedient Understanding of Jesus' Command to Serve the Lord's Supper to Discipled Nations: 14:13–21"). This application of the principle of transparency can also be seen in Gundry's comment concerning the addition of Peter walking on the water to Matthew's stilling of the storm pericope. He mentions that it is difficult to resist the conclusion that Matthew "composed it [vv 28–31] as a haggadic midrash on discipleship: confessing Jesus as Lord, obeying Jesus' command, being guilty of little faith in persecution, crying out for deliverance, and being rescued and rebuked by Jesus."[77]

Finally, van Aarde does not so confidently assert the transparency of the disciples for some reality in Matthew's community. This stems from his more eclectic (transitional) methodology. Since he is using redaction criticism as only part of his overall "narratological analysis," he shies away from speaking definitively of the transparency of the Matthean disciples. Rather, he speaks of the portrayal of the disciples as *suggestive* for the situation in Matthew's church. For van Aarde, the disciples are "inclined to deny their *helper function* on the pre-paschal temporal level. The narrator thus suggests that the same inclination exists on the post-paschal level."[78] This more tentative position regarding the relationship between the Matthean portrayal of the disciples and its function for the Matthean community is a tendency of narrative approaches over against redaction criticism.

To summarize, a review of the redaction critics surveyed who have dealt with the subject of the disciples' function shows that redaction criticism in general is quite confident in the transparency of the Matthean disciples for some extra-textual reality within Matthew's church. Nevertheless, there is disagreement over the exact nature of this transparent reality, namely, whether the disciples stand for the whole congregation or only its leadership.

Both Barth and Gundry understand the disciples in Matthew to illuminate the whole church. According to Barth, "Matthew sees the Church in general embodied in the μαθηταί."[79] For Gundry, the disciples stand for the true believers of Matthew's church who are a part of the larger *corpus mixtum*. In this view, the crowds are transparent for the whole, mixed body of professing believers.[80]

---

[77] Gundry, *Matthew*, 300.

[78] Cf. van Aarde, "The Disciples," 88.

[79] Barth, "Matthew's Understanding," 110, n. 2.

[80] Gundry, *Matthew*, 251.

Sheridan and Minear (and van Aarde more tentatively) understand the disciples to be transparent for the leadership of the Matthean church rather than for the whole church. Sheridan notes in this regard how Matthew heightens the mediation of the disciples in the feeding stories and affirms the role of the disciples in leading the "little ones" of chapter 18.[81] He concludes that "the disciples can be seen to represent the leaders in the church."[82]

Minear spends considerable time arguing this viewpoint in his article, "The Disciples and the Crowds in the Gospel of Matthew."[83] His focus in this article is the portrayal of the crowds (ὄχλοι) in Matthew, specifically their positive appraisal by Matthew,[84] and the function of both the disciples and crowds for the Matthean audience. Minear concludes that the crowds in Matthew represent followers of Jesus (i.e., the laypeople in Matthew's church). Corresponding to this, the disciples represent the leadership of the Matthean community.[85] "When...the modern reader finds Jesus speaking to the crowds, he may usually assume that Matthew was speaking to contemporary laymen. When he finds Jesus teaching the disciples, he may usually suppose that Matthew had in mind the vocation of contemporary leaders as stewards of Christ's household."[86]

Finally, Luz asserts that the question of whether the disciples are transparent for the church leaders or the entire Matthean community cannot be decided with certainty. Indeed, Matthew contains evidence for both positions, and this implies that such a distinction was relatively unimportant for Matthew's understanding of discipleship.[87] Thus, while there is redaction-critical consensus that the disciples are transparent for Matthew's community, there is disagreement as to whether the whole church or only its leadership is in view.

The third area in which redaction critics speak of the function of the disciples is in relation to Matthew's symbolic world, specifically, his view of discipleship. Luz contends that Matthew's portrait of the disciples directly contributes to his definition of discipleship. "The disciples are hearers of [the historical Jesus'] teaching and understand it. This is the presupposition for the

---

[81] Sheridan, "Disciples," 250.

[82] Ibid., 255.

[83] Paul S. Minear, "The Disciples and the Crowds in the Gospel of Matthew," *AThR Supplement* 3 (1974) 28–44. Minear provides no significant characterization of the disciples (focusing his attention on the portrayal of the crowds instead), so he was not cited in the earlier discussion of portrayal.

[84] Ibid., 40.

[85] Ibid., 31.

[86] Ibid., 41.

[87] Luz, "Disciples," 128.

definition of discipleship at Matt 12:50 as doing the will of God."[88] Gundry also believes that Matthew emphasizes the understanding of the disciples because he wants to stress understanding as necessary to discipleship.[89]

Sheridan connects the disciples' portrayal with Matthew's view of discipleship by asserting that the disciples are *exemplary* for Christians. While conceding that the disciples cannot completely be identified with the Christian community, Sheridan says that they are exemplary for Christians "in their understanding, in their need for trust, and in the fruit they bear."[90] Wilkins also speaks of the exemplary nature of the disciples:... "one is able to see that Matthew's portrait of the disciples...presents an example of discipleship for his church. The disciples are a positive example of what Matthew expects from his church, a negative example of warning, and a mixed group who are able to overcome their lack through the teaching of Jesus."[91] It should be noted, however, that Wilkins is not referring to the disciples as *ideal* examples, since they are both a positive and a negative example to the reader. Rather, he seems to be pointing to a representative function of the Matthean disciples (although he does not use this specific term). In fact, in the conclusion of his essay, Wilkins states that although *Jesus* is exemplary for Matthew's reader, the reader will more readily identify with the *disciples* (i.e., the disciples as representative for the reader). Thus he concludes, "[t]he stumbling disciples provide an example for the readers of how Jesus would work with them."[92]

---

[88] Luz, "Disciples," 123.

[89] Gundry, *Matthew,* 359; cf. also 534 where Gundry speaks of Matthew's portrayal of disciples (vs. *the* disciples) as knowledgeable and understanding. This move from Matthew's portrayal of the disciples as characters to his portrayal of disciples in general is a move from what is to what should be (i.e., the ideal disciple) and therefore may be seen as a move from narrative portrayal to symbolic world.

[90] In his conclusion, Sheridan reiterates this idea with a slight modification. "The disciples in Matthew remain exemplary for all Christians in that, with the help of Jesus, they overcome their lack of trust in his power and in the care of the Father" ("Disciples," 255).

[91] Wilkins, *Concept of Disciple,* 171–72.

[92] Ibid., 439. One problem in discerning Wilkins' perspective on the function of the disciples is his tendency to equate the actual activity of the disciples as a character group with the ideal disciple envisioned in Jesus' teaching. He notes that "[a]t the end of instruction to the disciples, they indicate that they now understand (13:51). True disciples will understand Jesus' teaching" ("Named and Unnamed Disciples," 423). These two sentences illustrate Wilkin's tendency to equate Matthew's *portrayal of the disciples* with Matthew's *view of discipleship*. In fact, his first sentence under the heading, "The disciples understand Jesus' teaching," displays this very same tendency: "More than the other evangelists, Matthew emphasizes that the essence of true discipleship lies in individuals who understand and obey Jesus' teaching" (Ibid., 422). This same problem can be seen in some narrative approaches to the disciples' characterization and Matthean discipleship.

In conclusion, the function of the Matthean disciples is a broad category within redaction criticism that includes their function within Matthew's story, their function in illuminating Matthew's church, and their function in disclosing Matthew's view of discipleship. While there is rather uniform agreement on their function within Matthew's story (to highlight Jesus as effective teacher), as well as their transparent function for Matthew's community, there is disagreement over the group to which they correspond in his community (the leaders or the church as a whole). In addition, there is a lack of clarity in the discussion of the disciples' function regarding the Matthean view of discipleship. At times, the character group of the disciples and their portrayal by Matthew is simply equated with Matthew's view of discipleship, while other scholars point to an exemplary or representative function of the disciples. In general, the function of the disciples as it relates to Matthew's view of discipleship has not been adequately addressed by redaction criticism.

Given the similarities and differences discussed in this section among redaction-critical views, how might one speak of the views proposed by redaction critics on the subject of the Matthean disciples? It would seem that Wilkins goes too far in speaking of "something of a consensus," especially as he is including in this consensus results of other methodologies (including narrative and sociological approaches).[93] The "prevailing views" of redaction criticism (Trotter's terminology) might be a better choice to describe the situation.

NARRATIVE CRITICISM AND ITS APPLICATION TO THE DISCIPLES IN MATTHEW

The Portrayal of the Matthean Disciples in Narrative Criticism

Narrative critics generally agree that the disciples in Matthew are portrayed in a mixed fashion, exhibiting at times positive but more often negative characteristics. First, narrative critics who have done substantial work on the portrayal of the disciples affirm what redaction critics have already noted, namely, that the disciples are characterized by "little faith." In addition (and counter to redaction criticism in general), narrative critics have seen a tendency to *misunderstand* as characteristic of the Matthean disciples. Since narrative discussion of the disciples weaves together these two character traits, they will not be separated in the following analysis (as in the analysis of redaction-critical studies above). Nevertheless, the issue of whether the disciples *progress*

---

[93] Wilkins, "Named and Unnamed Disciples," 419–20.

in their understanding as the narrative develops will be discussed separately, since this is an area in which there is significant disagreement.

Jack Kingsbury was one of the early narrative critics to work on the gospel of Matthew.[94] In his chapter on the disciples in *Matthew as Story*, Kingsbury sketches the contours of the "story of the disciples"[95] by tracing their portrayal through the major sections of Matthew.[96] In 4:17–11:1, which emphasizes Jesus' ministry to Israel, the disciples are first introduced through their call and their mission to Israel.[97] In their mission to Israel, however, the disciples are frequently susceptible to "little faith" (i.e., weak faith).[98] In 11:2–16:20, which focuses on Israel's repudiation of Jesus, the disciples are portrayed as recipients of divine revelation.[99] They receive insight into the mysteries of the kingdom and are granted knowledge that Jesus is Son of God.[100] Nevertheless, even though they receive this revelation, the disciples "on other occasions...show that they can falter in their understanding and this engenders conflict between Jesus and them" (e.g., 14:16; 16:7–12).[101]

According to Kingsbury, this conflict intensifies in 16:21–28:20, in which Matthew tells the story of Jesus' journey to Jerusalem and his ultimate suffering, death, and resurrection.[102] Here the disciples are portrayed in conflict with Jesus' point of view concerning his suffering Sonship and their suffering discipleship.[103] This conflict "has to do with the disciples' imperceptiveness, and at times resistance, to the notion that servanthood is the essence of discipleship."[104] Nevertheless, the disciples are eventually led to appropriate Jesus' point of view at the conclusion of the gospel (28:7, 10, 16–17) where they come to "full knowledge of Jesus and themselves."[105] In other words, they finally appropriate Jesus' evaluative point of view.

---

[94] Jack D. Kingsbury, *Matthew as Story*, 2d ed. (Philadelphia: Fortress Press, 1988). The first edition was published in 1986.

[95] Kingsbury speaks of the story of the disciples following the contours of Matthew's story of Jesus (Ibid., 129).

[96] According to Kingsbury, these are 1:1–4:16; 4:17–16:20; and 16:21–28:20.

[97] Kingsbury, *Matthew as Story*, 129.

[98] Ibid., 136.

[99] Ibid., 129.

[100] Ibid., 139.

[101] Ibid., 138.

[102] Ibid., 129.

[103] Kingsbury cites the following examples in this regard: 17:14–20, 22–23; 19:13–15, 23–26; 20:20–23; 26:47–50 (Ibid., 129).

[104] Ibid., 130.

[105] Ibid., 144.

Richard Edwards has written quite extensively on the subject of the Matthean disciples. His 1985 essay, "Uncertain Faith: Matthew's Portrait of the Disciples," was an early narrative analysis of Matthew's portrayal of the disciples. In it, Edwards describes the Matthean disciples as inconsistent followers who never live up to Jesus' standards.[106] They are portrayed as ambivalent, sometimes understanding and at other times clearly not comprehending Jesus' teaching. Edwards comes to the same conclusion in his more recent book, *Matthew's Narrative Portrait of Disciples.*[107] Edward's particular narrative methodology is to ask how the "text-connoted reader"[108] is informed and influenced by the narrative.[109] Analyzing eleven "character-shaping incidents" in the Matthean portrayal of the disciples, Edwards traces the positive and negative portrayals of the disciples which alternate through the narrative. He consistently speaks of the disciples as "limited" followers who are not able to meet Jesus' expectations of a high level of faith for them.[110] Besides having a limited faith, the disciples also fail to recognize Jesus' authority (at 8:18–27), express fear and doubt (Peter at 14:22–33), and lack understanding about what it means to be fishers of people (26:30–75).

Nevertheless, the disciples also exhibit positive characteristics, including following Jesus and accepting the task of becoming fishers of people (at 4:18–22), understanding Jesus' metaphorical teaching (at 13:51–52), recognizing Jesus as the Son of God (at 14:22–33 and 16:5–23), and understanding Jesus' teaching about John the Baptist (at 17:1–13). Edwards concludes his book by inferring from his analysis what the text-connoted author understands about the disciples. In terms of the alternating portrayal of the disciples, Edwards states that "[d]espite the disciples' positive and negative characteristics in the flow of the story, they have been followers in enough ways to be asked to be 'disciple makers.'"[111]

Warren Carter, in *Matthew: Storyteller, Interpreter, Evangelist,* utilizes a methodology which he terms "audience-oriented criticism." A type of reader-

---

[106] Richard A. Edwards, "Uncertain Faith: Matthew's Portrait of the Disciples," in *Discipleship in the New Testament,* ed. Fernando F. Segovia (Philadelphia: Fortress, 1985) 2.

[107] Richard A. Edwards, *Matthew's Narrative Portrait of Disciples* (Valley Forge: Trinity Press International, 1997).

[108] Similar to narrative criticism's implied reader.

[109] Edwards, *Portrait,* 10.

[110] Ibid., (1997) 39, 76, 125, 140. Edwards gives a partial presentation of this narrative/reader-response analysis in an earlier essay: idem., "Characterization of the Disciples as a Feature of Matthew's Narrative," in *The Four Gospels,* ed. F. Segbroeck, 2:1305–23 (Leuvan: University Press, 1992).

[111] Edwards, *Portrait,* 143.

response criticism, audience-oriented criticism involves trying to identify and read along with the readers which the author has in mind while writing the gospel. This audience, which is an authorial construct, is able to respond appropriately to and understand everything in the text, and so is an ideal audience.[112] In his discussion of the authorial audience, Carter is careful to distinguish it from the implied reader of many narrative approaches. Nevertheless, there seems to be little real difference between the two,[113] and Carter's approach quite closely resembles other narrative approaches reviewed here in many other ways.[114] For these reasons, Carter's work appropriately fits under the general rubric of narrative approaches.

In his chapter that focuses on the characterization of the disciples, Carter traces their portrayal as a group through five of the six narrative blocks in Matthew.[115] Carter asserts that an important aspect of the audience's understanding of the disciples has to do with their inconsistency.[116] The disciples have moments of insight but also fail to live out their identity at other times. Carter refers to their "growing understanding" as part of the reason for their frequent inconsistency.[117] He traces this inconsistency throughout the gospel, emphasizing particularly their moments of "little faith," misunderstanding/lack of understanding, and failure to live up to the ideals of

---

[112] Warren Carter, *Matthew: Storyteller, Interpreter, Evangelist* (Peabody, MA: Hendrickson, 1996) 4.

[113] Ibid., 278–79. For example, Carter claims that the concept of the implied reader is "essentially unrealistic…[since it] is impossible for any reader to grasp all the complex interrelationships that may occur within a text" (*Matthew*, 279). The problem with Carter's assessment is that the same could be claimed concerning the "authorial audience," since they too understand and respond appropriately to everything in the text (4). In addition, Carter complains that the concept of the ideal reader envisions a passive reader rather than one actively involved in producing meaning as in audience-oriented criticism (*Matthew*, 279). Nevertheless, while Carter affirms the view that meaning is produced in the interaction of text and reader, the application of his method differs very little from other narrative approaches, which utilize the implied reader concept. In other words, when push comes to shove, he can quite confidently speak of the audience recalling this or sensing that, as if meaning were determined by the text and the reader/audience was simply a responder to it (e.g. *Matthew*, 254).

[114] For example, Carter deals with typically narrative subjects in his analysis of Matthew, including point-of-view, plot, settings, and characters.

[115] Since the disciples do not appear until the second narrative block, Carter does not discuss the first narrative block in this chapter.

[116] Carter, *Matthew*, 243.

[117] Ibid., 243.

Jesus' teaching.[118] In his discussion of Matt 16:21–20:34, Carter states that "faith comes hard for the disciples....[T]hey struggle to exercise faith in casting out a demon (17:14–20, esp. 16). They thereby fail at the mission task which Jesus has commissioned them to do (10:1, 8)."[119]

In *Matthew's Inclusive Story*, David Howell uses a methodology that incorporates selected aspects of narrative criticism with a type of reader-response criticism in his study of Matthew.[120] One major chapter of his book deals with the temporal ordering and plot of Matthew's story. In this section, he frequently refers to the portrayal of the disciples throughout the plot of the gospel. He speaks of the ambiguity of this portrait, since the disciples exhibit positive characteristics (e.g., following Jesus, confessing Jesus as the Son of God, understanding some of Jesus' teachings, and progressing in their understanding of his identity) as well as negative characteristics (e.g., fear, doubt, wavering faith and wavering understanding). In relationship to their understanding, Howell observes their progress in understanding Jesus' identity shown at 14:33; their flawed understanding at 15:15–16, 16:12, and 17:13; the wavering nature of their understanding at 15:32–33; Peter's defective understanding at 16:13–14 as shown in events that follow; and their failure to comprehend the true nature of Jesus' ministry at 26:6–7. In a summary of the disciples' understanding in relationship to Matthew's plotting device of acceptance and rejection, Howell speaks of "the disciples' continued inability to comprehend fully the nature of Jesus' ministry and mission, despite the teaching and predictions [of Jesus]."[121]

In "The Faith of the Reader and the Narrative of Matthew 13:52–16:20," Donald Verseput uses a narrative-critical methodology to reexamine the relationship between the faith and understanding of the disciples in Matthew, focusing on Matt 13:52–16:20. Verseput notes Barth's "generally accepted" conclusion that the intellectual element has been excluded from Matthew's concept of πίστις and transferred to συνιέναι. Verseput then seeks to show by means of an analysis of Matthew's rhetoric in 13:52–16:20 that "the controlling

---

[118] For example, in his discussion of Matt 11:2–16:20, Carter speaks of the disciples' lack of understanding and trust at the second feeding miracle (15:33) and of further misunderstanding in 16:1–12 (Carter, *Matthew*, 248). Carter also reaffirms the disciples' misunderstanding in his *Households and Discipleship: A Study of Matthew 19–20*, JSNTSup 103 (Sheffield: JSOT Press, 1994) 206. This work, however, does not much deal with the portrayal of the disciples in Matthew. Rather, it focuses on discipleship as taught by Matthew's Jesus and understood by the authorial audience in Matt 19–20.

[119] Carter, *Matthew*, 249–50.

[120] David B. Howell, *Matthew's Inclusive Story: A Study in the Narrative Rhetoric of the First Gospel*, JSNTSup 42 (Sheffield: JSOT Press, 1990) 17.

[121] Ibid., 148.

purpose behind the narrative plot is the author's attempt to impart a certain cognitive understanding to the reader which might function as an antidote to the malady of 'little faith.'"[122] Verseput thus sees understanding as an essential component of the Matthean concept of faith.

Verseput analyzes the narrative of 13:52–16:20, focusing on the concepts of unbelief, faith, and "little faith," while examining the cognitive aspects of these concepts. He concludes at a number of points that the disciples' inadequate understanding of the power (δύναμις) and authority (ἐξουσία) of Jesus is central to their characterization as ones of "little faith."[123] In addition, he notes that from the reader's perspective this lack of understanding on the disciples' part is completely unwarranted and even foolish.[124] For Matthew, "little faith" is "the unjustified incapacity of the disciple to grasp and rely upon Jesus' inexhaustible power."[125] Verseput briefly moves beyond 13:52–16:20 to assert that the disciples do not achieve any kind of final insight, for, even at the end of the gospel, Matthew speaks of their hesitation (28:17; cf. also 17:14–20).

To conclude, almost all of the narrative critics reviewed here speak of the mixed nature of the disciples' portrayal.[126] In addition, they agree upon the disciples' characterization as those of "little faith" (also affirmed by redaction critics).[127] Regarding the understanding of the disciples, none of those narrative critics reviewed asserts that the Matthean disciples can be *characterized* by understanding (i.e., said to understand in any consistent sense). Rather, in some manner, they all speak of the insufficient understanding of the disciples. For Kingsbury, the disciples falter at times in their understanding and are imperceptive to discipleship as servanthood. Howell speaks of the disciples' failure to fully understand the true nature of Jesus' ministry and mission. Verseput emphasizes that the disciples do not understand Jesus' power and

---

[122] Donald J. Verseput, "The Faith of the Reader and the Narrative of Matthew 13:53–16:20," *JSNT* 46 (1992) 5.

[123] Ibid., 15, 19, 20–21. In his discussion of Matt 16:13–20, Verseput concludes that, while the Marcan disciples do not comprehend the *identity* of Jesus (until 8:27–30), the Matthean disciples do not sufficiently comprehend the greatness of his *power* (21).

[124] Ibid., 15, 19, 21.

[125] Ibid., 23.

[126] Edward's "alternating portrayal," Carter's "inconsistency," Howell's "ambiguity," and Kingsbury's "conflicting traits" all point to this mixed portrayal. Only Verseput does not mention this phenomenon. Rather, he emphasizes the negative aspects of their portrayal to illuminate the disciples' function as a foil for the implied reader.

[127] Kingsbury describes this as weak faith, and Edwards speaks of the disciples' inability to meet Jesus' expectations of a high level of faith. For Verseput, faith is closely tied to understanding (i.e., their "little faith" is primarily about their inability to grasp Jesus' authority).

authority. For Edwards, they lack understanding about what it means to be fishers of people. And, according to Carter, the disciples frequently demonstrate a lack of understanding.

Related to the disciples' tendency to misunderstand is the issue of whether they move toward a more complete understanding as the Matthean narrative progresses. For Kingsbury, the disciples have gained full knowledge of Jesus and themselves by the end of the narrative. "[I]n appearing to them as the risen Son of God who remains the crucified Son of God, [Jesus] leads them to comprehend both that death on the cross was the central purpose of his ministry and that servanthood is the essence of discipleship."[128] Edwards frequently asserts that the Matthean disciples make progress toward fulfilling Jesus' expectations (at Matt 13:51–2; 14:22–33; 15:5–23; 17:1–13; 19:23–20:28).[129] In his discussion of the Transfiguration, Edwards summarizes his analysis thus far and states that "[t]he information the [text-connoted reader] gains about the disciples thus resembles information provided in previous incidents. They are seen as far from ideal followers, but they are making progress toward fulfilling Jesus' expectations."[130] Carter speaks of the disciples' "growing under-standing," although he later more cautiously speaks of the disciples making little progress from Matt 14 onward.[131] Howard is also careful to specify how and where he observes a growth in the disciples' understanding, namely, they grow in their understanding of Jesus' identity between Matt 8 and 14. Only Verseput argues that the disciples do not progress *in any way* toward greater faith or understanding. "Matthew's purpose has thus not been to inform the reader of the disciples' progress towards greater faith—indeed, none is evident—but to use their blockishness as a foil to educate the reader in the mighty power of Jesus: in the light of the ἐξουσία present in God's son, 'little faith' such as theirs lacks all reasonable foundation."[132]

---

[128] Kingsbury, *Matthew as Story,* 145. For another summary of the disciples' characterization, cf. 17.

[129] Edwards, *Portrait,* 52, 63, 77, 85, 100.

[130] Ibid., 85. In line with this, Edwards elsewhere asserts that, while Jesus remains static through the narrative, the disciples are characters who undergo change; Richard Edwards, "Reading Matthew: The Gospel as Narrative" *List* 24 (1989) 255–56.

[131] Carter, *Matthew,* 246 and 253–54, respectively. However, in his recent commentary, Carter refers to the disciples' growth in understanding and growth in faith in Matthew 17; Warren Carter, *Matthew and the Margins: A Sociopolitical and Religious Reading,* The Bible and Liberation Series (Maryknoll, NY: Orbis Books, 2000) 353, 355.

[132] Verseput, "Faith of the Reader," 21.

The Function of the Matthean Disciples in Narrative Criticism

There is more variance among narrative perspectives concerning the function of the disciples in Matthew than regarding their portrayal. Since narrative critics have understood the function of the disciples in Matthew in a variety of ways, Syreeni's three-tiered model (the textual world, the concrete world, and the symbolic world) will be used to organize the variety of ways function has been discussed.

First, some narrative critics, in their focus on the disciples' function within the *textual* world of Matthew, delineate the relationship between the disciples and Matthew's implied reader.[133] Kingsbury, in "Reflections on 'The Reader' of Matthew's Gospel," speaks of the inaccuracy of *equating* the disciples (or any character group) with the implied reader.[134] Rather, the implied reader is free to "'draw near' or 'distance' himself...from any given character(s) as signalled by the implied author or narrator."[135]

Howell makes this point a major thesis of his work, and spends considerable space building a case against such an equation. He argues that the implied reader[136] receives more information and is able to observe the interaction among characters more than any character group in Matthew's story. Therefore, the implied reader is ultimately "called to stand with the implied author and Jesus and evaluate all characters, even the disciples, according to the ideological criterion of whether they accept Jesus and his teaching."[137] As a result, in Howell's view, the disciples do *not* function to illuminate the Matthean reader/community. Rather, the disciples function as a teaching tool for the implied reader regarding discipleship (as do the other characters). "The role of

---

[133] Kingsbury defines the implied reader as "that imaginary person in whom the intention of the text is to be thought of as always reaching its fulfillment" (*Matthew as Story,* 38). Because the implied reader is *a construct derived from the text itself,* narrative critics distinguish the implied reader from the gospel's real readers, either modern or ancient (see discussion which follows regarding concrete world for the relationship between the implied reader and Matthew's audience). See chapter 5 for a thorough discussion of the implied reader as understood in this work.

[134] Jack D. Kingsbury, "Reflections on 'The Reader' of Matthew's Gospel," *NTS* 34 (1988) 457.

[135] Ibid., 457–58.

[136] Defined by Howell as the one who is on the receiving end of all the textual strategies used by the implied author, representing the response which the author may have been aiming at for his audience (*Inclusive,* 42).

[137] Howell, *Inclusive,* 234.

the implied reader...[is] to be fully obedient to Jesus in ways in which the disciples have failed."[138]

Verseput, agreeing with Howell that the implied reader and the disciples cannot be equated[139] and that the disciples function to teach the implied reader, goes on to refer explicitly to the function of the disciples as that of a *foil* for the implied reader. The disciples act "as a foil to educate the reader in the mighty power of Jesus."[140] Their incomprehension of the authority and power of Jesus functions to teach the reader the folly of such "little faith" and, in turn, engender greater faith and understanding in the reader.[141]

While these narrative critics spend considerable space addressing the function of the disciples in relation to the implied reader (i.e., their function within the textual world), only two of the narrative critics reviewed speak of the function of the disciples regarding the *concrete* world, and these only in their earlier (transitional) narrative-critical work in more oblique fashion.[142] In fact, given the argument by narrative critics that the Matthean disciples cannot be

---

[138] Howell, *Inclusive*, 247.

[139] Verseput speaks of surrendering the "once fashionable conviction that the disciples in Matthew are 'transparent' for the Matthean community," since, although the implied reader will identify with the disciples, the reader is also "required to evaluate their shortcomings, learn from their mistakes" ("Faith of the Reader," 12; n. 4). Verseput cites Howell in this regard.

[140] Verseput, "Faith of the Reader," 21.

[141] Ibid., 19, 23.

[142] Kingsbury in his earlier narrative work on Matthew does suggest at one point that Matthew's portrayal of the disciples may indicate "that the intended readers were living in close proximity to Jews" (*Matthew as Story*, 154). By this he is referring to Matthew's use of "righteousness greater than that of the scribes and Pharisees" as a description of Christian piety. According to Kingsbury, Matthew may have had the Jew 'next-door' in mind here. This reference to the disciples indicates that Kingsbury understands the disciples as possibly transparent for the Matthean community. If the scribes and Pharisees can be understood as the "Jew next-door" (an application of the method of transparency), then are not the disciples, in this scenario, transparent for the Matthean community? This confirms that, while Kingsbury embraces narrative-critical methodology in his description of the portrayal of the Matthean disciples in *Matthew as Story*, his comments on the function of disciples as well as the function of the narrative in general closely resemble those of redaction criticism. Edwards also suggests at one point that the disciples might be read to illuminate the situation of the implied readers.

"Perhaps his implied readers, like the disciples themselves, have ambivalent attitudes toward Jesus which must be acknowledged as a fact of authentic discipleship" ("Reading Matthew," 258). This also sounds more like redaction criticism's principle of transparency than narrative criticism's implied reader. (Note that Edwards refers to the "implied readers" [plural], rather than the narrative construct of the 'implied reader' [singular]). However, this does not characterize Edwards' more recent work on Matthew (cf. *Portrait*, 8).

equated with the implied reader, it is not surprising that fully developed narrative criticism does not view the disciples as transparent for the Matthean community/first-century readers (or any other extra-textual reality for that matter).[143]

The third major way in which narrative critics address the function of the disciples is related to Matthew's *symbolic* world, specifically, the view of discipleship expressed in Matthew. While each of the narrative critics reviewed here makes this association, there is disagreement among them regarding the exact nature of the relationship between the disciples and Matthew's view of discipleship.

Edwards essentially equates the disciples' portrayal with the definition of Matthean discipleship. "The disciples never live up to Jesus' standards. Given the effect on the reader, discipleship will be viewed as a situation that is never completed, is likely to be in constant flux, and cannot be idealized."[144] Thus, it would seem for Edwards that the function of the disciples is to directly illuminate Matthew's view of discipleship. This is confirmed by Edwards' more recent work in which he concludes with the text-connoted author's perspective on the nature of discipleship based on the disciples' portrayal. "So a disciple... is not an ideal individual who meets Jesus' expectations, but one who recognizes Jesus and who will follow him, in a limited fashion, under most conditions."[145]

Carter also appears at first to equate the characterization of the disciples with Matthean discipleship. "The traits which the audience associates with the disciples form a vision of the identity and lifestyle of the audience's discipleship."[146] This is also confirmed by the title of his chapter on the disciples, "Characters: The Disciples—Prototypes of Believers." Nevertheless, Carter, early in this chapter makes an important distinction between "the disciples as they are [inconsistent], and, in Jesus' teaching, as they should be."[147] And indeed, Carter's chapter conclusion seems to focus on the disciples as they should be (as ideal) rather than on the disciples as portrayed by Matthew. According to Jesus' teaching: (1) disciples live faithfully in transition; (2) disciples live "an alternative existence" in obedience to Jesus;

---

[143] Some narrative critics do address how the implied reader might ultimately illuminate the actual/concrete reader of Matthew (i.e., the Matthean community). This topic will be discussed in more detail in chapter 5.

[144] Edwards, "Uncertain Faith," 52.

[145] Edwards, *Portrait*, 143.

[146] Carter, *Matthew*, 254.

[147] Ibid., 243.

and (3) disciples live "a marginalized, alternative social existence" in mission to mainstream society.[148]

Thus, although Carter seems to understand the function of the disciples to be closely tied to Matthew's view of discipleship, he is inconsistent in his correlation between the portrayal of the disciples and Matthean discipleship. As indicated, he concludes his chapter on disciples by describing three traits of *the* disciples drawn from the 'ideal disciple' of Jesus' teaching rather than from the portrayal of the disciples in Matthew. In his concluding chapter, however, he more closely applies the portrayal of the disciples ("as they are") to his understanding of Matthean discipleship. "Matthew does not present the community of disciples as perfect. Disciples fail and fear. They deny their calling. The gospel recognizes that faithfulness and faithlessness coexist."[149] So, while Carter does not simply equate Matthew's portrait of the disciples with Matthew's view of discipleship, he also does not adequately or consistently clarify the relationship between the two.

Both Kingsbury and Howell understand the portrait of the disciples to be *one part* of the larger education of the implied reader concerning discipleship. Both speak of the implied reader assessing the performance of the disciples (both positively and negatively), thereby adding to his/her view of discipleship. This is, however, only one part of the process of understanding Matthean discipleship, which also includes assessing all other characters and character groups in a similar fashion in terms of their stance toward Jesus.

Specifically, Kingsbury speaks of the disciples informing the reader of the values governing the life of discipleship in Matthew.

> Because the disciples possess conflicting traits, the reader is invited, depending on the attitude Matthew as narrator or Jesus takes toward them on any given occasion, to identify with them or to distance himself or herself from them. It is through such granting or withholding of approval on cue, therefore, that the reader becomes schooled in the values that govern the life of discipleship in Matthew's story.[150]

Similarly, for Howell the disciples function to illuminate certain aspects of Matthean discipleship. The implied reader is called to evaluate the disciples in relation to their acceptance of Jesus and his teaching and to add to his/her view of discipleship accordingly.[151] The implied reader can "learn about discipleship by observing all the characters in the Gospel and the stance they take in

---

[148] Carter, *Matthew*, 254–55.

[149] Ibid., 268. Note that Carter is referring to "disciples" rather than "*the* disciples." He has moved here from the character group to a generalization regarding Matthean discipleship.

[150] Kingsbury, *Matthew as Story*, 14.

[151] Howell, *Inclusive,* 233–34.

relationship to Jesus."[152] Finally, while Verseput does not utilize the term 'discipleship,' he clearly implies that the implied reader will be taught the true way to respond to Jesus by observing the disciples' unjustified misunderstanding of Jesus' power.[153]

In conclusion, regarding the function of the Matthean disciples within narrative criticism, there is substantial agreement concerning their function in relationship to the implied reader, namely, that the two cannot simply be equated. Rather, the implied reader may frequently distance herself from the disciples and their inadequate responses to Jesus. In terms of the disciples' function for the concrete world, most narrative critics (and *all recent* narrative-critical work) disavow (or at least avoid comment upon) any direct link between the disciples and Matthew's community. Finally, there is little consensus regarding the function of the disciples for Matthew's view of discipleship. While some seem to equate the disciples' characterization with Matthean discipleship (Edwards and, at times, Carter), others understand their portrayal to be one part of (and possibly a foil for) Matthew's view of discipleship (Kingsbury, Howell, and Verseput).

ISSUES THAT EMERGE

The Understanding of the Disciples

As has been demonstrated in this literature review, a prevailing view of redaction criticism answers "yes" to the question of whether the disciples understand. With the exception of Trotter, whose work has not impacted the majority viewpoint, redaction critics have affirmed that the disciples basically understand Jesus' teaching, his identity, and his mission. While some may qualify this by affirming that the disciples understand only after being taught by Jesus, this does not significantly alter their basic description of the disciples as those who understand.[154]

---

[152] Howell, *Inclusive,* 217.

[153] In fact, Verseput asserts that "Matthew is more than just a little concerned with the ongoing commitment of faith in the life of the believer"("Faith of the Reader," 23).

[154] Some examples of more recent Matthean scholars who continue to hold to this viewpoint include J. Andrew Overman, *Matthew's Gospel and Formative Judaism: The Social World of the Matthean Community* (Minneapolis: Fortress, 1990) 124–136; Patrick J. Hartin, "Disciples as Authorities within Matthew's Christian –Jewish Community," *Neot* 32 (1998) 389–404; B. Rod Doyle, "Disciples in Matthew: A Challenge for the Church Today," *East Asian Pastoral Review* 29 (1992) 306–29.

This conclusion, however, is problematic for a number of methodological reasons.[155] First, redaction criticism (especially earlier redactional work) has almost exclusively focused on the modifications Matthew has made to his source, tending to ignore what he has retained. For example, Barth can surmise that, since the disciples' question at 13:10 (parallel to Mk 4:10) is no longer asking about the meaning of the parable of the soils (but only about the reason for speaking to the crowds in parables), the Matthean disciples have no *need* of asking Jesus about the meaning of parables in general.[156] Nevertheless, their request at 13:36 for an explanation of another of Jesus' parables argues against this conclusion and shows that Barth is basing his results on what is modified by Matthew and not on what is retained from his sources.[157] This methodological tendency has been shown to be inadequate by more recent redaction criticism. (For example, Wilkins' composition criticism demonstrates the general movement toward viewing what is retained as significant for redaction approaches.)[158]

Second, redaction criticism has primarily focused on Matt 13–17 (where συνιέναι occurs as a descriptor for the disciples). The result has been to ignore chapters 18–20 as relevant to the question of the disciples' understanding. This can be seen in the work of Barth, Luz, and Sheridan, who provide virtually no analysis of Matt 18–20 to support their claims that the disciples understand Jesus' teaching and identity.[159] Yet this section of Matthew highlights the disciples just as consistently as Matt 13–17 and so should not be neglected in a full analysis of their characterization.

---

[155] For, as Trotter has demonstrated, redaction criticism as a method can provide quite different results on this issue.

[156] Barth, "Matthew's Understanding," 105.

[157] Matt 13:36–43 is M material and therefore not as easily analyzed in terms of redactional activity. Nevertheless, 13:36 clearly would *not* fit under the category of Matthew's modifications to his Marcan source (as would 13:10).

[158] Perrin also defines the redaction-critical task more widely, focusing on the Evangelist's theological motivation as seen in part in the modification and *collection* of traditional material, i.e., in what is retained as well as what is changed. (Perrin, *Redaction Criticism*, 1). Cf. also Graham N. Stanton, *A Gospel for a New People: Studies in Matthew* (Louisville: Westminster/John Knox Press, 1992) 41–42.

[159] Gundry, of course, deals with the whole of Matthew in his commentary. However, his analysis of the disciples' portrayal in Matt 18–20 often suffers from an over-idealism derived, it seems, from his conclusion of a thoroughgoing program in Matthew which removes the disciples' misunderstanding; e.g., *Matthew*, 359, 384, 381. Cf. also Zumstein, whose brief survey of the disciples' understanding focuses exclusively on Matt 13–17; Jean Zumstein, *La condition du croyant dans l'Evangile selon Matthieu*, OBO 16 (Göttingen: Vandenhoeck & Ruprecht, 1977) 41–42. Zumstein concludes that the disciples rightly understand "the preaching, destiny, and identity of Christ" (42; my translation).

Finally, closely related to the neglect of certain portions of Matthew in sketching the disciples' portrayal, redaction criticism has tended to tie the issue of the disciples' understanding primarily to the use of the words for understanding (e.g., συνιέναι and νοέω).[160] This focus on individual words rather than on whole narratives/discourses provides a skewed perspective on the portrayal of the disciples, since the assumption that the only relevant material for discerning the understanding of the disciples occurs in passages which use συνιέναι or its synonyms is much too atomistic and does not allow the whole of Matthew's story to speak to this issue.[161] It is in this regard that narrative approaches offer a needed corrective to the way in which redaction criticism has often been carried out in Matthew.

The result of these methodological problems is that many redaction critics attribute a consistency of understanding to the Matthean disciples (e.g., "essentially they understand" or "when taught by Jesus, they understand") that the evidence does not warrant, even the evidence gathered solely from redactional analysis. Trotter, a thoroughgoing redaction critic, obtains results that prove this point. Using a redaction approach which does *not* focus exclusively on Matt 13–17[162] and which examines what is *retained* as well as what is modified by Matthew,[163] Trotter concludes, quite differently than most redaction critics, that the disciples cannot be characterized by understanding.[164]

Narrative critics exhibit a greater degree of agreement concerning this issue, in some way attributing to the disciples a tendency to *misunderstand* Jesus. They also agree in assessing the general portrayal of the disciples as mixed or inconsistent. This fits the evidence more adequately than the prevailing redaction-critical viewpoint already discussed above. However, most of the narrative critics reviewed see some sort of progression in the disciples'

---

[160] This is a major reason why redaction critics typically do not examine this issue in chapters 18–20, since the term συνιέναι does not occur there in regard to the disciples. Even Trotter limits his study of the disciples' understanding primarily to 13–17, since this is where redaction criticism has traditionally focused its energies on the topic ("Understanding," 27).

[161] In addition, the influential work of Barr affirms that meaning adheres not in individual words but in propositions, sentences, and discourses. Cf. James Barr, *The Semantics of Biblical Language* (London: Oxford University Press, 1961).

[162] Trotter primarily examines 13–17 to illuminate the disciples' understanding but also expands his study to texts which talk about the stumbling of the disciples (e.g., 11:16; 24:10), as well as texts which have often been used to prove that the disciples understand across the whole of the gospel (e.g., 19:25; 20:17).

[163] For example, see his discussion of Matt 19:25 (Trotter, "Understanding," 125).

[164] Trotter does focus on individual words, but seems to pay close attention to their context in the narrative.

understanding as the narrative unfolds.[165] As will be shown, this conclusion is not supported by a character analysis of the disciples in 16:21–20:28 in light of their overall portrayal in Matthew.

Inattention to Mt. 16:21–20:28 in the Characterization
of the Disciples' Understanding

As has already been noted, redaction critics have focused primarily on Matt 13–17, while virtually ignoring Matt 18–20 as relevant for the issue of the disciples' understanding. In addition, while narrative critics cannot be said to ignore this section of Matthew, there is a surprising lack of any sustained treatment of the disciples' understanding derived from Matt 18–20 in narrative analyses.[166] That this should be the case, despite Kingsbury's convincing argument for the disciples' prominence beginning at 16:21, is problematic for a complete character analysis of the Matthean disciples.[167] Thus, the centerpiece of this book will be a narrative analysis of 16:21–20:28, focusing on the portrayal of the disciples as they interact with Jesus and his teaching concerning himself and the kingdom of heaven.

Relationship between Faith and Understanding in Matthew

While the characterization of the disciples as those of "little faith" is widely recognized by both redaction and narrative critics, a complete analysis of the ways in which the disciples exhibit and do not exhibit faith in Matthew has yet to be done. In other words, a *narrative* analysis of faith in Matthew (versus merely a word analysis of ὀλιγοπιστία) and how this illuminates the "little faith" of the disciples in still needed to understand more fully the portrayal of the Matthean disciples.

---

[165] See p. 24 of this chapter.

[166] The one exception to this is Carter's extended analysis of Matt 19–20 in *Households*. Nevertheless, this analysis is much less of a narrative analysis than a sociological/comparative analysis of these pericopes in light of first-century Greco-Roman household codes. As a result, Carter speaks little to the issue of the disciples' understanding in this work. In addition, his narrative analysis of Matthew (in *Matthew*) reverts at a number of points to his conclusions from *Households and Discipleship* when he deals with Matt 19–20. This explains, in part, his tendency to distinguish inadequately between the disciples' portrayal and the 'ideal disciple' of Matthean discipleship in this part of *Matthew: Storyteller, Interpreter, Evangelist.*

[167] See chapter 2 for a rationale of 16:21–20:28 as a discreet unit focusing on the disciples in their relationship to Jesus.

In addition, from Barth to the numerous scholars influenced by him, the redaction-critical view that Matthew has removed the noetic element from his concept of faith has become popular and at times assumed. Yet Matthew's supposed removal of the cognitive element from his concept of πίστις does not fit the entirety of the evidence. Thus, the issue of the relationship between faith and understanding in Matthew deserves another look.

The Function of the Disciples: Two Basic Problems

A Lack of Argumentation for Conclusions

In general, many redaction and narrative critics simply assume the validity of their perspective on the disciples' function. For most redaction critics, it is assumed that the disciples function to illuminate the situation of the Matthean church. Specifically, the disciples are transparent for either the church as a whole or its leadership. Nevertheless, this viewpoint is seldom supported by solid argumentation. Instead, it is one of the fundamental assumptions of the redaction-critical method. In fact, the argument is often circular, since the 'fact' that the disciples understand is often used to demonstrate that the disciples stand for the Matthean church, while the 'fact' that they stand for the church is often supported by their understanding! Furthermore, the more basic assumption of this view of transparency is that the disciples (in their portrait as understanding) are to be *identified* with the Matthean community.

Some narrative critics also assume rather than argue for the identification of the disciples' portrayal and their function at some level (even though arriving at a different portrait). For example, Edwards essentially *identifies* the portrayal of the disciples with Matthean discipleship (so that their "alternating portrayal" demonstrates the non-idealized nature of Matthean discipleship). Carter also speaks at times as if the portrayal of the disciples is to be *identified* with Jesus' view of discipleship (i.e., the ideal disciple of Jesus' teaching).[168]

This tendency among both redaction and narrative critics simply to assume that the disciples are to be identified with either a Matthean textual or extra-textual reality demonstrates that there is a need for a thorough and integrative discussion of the function of the disciples. While some narrative critics do argue against such a one-to-one correspondence between the disciples' portrayal and function (thereby demonstrating an awareness of the need to argue their conclusions regarding the disciples' function), there is room for a sustained analysis of the range of viewpoints on this issue as well as a more

---

[168] See pp. 27–28 of this chapter for a more complete summary of Carter's perspective.

complete assessment of the ways in which the disciples function (and do not function) within and outside of the narrative. In particular, there is a need to examine *how* the portrayal of the disciples contributes to Matthew's view of discipleship. That is, how can one take both narrative and discourse texts seriously in developing a complete view of Matthean discipleship?

A Lack of Clarity in Discussion

Related to the lack of argumentation for conclusions regarding the function of the Matthean disciples is a lack of clarity. First, how is the term/concept 'function' being used? Without much clarification, scholars of both methodologies move among various levels related to the disciples' function. This is where Syreeni's three-tiered model has provided clarity where there has been a certain amount of ambiguity. Assessing the function of the disciples in the *textual world* of Matthew, some redaction critics assert that the disciples' understanding functions to highlight Jesus as a successful teacher. Also related to the *textual world*, some narrative critics speak of the effect or function of the disciples upon the implied reader. Related to the *concrete world*, redaction critics typically affirm a situation outside of the text that is illuminated by the disciples (while narrative critics are much more hesitant in this area).

Finally, both redaction and narrative critics affirm the function of the disciples in relation to Matthew's *symbolic world*, specifically, his view of discipleship. The particular relationship between the disciples and Matthean discipleship, however, is not at all agreed upon. There are in fact numerous questions to explore in this final area of the disciples' function. For example, how do the disciples as a character group relate to *other "disciples"* in Matthew (individuals who follow Jesus or exhibit characteristics of disciples as defined by Jesus in his teaching)? How do the disciples as a character group relate to *Jesus' teaching* about disciples and discipleship? Finally, how do the disciples as a character group relate to *the Matthean view of discipleship* in general, and how might Matthean discipleship be defined in a way that integrates both the narrative and discourse sections of the gospel? Clarification of these issues is essential for a complete and adequate discussion of Matthean discipleship and the function of the Matthean disciples in general.

TASK, METHOD, AND THESIS

The *task* of this work is to examine the portrayal of the disciples in Matthew. After briefly defining the disciples as character group, discussing Peter's relationship to this character group, and arguing for 16:21–20:28 as a discreet unit which focuses on the relationship between Jesus and the disciples, a narrative analysis of 16:21–20:28 will be done. It will focus primarily on the characterization of the disciples in regard to their understanding. Then an attempt will be made to integrate these results with their broader characterization across the entire story of Matthew. Finally, the implications of their characterization for an understanding of the function of the disciples in Matthew will be discussed.

The *method* employed in this study will be narrative criticism and specifically the analysis of characterization.[169] Narrative criticism has been variously described and practiced. However, a centerpiece of much narrative-critical work is the distinction between story and discourse.[170] The story is focused on the events, characters, and setting of the narrative, the interaction of which can be referred to as the plot of the story.[171] The discourse (or the narrative's rhetoric) is the means by which the story is told. Factors in a narrative's discourse include point of view, narration, plottedness/time, and stylistics. For example, a single story can be told from numerous points of view, significantly affecting the meaning of the narrative. In addition, various poetic devices (stylistics) might be used to enhance the story (e.g., the repetition of fulfillment quotations in Matthew). These factors intermingle as the implied author communicates via the whole of the narrative (story joined to discourse) with the implied reader.[172] These last two terms require particular definition,

---

[169] The method used to analyze characterization will be discussed in chapter 2.

[170] Numerous biblical scholars rely on Seymour Chatman's description of these two aspects of narrative for doing narrative criticism. Cf. Chatman's *Story and Discourse: Narrative Structure in Fiction and Film* (Ithaca, N.Y.: Cornell University Press, 1978), as well as usage of this model for gospel studies in Kingsbury (*Matthew as Story*, 1988); David M. Rhoads and Donald Michie, *Mark as Story: An Introduction to the Narrative of Gospel* (Philadelphia: Fortress Press, 1982); and Mark Allan Powell, *What is Narrative Criticism?* GBS (Minneapolis: Fortress Press, 1990).

[171] Mark Allan Powell, "The Bible and Modern Literary Criticism: A Critical Assessment," in *The Bible and Modern Literary Criticism: A Critical Assessment and Annotated Bibliography* (New York: Greenwood Press, 1992) 9.

[172] In terms of this study, the portrayal of the disciples is an aspect of the story of Matthew (relating to one of the character groups of the story), while the function of the disciples is an aspect of Matthew's discourse, especially as it relates to the effect of the disciples on Matthew's implied reader. Nevertheless, Moore has rightly warned against artificially separating these two aspects of narrative, since there is no unmediated story, only "discoursed" story (or as Moore puts it discourse + discourse, rather than story + discourse). Cf. Stephen Moore, *Literary Criticism and the Gospels: The Theoretical Challenge* (New Haven: Yale University Press, 1989) 62–68. Thus, while it may be helpful for analytical reasons to separate issues of portrayal and function, one must realize that characterization itself is a discourse-level activity.

since, while integral to narrative criticism, they are frequently and understandably misconstrued.

The implied author is the author that can be known through the reading of the narrative alone. The implied author is thus distinct from the real author of Matthew, i.e. the historical figure who wrote the first gospel. While questions concerning the real author might draw upon early church tradition and source material for indication of the author's identity, time of writing, the nature of his community, etc., questions about the implied author might instead focus on his vantage point in narrating the gospel (e.g., his omniscience in terms of the events of the story) or his viewpoint regarding true discipleship.[173] The implied author is the one who tells the story using various narrative devices to communicate with and persuade the implied reader.

The definition of the implied reader used in this study will be more fully discussed in chapter 5. Nevertheless, a working definition will be introduced at this point, namely, the implied reader as the reader presupposed by the narrative.[174] Important to this definition is the implied reader as a *textual construct* (versus a construct created by actual readers), which can be derived from the narrative itself.[175] Thus, this definition affirms that the text itself provides the boundaries for its own reading. More specifically, Kingsbury defines the implied reader as "that imaginary person in whom the intention of the text is to be thought of as always reaching its fulfillment."[176]

The *thesis* of this work is that, although they confess Jesus to be Messiah and understand certain aspects of his teaching, the disciples in Matthew consistently *misunderstand* Jesus' mission (and therefore their own as well) and his message of the kingdom (and consequently their place in it). In 16:21–20:28 specifically, the disciples are inappropriately preoccupied with their own status within the coming kingdom in contrast to Jesus' teaching on the nature of true discipleship. In addition, the disciples are characterized by "little faith" in regard to Jesus' ability to act in concert with his true identity; and they do not progress in their faith and understanding in any significant way as the narrative moves toward its climax.

---

[173] Kingsbury and others convincingly argue that the further distinction between implied author and narrator is not necessary in the biblical narratives, in which the narrator is reliable and therefore can be equated with the implied author; e.g., Kingsbury, *Matthew as Story,* 31–33.

[174] This is the definition used by Powell. Cf. Mark Allan Powell, "Expected and Unexpected Readings of Matthew: What the Reader Knows," *AsTJ* 48 (1993) 32.

[175] This is also true for the implied author described above.

[176] Kingsbury, *Matthew as Story,* 38. Note that Kingsbury's definition is also a textually-based one.

With this characterization in mind, the disciples do *not* function as transparent for the Matthean community, since their lack of understanding and "little faith" cannot be demonstrated to refer to any extra-textual group, and their less than ideal portrayal does not engender complete identification with them by the Matthean audience/reader. The characterization of the disciples as those who misunderstand and have "little faith" does not support their function as the index of Matthean discipleship either. Rather, the disciples function to illuminate aspects of Matthean discipleship by providing at times a negative example of (a foil to) discipleship for the reader. In addition, the portrayal of the disciples (in both their positive and negative qualities) functions as just one part of the larger composite of Matthean discipleship, which includes Matthew's use of other characters as examples of discipleship and Jesus himself as a model for it.

CHAPTER 2

INTRODUCTION TO THE PORTRAYAL
OF THE DISCIPLES IN 16:21–20:28

"THE DISCIPLES" IN MATTHEW

The disciples in Matthew will be defined in this work as the character group that consists of the twelve men who are disciples of Jesus in Matthew's narrative (see name list in 10:2–4). The reason for the identification of the disciples with the twelve is Matthew's consistent representation of these twelve men as "the disciples" (οἱ μαθηταί). As Wilkins notes, "Matthew has basically intended μαθητής to be linked with οἱ δώδεκα."[1] At a number of points, the term "twelve disciples" is used to indicate this (10:1; 11:1; 20:17; and 26:20[2]). At other points, the word "twelve" is used as an independent appellation for this

---

[1] Michael J. Wilkins, *The Concept of Disciple in Matthew's Gospel*, NovTSup 59 (Leiden: E. J. Brill, 1988) 171. Wilkins also speaks of the close identification of the term "disciple" with the title "the twelve" in "Named and Unnamed Disciples in Matthew: A Literary/Theological Study," in *1991 SBLSP* (Atlanta: Scholars Press, 1991) 421. Luz states that "if Matthew can omit Mark's *dōdeka* in replacing it with *mathētai*, this shows not that the number of the disciples being twelve was important to him, but that he took it for granted;" Ulrich Luz, "The Disciples in the Gospel according to Matthew," in *The Interpretation of Matthew*, ed. Graham Stanton, 2d ed. (Edinburgh: T&T Clark, 1995) 116. Contra Freyne, who argues for a different group referent for "the disciples" and "the twelve" at 9:37–10:1 and allows for the possibility elsewhere in Matthew; Sean Freyne, *The Twelve: Disciples and Apostles: A Study in the Theology of the First Three Gospels* (London: Sheed and Ward, 1968) 186.

[2] In the latter two examples, there is some textual uncertainty about the inclusion of "disciples" in addition to the "twelve."

same group (10:5; 26:14, 47). Finally, at 19:28 it is clear "the disciples" that have been mentioned throughout the chapter are the twelve, since Jesus refers to them judging Israel from twelve thrones.

In contrast, when an indefinite disciple (μαθητής without the article) is mentioned in the text, it is always in the context of Jesus' teaching about discipleship in general rather than a specific reference to this twelve-member group (10:24 with 10:25; 10:42; see also 13:52 for the verbal cognate, μαθητητεύθεις).[3] The single use of μαθητής that may refer to specific members of Jesus' disciples outside of the twelve occurs at 8:21.[4] In 8:18–22, a scribe comes to Jesus and expresses a desire to follow Jesus. Shortly thereafter, "another of the disciples" expresses a similar desire but with a qualification to be allowed to bury his father. Given that this text precedes the formal introduction of the "twelve disciples" at 10:1 and that there is no attempt by Matthew to connect either of these characters with the twelve, it would seem best to view these disciples (or potential disciples[5]) as outside of the character group, disciples. In other words, "the disciples" in Matthew refers specifically to the character group that consists of the twelve disciples of Jesus.

This character group should then be distinguished from the *ideal disciple* projected in Jesus' discipleship teaching throughout Matthew.[6] Who the disciples as a character group show themselves *to be* in the narrative might be quite different from what all disciples *should be* according to Jesus. Thus, whether Jesus uses the term "disciple" in his teaching at a particular point, he is often describing his expectations for his disciples both generically, as well as for the character group specifically (e.g., 16:24–27, where the term "disciple" is not used but where the requirements of following Jesus are described).[7]

---

[3] The reference at 27:57 to Joseph of Arimathea as one who had become a disciple of Jesus involves the cognate of μαθητής (μαθητεύω) rather than the noun that occurs wherever the disciples as character group are indicated.

[4] This is the only occurrence of μαθητής in Matthew (8:21) as a definite noun that infers anything other than a direct correspondence between the character group of the disciples and Jesus' twelve disciples or representatives thereof (out of 66 occurrences).

[5] Kingsbury's interpretation of the passage points to the first as a "would-be disciple" and the second as a true, though reluctant, disciple; in Jack D. Kingsbury, "On Following Jesus: The 'Eager' Scribe and the 'Reluctant' Disciple (Matthew 8:18–22)," *NTS* 34 (1988) 45–59. Gundry's interpretation understands the first to be a true disciple and the second to be a false one; in Robert H. Gundry, "On True and False Disciples in Matthew 8:18–22," *NTS* 40 (1994) 433–41.

[6] Daniel Patte helpfully distinguishes between "actual disciples" and "ideal disciples" in this regard in *The Gospel according to Matthew: A Structural Commentary on Matthew's Faith* (Philadelphia: Fortress Press, 1987) 119 and related endnote (136, n.16).

[7] An apparent problem with Carter's construction of Matthean discipleship is his tendency to intertwine discussion of the disciples as character group and Jesus' teaching on discipleship (an "ideal" disciple). While distinguishing between the characterization of the

This character group should also be distinguished from numerous *disciple-type characters* in Matthew's gospel. That is to say, there are a number of characters in Matthew that exhibit qualities of discipleship as defined by Jesus elsewhere. For example, the centurion who requests healing for his servant (8:5–13) exhibits greater faith than any Jew Jesus has yet encountered. The same is true of the Canaanite woman whom Jesus describes as having great faith at 15:28 (and see Jesus' teaching on the importance of faith at 17:20 and 21:21–22).[8] These characters appear only briefly in the narrative and are not included in the *character group* of the disciples. Nevertheless, they often are more exemplary "disciples" than the specific character group known as "the disciples." In fact, these disciple-type characters play an important role in the formation of Matthew's concept of discipleship.[9]

Therefore, the disciples are the character group that consists of the twelve men who follow Jesus throughout his earthly ministry in Matthew's narrative. According to Kingsbury, this group "may be treated as a single character."[10] This means that they exhibit identifiable characteristics as a group in the story. This also means that one or more of these disciples can function as representative for the entire character group.[11] For example, in Gethsemane

---

disciples and Jesus' instruction about disciples in 16:21–20:34 in his analysis of the disciples' portrayal, Carter's final summary paragraph draws no distinction between the two; Warren Carter, *Matthew: Storyteller, Interpreter, Evangelist* (Peabody, MA: Hendrickson, 1996) 254–55. (Cf. my discussion on pp. 27–28.)

[8] I would also place Joseph of Arimathea in this category, since he is not referred to as one of the μαθηταί but is described as one who had become a disciple (ἐμαθητεύθη) of Jesus (27:57). In addition, Joseph is clearly shown to be distinct from the character group of the disciples, who are conspicuously absent from the crucifixion and burial scenes but are reintroduced explicitly as "the eleven disciples" at 20:16. Wilkins confirms this delineation as well ("Named and Unnamed Disciples," 435).

[9] See chapter 5 for further discussion of this important issue. The numerous women who follow Jesus and appear briefly but significantly at various points in the narrative are part of this larger group of "disciple-types." See Wainwright's discussion of the relationship between the twelve disciples as a group and the women who are faithful to Jesus' vision of discipleship in Elaine Mary Wainwright, *Towards a Feminist Critical Reading of the Gospel according to Matthew* (New York: Walter de Gruyter, 1991) 330–39.

[10] Jack D. Kingsbury, *Matthew as Story*, 2d ed. (Philadelphia: Fortress Press, 1988) 13. Donaldson also notes that "the disciples…appear in the great majority of instances as an undifferentiated group;" in Terence L. Donaldson, "Guiding Readers—Making Disciples: Discipleship in Matthew's Narrative Strategy," in *Patterns of Discipleship in the New Testament*, ed. R. Longenecker (Grand Rapids: Eerdmans, 1996) 32.

[11] For Syreeni, the four disciples at 4:18–22 are given a representative role for the larger group of disciples (see 5:1). See Kari Syreeni, "Peter as Character and Symbol in the Gospel of Matthew," in *Characterization in the Gospel: Reconceiving Narrative Criticism*, ed. David Rhoads and Kari Syreeni, JSNTSup 184 (Sheffield: Sheffield Academic Press, 1999) 122.

three of the eleven disciples (Peter and the two sons of Zebedee) go with Jesus to pray while the rest of the group remains together (26:36–46). Yet when Jesus returns to find "the disciples" sleeping, he admonishes Peter specifically for sleeping (although using the plural pronoun). This would seem to infer that the designation "the disciples" at 26:40 refers to the subgroup of three. But when Jesus returns for a third time to find "the disciples" sleeping, he tells them to rise and go with him to his betrayal (26:46). At this final moment, it seems that the whole of the disciple group is in view. This intertwining of referents for the term "the disciples" argues for a uniform characterization of the disciples and any particular individual or group from among them who represents the larger group.[12]

In addition, Peter specifically functions as a representative of the character group of the disciples. Given the frequent reference to Peter in Matthew's gospel, it is a fair question whether Peter should be understood primarily as representative of the disciples or as a unique character in his own right. In fact, Peter's role in the gospel has been dealt with extensively in Matthean scholarship.[13] There are two significant reasons for viewing Peter as basically a representative of the disciples.

First, Peter's characterization parallels that of the disciples as a character group. In other words, the disciples are consistently given the same characteristics as Peter by Matthew. For example, Peter individually (14:31) and the disciples in general (8:26; 16:8; cf. 17:20) are portrayed as those of "little faith" ($\dot{o}\lambda\iota\gamma\acute{o}\pi\iota\sigma\tau\sigma\varsigma$). There is no indication by Matthew that Peter is to be understood differently in this regard than the disciples. In fact, commentators typically list the reference to Peter's "little faith" at 14:31 in their discussion of the *disciples'* characterization as those of "little faith."[14] Other examples of this parallel characterization include the portrayal of the disciples as fearful (at 14:26 with Peter described so at 14:30) and their portrayal as misunderstanding

---

[12] For another example of this intertwining of references to the disciples as a whole and as a representative sub-group, see 17:1–13, especially 9–13.

[13] For a brief and helpful overview of the issue from a historical-critical perspective, see William D. Davies and Dale C. Allison, *A Critical and Exegetical Commentary on the Gospel according to St. Matthew*, ICC (Edinburgh: T&T Clark, 1988–97) 2:647–52. Narrative readings of Matthew do not typically argue for Peter's representational role but instead assume it. For example, Howell understands "Peter's difficulty in accepting the way of suffering" as typifying the conflict between Jesus and his disciples; David B. Howell, *Matthew's Inclusive Story: A Study in the Narrative Rhetoric of the First Gospel*, JSNTSup 42 (Sheffield: JSOT Press, 1990) 145–46.

[14] E.g., Luz, "Disciples," 119; Joachim Gnilka, *Das Matthäusevangelium*, HTKNT (Freiburg: Herder, 1986) 2:108.

the true nature of discipleship (at 18:1 with Peter portrayed similarly at 18:21).[15] "Almost everything that is said of Peter is elsewhere said of the disciples."[16] An exception may be Peter's portrayal as impulsive at a number of points in the narrative, which seems less characteristic of the disciples in general (e.g., 14:28–30; 17:4, 24–25).

Second, Peter asks questions in which any or all of the disciples would share an interest (e.g., 17:24–27; 18:21–22; 19:27–29; also the statement at 15:15).[17] This is quite clearly demonstrated at 19:27–29 where Jesus answers *Peter's* question by addressing *all the disciples* (ὁ δὲ Ἰησοῦς εἶπεν αὐτοῖς—"and Jesus said to them"). In this way, Peter is a kind of spokesperson for the disciples. "Peter is predominantly a type who represents the characteristics of the disciples as a group...evident primarily in Peter's role as spokesperson for the group."[18] This is not to deny that Peter is highlighted at numerous points in Matthew (especially in 13:53–19:30[19]) and that he is one of Jesus' closest companions in the story. Rather, the argument is that Peter functions primarily as representative for the disciples as a whole, and, as such, the reader is encouraged to assign the characteristics given to Peter to the disciples in general.[20]

RATIONALE FOR ANALYZING THE DISCIPLES' PORTRAYAL IN 16:21–20:28

Although I have demonstrated in chapter 1 that Matt 13–17 has received much more attention than Matt 18–20 regarding the disciples' portrayal in redaction and even narrative studies, it is still necessary to defend the delimitation of this particular section for a narrative analysis of the disciples.

---

[15] The latter, indirect characterization will be the primary focus of the narrative reading in the following chapter.

[16] Wilkins, *Concept of Disciple*, 215.

[17] Eduard Schweizer, "Matthew's Church," in *The Interpretation of Matthew*, ed. Graham Stanton, 2d ed. (Edinburgh: T&T Clark, 1995) 156.

[18] Fred W. Burnett, "Characterization and Reader Construction," in *Semeia* (1993) 20. Burnett does argue, however, that Peter moves beyond a representative role in the denial scene, since the extensive focus on his denial is not necessary for Matthew's plot (cf. "Characterization," 20–23). Kingsbury [Jack Dean Kingsbury, "The Figure of Peter in Matthew's Gospel as a Theological Problem," *JBL* 98 (1979) 74]; Carter (*Matthew*, 249); Powell [Mark Allan Powell, "The Plot and Subplots of Matthew's Gospel," *New Testament Studies* 38 (1992) 203]; Wilkins (*Concept of Disciple*, 212); and Anderson [Janice Capel Anderson, *Matthew's Narrative Web: Over, and Over, and Over Again*, JSNTSup 91 (Sheffield: JSOT Press, 1994) 92–93] also speak of Peter as the disciples' spokesperson.

[19] Davies and Allison (*Matthew*, 2:649) speak of Peter's prominence as a function of ecclesiology given its concentration in 13:53–17:27.

[20] "[A]lthough given personal function, [Peter] still basically represents the others" (Wilkins, *Concept of Disciple*, 210).

This will involve defending my reasons both for viewing 16:21–20:28 as a discreet unit within the Matthean narrative as well as for analyzing this section as an important source of information concerning the disciples' characterization.

Much debate has gone on related to the structure of Matthew's gospel. Most recent commentators favor viewing one of two structural indicators as defining the overall movement of the gospel.[21] Following the lead of Bacon, some commentators, including Hagner and Davies/Allison, emphasize the alternation between narrative and discourse, signaled by the five-fold repeated formula (7:28; 11:1; 13:53; 19:1; and 26:1) at the end of Matthew's five major discourses, as the primary structural indicator. Others, such as Kingsbury and Bauer, emphasize the importance of the structural marker at 4:17 and 16:21 for dividing the narrative into three major sections.[22]

The latter viewpoint is more convincing for a number of reasons. First, as Kingsbury has pointed out, the three-fold division (1:1–4:16; 4:17–16:20; 16:21–28:20) affirms the basic narrative quality of Matthew.[23] While containing much more teaching material than Mark, Matthew remains essentially a narrative and the repeated formula at 4:17 and 16:21 emphasizes Matthew's *story* of Jesus ("From that time, Jesus began to preach/show..."). This does not mean that the inclusion of blocks of teaching signaled by the five-fold formula is unimportant structurally. It simply means that greater emphasis should be placed upon the formula that signals the major shifts in Matthew's *plot*. This fits the overall movement in Matthew from Jesus' proclamation to Israel to his narrowed focus on the disciples to the events of his passion and resurrection.

Second, there does not seem to be enough warrant from Matthew's literary context to understand his structure *primarily* in terms of a narrative-discourse alternation pattern. As Bauer points out, Matthean narrative and discourse cannot be sharply distinguished at all points, since there is discourse material in sections typically identified as narrative and narrative elements within the great

---

[21] Some exegetes have identified chiastic or geographic indicators of Matthew's overall structure, but these proposals have been less than convincing to most recent commentators.

[22] To some extent, Gnilka and Luz fit here as well. Gnilka sees major breaks in the narrative at 4:17 and 16:21 but also at 26:1 (*Matthäus*, 2:423–24). Luz understands a major break to occur at 16:21 but divides the earlier part of the gospel after 4:22 (instead of 4:17) as well as after 11:30. Gundry is more cautious about imposing a simple three-part outline upon Matthew because of the presence of the five-fold formulae as well as themes that permeate all sections of the gospel. In the end, he concludes that Matthew is "structurally mixed;" Robert H. Gundry, *Matthew: A Commentary on His Handbook for a Mixed Church under Persecution*, 2d ed. (Grand Rapids: Eerdmans, 1994) 11.

[23] Kingsbury, *Matthew as Story*, 40.

discourses.[24] In fact, an important narrative device in 16:21–20:28, the use of questions posed to Jesus, also characterizes the fourth Matthean discourse lying within this larger narrative section (cf. 18:1, 21). In addition, although the five-fold formula would seem to indicate the presence of five major teaching blocks in Matthew, there is still some question as to the exact number of discourses. Gnilka, for example, identifies six discourses in Matthew (with chapter 23 distinct from 24–25).[25]

Finally, as Bauer helpfully points out, the five-fold formula is transitional rather than concluding in nature. In each case, the formula itself clearly connects the preceding discourse with what follows.[26] In addition, the often seamless way in which the discourses emerge from their antecedent narrative (i.e., the lack of a clear starting point for the discourses) demonstrates a close connection with what has preceded. This is certainly the case in the section under discussion, 16:21–20:28. The fourth Matthean discourse (18:1–35) begins with a distinctly narrative question posed by the disciples to Jesus, blurring the exact beginning point of the discourse proper.[27] As in the surrounding context, Peter continues to be a spokesperson for the disciples in chapter 18. In addition, numerous major and minor themes of the narrative in 16:21–20:28 run through chapter 18. The identification of true discipleship with denial/servanthood/humility (16:24; 18:4; 20:26), the stumbling block theme (16:23; 17:27; 18:5, 7), the presence of kingdom parables (18:23; 20:1), and the unexpected teaching of Jesus regarding status within the kingdom (18:1–5; 19:13–15; 19:24–25; 19:30; 20:16, 25–27) can be seen in the discourse of chapter 18 as well as in the material surrounding it.

While the five-fold formula is transitional, the two-fold formula at 4:17 and 16:21 is a summary statement and thus the more important structural marker. In

---

[24] David R. Bauer, *The Structure of Matthew's Gospel: A Study in Literary Design*, JSNTSup 31 (Sheffield: Almond Press, 1988) 131.

[25] Gnilka, *Matthäus*, 2:269. While acknowledging the close connection between chapters 23 and 24–25, Gnilka argues (*Matthäus*, 2:309) for distinguishing them as two discourses given their distinct opening scenes as well as their different circles of address (23 to the crowds and disciples; 24–25 to the disciples privately).

[26] Bauer notes that the subordinate clause in the formula ("and when Jesus had finished these [words]") points back to the discourse material, while the main clause (subject + verb, etc.) points ahead to what follows (*Structure*, 129).

[27] Thompson argues for 17:24–18:35 as a distinct section of Matthew in William G. Thompson, *Matthew's Advice to a Divided Community: Matthew 17:22–18:35* (Rome: Biblical Institute Press, 1970) 25, 251. So also David Garland, *Reading Matthew: A Literary and Theological Commentary on the First Gospel* (New York: Crossroad, 1993) 186; and Kingsbury, *Matthew as Story*, 109. To give another example, commentators disagree over the starting point of the missionary discourse, citing anywhere from 9:35–10:5 as its beginning (Bauer, *Structure,* 129–30).

each occurrence, the formula summarizes the narrative that follows. 4:17 encapsulates 4:17–16:20 by introducing the proclamation of Jesus; and 16:21 summarizes 16:21–28:20 by introducing the theme of the passion of Jesus as well as the more immediate discipleship focus of 16:21–20:28. In the same vein, according to Kingsbury, 1:1 functions as a superscription for 1:1–4:16, in that it introduces and summarizes the first section of Matthew, focusing on the identity of Jesus.[28]

If 16:21 is a key turning point in the gospel, after which Jesus focuses on demonstrating to his disciples the nature of his role as Messiah, how is this section best subdivided? Kingsbury speaks of 16:21–20:34 as a unit that focuses on Jesus' journey to Jerusalem, emphasized in his three passion predictions (two of which mention Jerusalem specifically). "[T]he entire section of 16:21–20:34... is to be understood as part and parcel of Jesus' 'journey to Jerusalem.'"[29] In addition, this section is tied together by its consistent emphasis on Jesus' teaching of his disciples.

While many understand this section to end at 20:34,[30] I argue that it is better to delimit the section as 16:21–20:28.[31] First, the unifying plot-focus on Jesus teaching and interacting with his disciples ends at 20:28. The disciples are not mentioned in 20:29–34 (the healing of the two blind men). This is the first pericope that does not in some way draw in one or more of the disciples since 16:21.[32]

---

[28] Jack D. Kingsbury, *Matthew: Structure, Christology, Kingdom* (Philadelphia: Fortress, 1975) 9–11.

[29] Kingsbury, *Matthew as Story*, 78, cf. also 106. Others who understand 16:21–20:34 to be a distinct section in this part of Matthew include Carter, *Matthew*, 167; and Howell, *Inclusive*, 145. Bauer expands upon the recurrence of "Jerusalem" (at 16:21; 20:17–19) to speak of a geographical framework for 16:21–20:34 (17:22; 17:24; 19:1; 20:29) that is closely related to the passion predictions (*Structure*, 97).

[30] All those mentioned in the previous footnote, for example.

[31] Davies and Allison argue that 20:28 (rather than 20:34) completes the section beginning at 19:1, with the entire section focusing on the overturning of traditional values. In contrast, in 20:29–21:23... "we leave behind the eschatological sage with his commands for Christian behavior and meet instead the kingly Son of David who shows Jerusalem his prophetic *exousia*" (*Matthew*, 3:1–2). Verseput, tying 20:29–34 closely with 21:1–11, speaks of the "narrative unit effectively begin[ning] already in 20:29–34;" Donald Verseput, "The Davidic Messiah and Matthew's Jewish Christianity," SBLSP (1995) 113. Cf. also Grundmann's understanding of a major division between 20:28 and 20:29; Walter Grundmann, *Das Evangelium nach Matthäus*, THKNT I (Berlin: Evangelische Verlagsanstalt, 1968) 445–46.

[32] Rather, the crowds again become more significant in the storyline in 20:29–34 and the following chapters. Their appearance in 16:21–20:28 is limited to 17:14 and 19:2, while references to the crowds in the following section are numerous (e.g., 21:8, 9, 11, 46; 22:33; 23:1).

Second, I would argue that 20:28 brings together a number of key themes throughout 16:21–20:28, functioning as climactic in some ways to the entire section. The final pericope (20:20–28) provides a particularly clear example of the clash between the disciples' understanding of their role in the kingdom and Jesus' ideological stance (they essentially quarrel over their priority seating in the coming kingdom). Matt 20:20–28 also reintroduces the explicit reference to kingdom greatness first introduced at 18:1–5 but explored throughout chapters 18–20. In addition, the "references in 16:21–20:34 to the approaching death and resurrection of Jesus reach their *high point* in the declaration Jesus makes just before entering Jerusalem regarding the purpose of his coming: to give his life as a ransom for many (20:28)" (emphasis mine).[33]

Third, Luz has rightly acknowledged that 20:29–34 is transitional[34] and thus could be understood without difficulty to be a part of what follows. The repeated phrase "Son of David" (at 20:30, 31 and at 21:9) ties 20:29–34 rather closely with 21:1–11. Finally, the common argument that the shift between major sections occurs at 21:1 because Jesus here begins his time in Jerusalem does not actually support breaking the narrative at 21:1, since Jesus only enters Jerusalem officially at 21:10–11.[35] No commentator, however, has proposed dividing the narrative between 21:9 and 21:10. To sum up, 20:29–34 is best understood as beginning a new section of Matthew that turns the reader's attention to Jesus' approach to and final days in Jerusalem, while 20:20–28 completes the previous section beginning at 16:21.

In addition to being a discreet unit within the overall structure of the gospel, 16:21–20:28 is also an important source for Matthew's characterization of the disciples.[36] Not only are the disciples narratively present with Jesus throughout this section,[37] they are almost always Jesus' *primary* dialogue partners. In fact,

---

[33] Bauer, *Structure*, 98.

[34] Ulrich Luz, *Das Evangelium nach Matthäus*, EKKNT (Zurich: Benziger/ Neukirchener, 1985–1997) 3:167.

[35] Bauer rightly notes that Jesus reaches "the environs of Jerusalem in 21.1 and Jerusalem itself in 21.10" (*Structure*, 97).

[36] "Disciple instructions and disciple stories" ("*Jüngerunterweisungen und Jünger-geschichten*") dominate this section, according to Luz, *Matthäus*, 2:484; cf. also Wainwright, *Feminist Reading*, 119. A redaction-critical reading of this section of Matthew confirms this theme. Matthew has added to Mark, for example, the pericope on Peter's interaction with Jesus concerning the temple tax as well as the extension of the divorce controversy, which places the emphasis of the entire passage (19:1–12) upon the interaction between Jesus and the disciples. Note also the disciple-oriented addition at 18:22–23 as well as the frequent addition of the term οἱ μαθηταί at 16:21; 17:6, 10; 18:1; 19:25; 20:17 to the Marcan source material.

[37] Either as a whole group or by representation. Weaver affirms this to be the case for 16:21 through Jesus' entry into Jerusalem; in Dorothy Jean Weaver, *Matthew's Missionary*

characteristic of this section are the 'debriefing moments' that Jesus has with his disciples at the climax of many of the individual narrative units. Even those sections that focus initially on Jesus' interaction with non-disciples typically end with a 'debriefing moment.' For example, Jesus' only interaction with the Jewish authorities (in this case, the Pharisees) in 16:21–20:28 moves from a controversy with them on divorce to a concluding teaching with his disciples (19:1–9, 10–12).[38] This is also the case at 17:14–20 (with debriefing occurring at 17:19–20) and 19:16–26 (with debriefing occurring at 19:23–26).

My subdivision of 16:21–20:28 is based on this observation regarding the prominence of the interaction between Jesus and the disciples. In many cases, I have delimited sections that are larger than those typically defined in form and redactional approaches. In doing so, I have tried to attend to the narrative and thematic connections that tie these larger sections together. The debriefing between Jesus and the disciples in what some have labeled separate accounts, I typically understand as climactic to the preceding narratives (see asterisk-marked sections below). In addition, I have assigned a significant role to the disciples' questions which punctuate the narrative of 16:21–20:28. My divisions often begin with a question (or implied question; see 17:24 and 20:20) raised by the disciples and then answered by Jesus (see double asterisk-marked sections below).[39]

16:21–28	First Passion Prediction and Peter's Response/Jesus' Teaching
17:1–13	The Transfiguration and Debriefing on Elijah*
17:14–20	Exorcism and Debriefing on Faith
17:22–23	Second Passion Prediction and Disciples Response
17:24–27	Jesus Teaches Peter about Freedom/Stumbling**
18:1–20	Jesus Teaches the Disciples about Stumbling and Restoration of Little Ones**
18:21–35	Jesus Teaches Peter about Forgiveness**
19:1–12	Controversy on Divorce and Debriefing on Celibacy*
19:13–15	Jesus Teaches Disciples about Children and Status

Discourse: A Literary Critical Analysis, JSNTSup 38 (Sheffield: JSOT Press, 1990) 140. For example, Peter, James, and John are present at the transfiguration, representing the character group of the disciples. In addition, Peter frequently acts as a representative of the disciples throughout this section (cf. 17:24–27; 18:21–35; 19:27–30). See previous section of this chapter for a defense of Peter as representative of the disciples.

[38] This is confirmed in Jack D. Kingsbury, "The Plot of Matthew's Story," *Int* 46 (1992) 353.

[39] In other cases, the disciples' question provides the transition from interaction between Jesus and other characters to the central interaction between Jesus and the disciples (e.g., 17:19; cf. also their statement at 19:10).

19:16–26	The Rich Man and Jesus with Debriefing on Salvation*
19:27–20:16	Jesus Teaches on Reward and Status**
20:17–19	Third Passion Prediction
20:20–28	Jesus Teaches on and Status and Servanthood**

Given the consistent highlighting of their interaction throughout 16:21–20:28, it is clear that the subplot between Jesus and the disciples comes to the forefront in this section of Matthew.[40] Thus, an examination of 16:21–20:28 should significantly enhance a full character analysis of the Matthean disciples.

CHARACTERIZATION METHODOLOGY

Before undertaking a narrative reading of the disciples and their portrayal in Matthew 16:21–20:28, it is essential to clarify my perspective on characterization in the Gospels. What follows is a brief description of characterization theory and method as applied to the Gospels as well as the delineation of the method of character analysis that I will be using in chapter 3.

Character Theory

The tendency of characterization theory applied to the Gospels is either toward viewing characters as a function of the plot (and therefore subordinate to the plot) or as personalities that are multi-faceted who undergo development as the story progresses. Those who argue that characters are essentially functional often take their cue from analysis of other ancient literature, observing the tendency in ancient literature for characters to function more generally as types of a larger category of people.[41] Those who argue that this quality of ancient (Greco-Roman) literature should be applied to the reading of characters in the Gospels provide a reading of characters that emphasizes their more static quality as well as their subordination to plot considerations.

On the other side of the issue are those who generally view characters as personalities who exhibit a more complex set of traits and may very well develop from the beginning to the end of the story. Chatman argues that a "viable theory of characterization should preserve openness and treat characters

---

[40] Powell considers the story of the disciples' relationship with Jesus as one subplot that is related to the main plot of God's plan and Satan's challenge; Mark Allan Powell, "Plot and Subplots," 203.

[41] For example, Mary Ann Tolbert, "How the Gospel of Mark Builds Character," *Int* 47 (1993) 348.

as autonomous beings, not as mere plot functions."[42] Chatman's work in the area of character theory has been appropriated in a number of influential narrative-critical works on the Gospels.[43]

Recognizing the differences between ancient and modern use of characters is a helpful starting point in this discussion. Stanton observes that it is *not* the tendency of ancient biographical writing to emphasize character development.

> Early encomiasts, such as Isocrates and Xenophon, were not interested in development of character, for they attempted to delineate their subjects in terms of their own notions of exemplary character traits. Nor did the Peripatetic biographers, and those who later inherited their techniques, trace development of character and personality, though it is an exaggeration to claim that the phenomenon of human alteration was unknown. Even in Philostratus' *Life* there is no trace of development of character. The idea that a person is understood only through development is modern, and is hardly found in the ancient world.[44]

Russell, analyzing Plutarch's concept of character, identifies the "common ancient view" of character change as "simply a progressive revelation of latent characteristics" (i.e., less a change in nature or φύσις than a gradual revelation of what was there from the beginning).[45] Scholes and Kellogg affirm more generally that the "concept of the developing character who changes inwardly is quite a late arrival in narrative."[46]

Instead of character development, ancient characterization tended toward the illumination of the typical. Tolbert refers to ancient characterization as the "practice of particularizing the universal or individualizing the general."[47] Halliwell, analyzing Isocrates' *Evagoras*, concludes that writings which primarily rely on a narrative mode of characterization tend "to give us more

---

[42] Seymour Chatman, *Story and Discourse: Narrative Structure in Fiction and Film* (Ithaca, NY: Cornell University Press, 1978) 119.

[43] Rhoads and Michie, in their discussion of characters, refer their readers especially to Chatman; David M. Rhoads and Donald Michie, *Mark as Story: An Introduction to the Narrative of Gospel* (Philadelphia: Fortress Press, 1982) 101, with endnote on 154. Powell cites Chatman when he speaks of characters as "open constructs;" Mark Allan Powell, *What is Narrative Criticism?* GBS (Minneapolis: Fortress, 1990) 51–52. For Matthew in particular, see Kingsbury, *Matthew as Story*, 9–10.

[44] Graham Stanton, *Jesus of Nazareth in New Testament Preaching*, SNTSMS 27 (Cambridge: Cambridge University Press, 1974) 121. Carter applies a similar understanding of ancient characterization to his study of Matthew's characters (*Matthew*, 190–91).

[45] D. A. Russell, "On Reading Plutarch's *Lives*," GR 13 (1976) 146, as well as n. 2.

[46] Robert Scholes and Robert Kellogg, *The Nature of Narrative* (New York: Oxford University Press, 1966) 165.

[47] Tolbert, "Character," 348.

'distanced', sometimes moralistic, images of individuals set firmly in the terms of general ethical categories."[48]

In the gospel narratives specifically, Culpepper has noted that in John "[t]he evangelist is not a novelist whose great concern is full-blown development of his characters... [O]ne is almost forced to consider the characters in terms of their commissions, plot functions, and representational value."[49] Similarly, Lehtipuu emphasizes that "little or no psychological development" was involved in ancient characterization, seeming to support a more functional view in which "most biblical characters serve more as plot functions than as credible people."[50]

Given that the evidence from ancient literature points to a more functional role for its characters, caution should be exercised before sketching a full-blown personality-based characterization from the gospel narratives. As Scholes and Kellogg state, "The ideal reader of narratives—ancient or modern—must be prepared to respond to the emphasis of the narrative with respect to character, placing individuality or "typical" connection foremost to the extent which the narrative itself calls for such priority."[51] In the case of the Gospels, the disciples are likely to be used more typically (i.e., as functionaries in service of the plot) than as the means of psychological development. Nevertheless, there may be reason to view characterization in the Gospels beyond the boundaries of function alone.

First, more recent character theories have emphasized a more nuanced view, allowing for a broader conception of the role of characters in the narrative. Ginsberg, in his analysis of some ancient and medieval narratives, concludes that the authors analyzed "all found different ways to create figures who express a great deal more than their typicality."[52] Burnett, while acknowledging that in ancient literature characters were types much more than individuals, argues for viewing characters on a continuum, using Adele Berlin's categorization in this regard. There are agents whose sole purpose is plot-

---

[48] Stephen Halliwell, "Traditional Conceptions of Character," in *Characterization and Individuality in Greek Literature*, ed. C. Pelling (Oxford: Clarendon Press, 1990) 58.

[49] R. Alan Culpepper, *Anatomy of the Fourth Gospel: A Study in Literary Design* (Philadelphia: Fortress, 1983) 102. Culpepper notes that Tannehill finds a similar situation to be the case in Mark; cf. Robert C. Tannehill, "Tensions in Synoptic Sayings and Stories," *Int* 84 (1980) 148.

[50] Outi Lehtipuu, "Characterization and Persuasion," in *Characterization,* ed. Rhoads and Syreeni, 75.

[51] Scholes and Kellogg, *Nature of Narrative*, 206.

[52] Warren Ginsberg, *The Cast of Character: The Representation of Personality in Ancient and Medieval Literature* (Toronto: University of Toronto Press, 1983). His analysis includes works by Ovid (43 B.C.E.–17 C.E.), Boccaccio, and Chaucer.

related. Then there are types which represent an entire class of people. Finally, one can speak of characters who possess a broader range of traits and about whom the reader knows more than necessary for development of the plot.[53] Burnett applies this to a character analysis of Peter in Matthew, concluding that, while "Peter is a secondary character who functions as a type," he also approaches "characterhood" in the denial scene (which is not essential to the plot, having nothing to do with Jesus' trial and fate).[54]

Second, the history of interpretation argues for a more nuanced way of viewing biblical characters. The way that readers of the Gospels through the centuries have read specific characters as highly significant in their own right seems to suggest the possible validity of understanding these characters as more than simply plot functionaries.[55] Lehtipuu's analysis is insightful in this regard. He identifies the difference between those characters that are plot-centered and those that might be termed "complex" as deriving from their varying impact on the reader. "Not all biblical characters are equally presented and equally important. However, the greatest difference between them is on the *symbolic* level. That is, some characters have greater significance for the reader than others."[56] The disciples in Matthew (and Peter individually) seem to have greater symbolic significance for the reader than, say, the Jewish authorities. This issue of the *symbolic significance* of the disciples as a character group, although closely connected to characterization, will be discussed in chapter 5.[57]

In conclusion, in relation to character theory, it would seem helpful to proceed with the provisional assumption that the disciples provide primarily a functional role in the Matthean narrative. In other words, the central goal of their characterization by Matthew might very well be to highlight plot considerations. In this vein, my narrative analysis of the disciples' portrayal

---

[53] Burnett, "Characterization," 15–16.

[54] Ibid., 21–23.

[55] For example, Luz defines Origen's understanding of Peter as "the type of the true, spiritual, and perfect Christian" in Ulrich Luz, *Matthew in History: Interpretation, Influence, and Effects* (Minneapolis: Fortress, 1994) 58.

[56] Lehtipuu, "Characterization," 81.

[57] Syreeni does a character analysis of Peter in Matthew by weaving together his commentary on the textual world and the symbolic world (in which he also seems to include comments on the concrete world of Matthew's audience) ("Peter as Character," 120). I have chosen to separate my analysis of these two worlds because I believe it is important to first analyze the whole of the narrative world (as best as possible) in order to better see how the symbolic is functioning in relationship to the reader of Matthew. In this I follow Kingsbury who argues for "a sustained reading" of Matthew's story before moving to any reconstruction of the social situation of Matthew's community; Jack D. Kingsbury, "Conclusion: Analysis of a Conversation," in *Social History of the Matthew Community: Cross Disciplinary Approaches*, ed. D. Balch (Minneapolis: Fortress Press, 1991) 269.

will include discussion of how the disciples contribute to the plot in addition to an analysis of the way the disciples are portrayed. The question of whether the disciples exhibit multi-faceted traits, moving toward a more personality-centered characterization, and whether they change or develop as the narrative progresses will be left as an open-ended question. Indeed, one of the purposes of the narrative reading of the disciples in 16:21–20:28 is to answer that very question.

Method of Matthew's Characterization

There is general agreement that ancient characterization is accomplished primarily via indirect means. Burnett speaks of the "indirect, minimal method of [ancient] characterization."[58] This was routinely accomplished by focusing on a character's words, actions, and relationships as a summary of his/her disposition, rather than relying on direct narration.[59] This is certainly true for Matthew's characterization in general and of the disciples in particular.[60] The portrayal of the disciples is accomplished primarily through what the disciples say and do as well as what others in relationship with them say and do. Less frequently, Matthew as narrator comments directly on the disciples' attributes or motivations. In Matt 16:21–20:28, in which the disciples are consistently present and interacting with Jesus, there are only five direct characterizations made by Matthew concerning the disciples (they were afraid at 17:6; they understood at 17:13; they were deeply grieved at 17:23; they were astonished at 19:25; and they were indignant at 20:24).

Method for Character Analysis in This Study

Given the conclusions drawn above, the following method of character analysis will be utilized in chapter 3. First, the portrayal of the disciples will be discerned by analyzing five categories of narration: the disciples' actions, their words, Jesus' actions toward the disciples, Jesus' words to them, and the narrator's comments.[61] These categories will be used to assess the disciples'

---

[58] Burnett, "Characterization," 14.

[59] Stanton, *Jesus of Nazareth,* 122; cf. 167–68 regarding Jesus' portrayal in the Gospels.

[60] Kingsbury speaks of Matthew's preferred method as "showing" the reader about his characters, with less emphasis on "telling" (*Matthew as Story,* 10).

[61] This method is similar to Edwards' delineation of five narrative features which highlight characterization: action, words spoken, (narrator's) description, reaction of other characters in the story, and the expectation expressed by other characters in the story; Richard A. Edwards, *Matthew's Narrative Portrait of Disciples* (Valley Forge: Trinity Press International, 1997) 12–13. Since Jesus is the only character who interacts directly with the

implied beliefs, values, and motivations, which will then inform the question of whether the Matthean disciples possess understanding. Second, the information regarding the disciples' portrayal will be viewed in relation to Matthew's plot development. Thus, the question of how the characterization of the disciples contributes to the plot of Matthew in 16:21–20:28 will be addressed in tandem with an analysis of the characterization itself.

The table which follows is a summary analysis of 16:21–20:28 using the five categories delineated, as well as the final category assessing the implied beliefs and values of the disciples.

---

disciples in this section of Matthew (except at 17:24), only his actions and words toward them will be analyzed. I also acknowledge the helpfulness of Uspensky's four-fold typology of analysis: the phraseological plane (speech), the spatial/temporal plane (actions), the psychological plane (motives), and the ideological plane (values and beliefs); cf. Mark Allan Powell's description of Uspensky's typology in "Characterization on the Phraseological Plane in the Gospel of Matthew," in *Treasures New And Old: Recent Contributions to Matthean Studies,* SBLSS 1, ed. D. Bauer and M. Powell (Atlanta: Scholars Press, 1996) 165. Since the latter two categories of motives and values/beliefs are frequently implicit rather than explicit in the Gospels, the initial focus of my analysis will be on the former two categories.

Table 1: Analysis of Disciples' Characterization in Matthew 16:21–20:28

Narrative Block	Disciples' Actions	Disciples' Words	Narrator's Commentary	Jesus' Words	Jesus' Actions	Disciples' Implied Beliefs/Values
16:21–28		Peter rebukes Jesus in response to passion prediction: "This must never happen to you."		In response to Peter's rebuke, Jesus refers to Peter as Satan and a stumbling block.		Peter is shown to hold a belief about Messiah that does not include suffering and death.
17:1–13	② In response to voice from cloud ("This is my Son… Listen to him."), the disciples fall on their faces.	① Peter proposes three dwellings for Jesus, Moses, and Elijah. ⑥ *Question:* "Why, then, do the scribes say that Elijah must come first?"	③ The disciples "fell to the ground and were overcome by fear." ⑦ After Jesus' explanation, "the disciples understood that he was speaking to them about John the Baptist."	④ To the disciples, "Get up and do not be afraid." ⑤ Afterwards, he tells the disciples to speak to no one about the vision.		

Table 1: Analysis of Disciples' Characterization (cont.)

Narrative Block	Disciples' Actions	Disciples' Words	Narrator's Commentary	Jesus' Words	Jesus' Actions	Disciples' Implied Beliefs/Values
17:14–20		*Question:* "Why could we not cast it out?"		Hearing that disciples couldn't heal: "You faithless... generation, how much longer must I be with you... put up with you?" <u>"Because of your little faith."</u>		
17:22–23			In response to passion prediction, the disciples "were greatly distressed."			Implies that they don't understand resurrection part of prediction.
17:24–27		Peter answers yes to the question about Jesus' payment of temple tax.		Jesus tells Peter to give money found in mouth of fish for both of their taxes.		
18:1–20		*Question:* "Who is the greatest in the kingdom of heaven?"		Jesus corrects them implicitly by his words.		Belief in a status-focused kingdom. Value of being greatest.

Table 1: Analysis of Disciples' Characterization (cont.)

Narrative Block	Disciples' Actions	Disciples' Words	Narrator's Commentary	Jesus' Words	Jesus' Actions	Disciples' Implied Beliefs/Values
18:21–35		*Peter's Question:* "Lord... how often should I forgive? As many as seven times?"		Jesus corrects him explicitly by his words.		Belief that there is limit to the number of times one is obligated to forgive.
19:1–12		In reaction to Jesus' teaching on divorce, the disciples state that it would be better not to marry.		Jesus clarifies the place of the unmarried in the kingdom.		Belief that the teaching on the permanence of marriage is too difficult to follow.
19:13–15		Disciples rebuke those bringing children to Jesus.		Jesus corrects them explicitly by his words.		Belief that children aren't worth Jesus' time. Do not value them.
19:16–26		② *Question* (after words on the rich): "Then who can be saved?"	① The disciples "were greatly astounded..." at words of Jesus about the rich.	③ Jesus corrects them with his words about salvation.		Belief that the rich are the most likely to be saved.

Table 1: Analysis of Disciples' Characterization (cont.)

Narrative Block	Disciples' Actions	Disciples' Words	Narrator's Commentary	Jesus' Words	Jesus' Actions	Disciples' Implied Beliefs/Values
19:27–20:16		*Peter's Question:* "Look, we have left everything and followed you. What then will we have?"		Jesus assures disciples of their role in coming judgment but qualifies it by parable & bracketing sayings.		Motivation related to reward for following Jesus.
20:17–19			② No response given for disciples after passion prediction.		① Jesus takes them aside privately to predict his passion.	
20:20–28	① Mother and sons kneel before Jesus.	② *Request by mother and 2 sons:* "Declare that these two sons of mine will sit… at your right … and… left in your kingdom." ④ *Sons answer:* "We are able."	⑤ "When the ten heard it they were angry with the two brothers."	③ Jesus asks if they are able to drink the cup he is about to drink. ⑦ Jesus teaches on greatness in the kingdom.	⑥ Jesus calls them to himself.	Continued belief in a status-ranked kingdom. Value of being at top.

CHAPTER 3

Narrative Analysis of Matthew 16:21–20:28

In keeping with the issues defined and methodology proposed in the previous chapter, I will discuss 16:21–20:28 by first examining how the disciples are portrayed in each section, followed by a description of how the characterization contributes to Matthew's plot.

Matthew 16:21–28

Jesus has just commended Peter for his confession (16:16–17). Peter has rightly identified Jesus to be Messiah by means of divine revelation. Given that confession, Jesus now turns to the task of showing his disciples "that he must go to Jerusalem and undergo great suffering at the hands of the elders and chief priests and scribes, and be killed, and on the third day be raised" (16:21).[1] In response, Peter rebukes Jesus and asserts that this will never happen to him (16:22), thereby showing that suffering and death do not fit Peter's conception of Messiah.

While it is common to see Peter's confession at 16:16 to be evidence that the disciples understand Jesus and his identity, the following story beginning at 16:21 clearly modifies that assessment at the least, possibly even contradicting

---

[1] Jesus progressively reveals the kind of Messiah he is through both his words *and his actions* (thus the word, δεικνύειν, "to show"). His words in the passion predictions set the tone for his identity and mission, but his actions also function to demonstrate his person and mission (e.g., his actions toward children at 18:1–5 and 19:13–15). [The NRSV will be utilized in all quotations unless otherwise noted.]

it.[2] Matthew shows in Peter's rebuke that, while Peter has come to know and confess Jesus to be Messiah, he certainly does not agree with Jesus as to what being Messiah is all about.[3] This is borne out by the statement of Jesus that follows. "Get behind me, Satan! You are a stumbling block to me; for you are setting your mind not on divine things but on human things." Peter's understanding of Jesus' Messiahship is not only quite misguided, it is a stumbling block to Jesus himself. By calling Peter "Satan," Jesus is identifying Peter's viewpoint as one that is anti-God.[4] Jesus reaffirms this in his contrast between setting one's mind on divine things (his own perspective) and setting the mind on human things. This contrast sets up an ideological conflict that plays out in the rest of the narrative between the divine perspective that Jesus consistently illuminates in his teaching and the human (contra-divine) perspective of the disciples.[5] In this first pericope, Peter demonstrates by his response that he truly does not understand the core of Jesus' agenda.

Examining how the disciples' portrayal (here, Peter) contributes to Matthew's plot, Peter's misunderstanding about the kind of Messiah Jesus conceives himself to be provides a teaching opportunity. In 16:24–28, Jesus instructs the disciples on the true nature of discipleship. The divine intention for discipleship is of the same cloth as the divine intention for Messiahship.[6] The cross is at the center of both. Denying self, taking up the cross, losing one's life are at the center of following Jesus (cf. also 10:38–39), because Jesus as Messiah is first called to the same. So Matthew's characterization of Peter as

---

[2] Howell speaks of defective understanding at 16:13–20 given what occurs at 16:21–23; David B. Howell, *Matthew's Inclusive Story: A Study in the Narrative Rhetoric of the First Gospel*, JSNTSup 42 (Sheffield: JSOT Press, 1990) 144. Luz calls the rebuke text "an antithetical and chiastic reprise" of the confession text; Ulrich Luz, *Matthew in History: Interpretation, Influence, and Effects* (Minneapolis: Fortress Press, 1994) 65.

[3] Boyce suggests that, "...even though Peter has the name right, it is a confession that rings false if not connected to suffering and the cross;" James L. Boyce, "Transformed for Disciple Community: Matthew in Pentecost," *WW* 13 (1993) 312.

[4] "...going against the will of God;" Donald A. Hagner, *Matthew*, WBC (Dallas: Word Books, 1993) 480.

[5] Kingsbury identifies this ideological conflict and speaks of it intensifying in 16:21–28:20; Jack D. Kingsbury, *Matthew as Story*, 2d ed. (Philadelphia: Fortress Press, 1988) 130. The disciples have difficulty understanding and accepting Jesus' evaluative point of view that "servanthood is the essence of discipleship." They miss the central purpose of Jesus' ministry (78). Cf. also Efird, who speaks of Jesus' challenge to the perspective of the disciples regarding the nature and work of the Messiah; James M. Efird, "Matthew 16:21–27," *Int* 35 (1981) 284–89.

[6] This section (16:21–28) "introduces two significant developments in the plot, one concerning Jesus' task, the other concerning the nature of discipleship;" Warren Carter, "Kernels and Narrative Blocks: The Structure of Matthew's Gospel," *CBQ* 54 (1992) 477.

one who misunderstands the nature of Messiahship functions as a mouthpiece for Jesus' divine perspective on Messiahship and discipleship.[7]

MATTHEW 17:1–13

In the next section of the narrative, Jesus takes three of the disciples, Peter, James, and John, with him to a high mountain where he is transfigured before them. When Peter sees Moses and Elijah appearing alongside of Jesus, he responds by proposing that they stay and offers to build a dwelling for each of the three figures. It is unclear whether this suggestion is meant to provide insight into Peter's character. (E.g., is Peter rash and impulsive?[8]) What is clear is that the voice from the cloud *corrects* Peter's perspective. The transfigured state of Jesus is not meant to be an end in itself. Rather, the whole event is meant to confirm Jesus as beloved Son and to admonish the disciples present to listen to him, i.e., to heed what he says (17:5). As in 16:21–28, Peter's words seem to demonstrate an inadequate understanding of what is happening in and through Jesus.[9]

While Peter is characterized indirectly at 16:22 and 17:4 through his own words, Matthew provides direct characterization about the three disciples in their response to the heavenly voice. "When the disciples heard this, they fell to the ground and were overcome by fear" (17:6). This is not the first time

---

[7] The final verse of chapter 16 connects the theme of the kingdom with the discipleship just described. The kingdom of heaven is the reign of God that is defined by Jesus' dying-kind of Messiahship and so is to be prepared for by a dying-kind of discipleship. Matthew seems to understand the transfiguration (which immediately follows 16:28) as at least part of what is referred to by Jesus as "see[ing] the Son of Man coming in his kingdom." "Probably the transfiguration proleptically introduces the whole eschatological sphere, which Jesus' resurrection inaugurates and his return consummates...," Craig S. Keener, *A Commentary on the Gospel of Matthew* (Grand Rapids: Eerdmans, 1999) 436. Cf. also David E. Gardner, *Reading Matthew: A Literary and Theological Commentary on the First Gospel* (New York: Crossroad, 1993) 181. For other points of view, cf. Hagner's discussion (*Matthew*, 485–87).

[8] See 17:24–25 for another instance where Peter might be viewed as rash. Although I have argued that the major features of Peter's characterization contribute to the overall portrayal of the disciples, this does not mean that Peter is only portrayed with traits that all the disciples exhibit. If there is a trait that is identified with Peter specifically, it seems to be his impulsiveness (see also 14:28); William Hendriksen, *Exposition of the Gospel according to Matthew*, New Testament Commentary (Grand Rapids: Baker, 1973) 601. Wilkins refers to Peter at 17:4 as "humanly foolish;" Michael J. Wilkins, *The Concept of Disciple in Matthew's Gospel*, NovTSup 59 (Leiden: E. J. Brill, 1988) 203.

[9] James A. Penner, "Revelation and Discipleship in Matthew's Transfiguration Account," *BSac* 152 (1995) 203.

Matthew portrays the disciples as fearful (see 14:26, 30).[10] Jesus' exhortation to stop being afraid also draws attention to their fearful state. Their fear at the divine voice functions to emphasize the words of the Father concerning Jesus and the command to listen to him.[11]

As I have argued in chapter 2, we need to resist the tendency to break the narrative at this point (after 17:8). Instead, 17:9–13 should be read in conjunction with 17:1–8, since it continues the theme of seeing Jesus transfigured ("the vision" spoken of in 17:9) and expands on the appearance of Elijah (17:10–13).[12] After Jesus orders the disciples to "tell no one about the vision until after the Son of Man has been raised from the dead" (17:9), the disciples ask Jesus a question. This is the first of many questions the disciples (together or through one of their members) ask of Jesus in this section of Matthew (e.g., 17:19; 18:1, 21; 19:25, 27). Their questions typically elicit a response from Jesus that centers on either his own Messianic role or the nature of the kingdom that he will bring and consequently the discipleship he now requires.[13] In this case, their question about the prophetic reference to Elijah preceding the Messiah introduces a reaffirmation by Jesus of his own impending suffering. As the already-on-the-scene Elijah has suffered, "so also the Son of Man is about to suffer at their hands" (17:12). Matthew's direct

---

[10] In fact, Matthew frequently connects the response of fear with miraculous, divinely-empowered events (see 9:6; 14:26, 30; 17:6; 27:53; and 28:4, 8) often with a corresponding exhortation to cease being afraid (14:27; 17:7; 28:5, 10).

[11] The disciples need to hear this word "for they do not yet understand or accept the truth which Peter has just repudiated" at 16:22; David R. Bauer, *The Structure of Matthew's Gospel: A Study in Literary Design*, JSNTSup 31 (Sheffield: Almond Press, 1988) 98.

[12] Ulrich Luz, *Das Evangelium nach Matthäus*, EKKNT (Zurich: Benziger/ Neukirchener, 1985–1997) 2:512.

[13] The kingdom and the church are not to be understood as synonymous. For Matthew, the kingdom is a future reality that Jesus nonetheless proleptically inaugurates *in his own life, death, and resurrection.* "Jesus' message is that in his own person and mission God has invaded human history and has triumphed over evil, even though the final deliverance will occur only at the end of the age;" George E. Ladd, *A Theology of the New Testament* (Grand Rapids: Eerdmans, 1974) 67–68.

Jesus' expectations for his followers (for the church: 16:18; 18:18) are based on the values that will be fully enacted in the eschatological kingdom. So while his followers (and the church in Matthew's setting) are not synonymous with the kingdom, they are to be shaped by "kingdom values" here and now. The phrase "kingdom of God" did not "*denote* a community, though it would *connote* the birth of a new covenant community;" N. T. Wright, *The New Testament and the People of God* (Minneapolis: Fortress, 1992) 307. Texts that seem to imply the present nature of the kingdom (e.g., 17:25–26; 18:1; 19:12) can be understood as exploring the implications of the future kingdom on the life of the believing community, which awaits the consummation of the kingdom. Cf. William D. Davies and Dale C. Allison, *A Critical and Exegetical Commentary on the Gospel according to St. Matthew*, ICC (Edinburgh: T&T Clark, 1988–97) 2:755–56.

narration in the following verse indicates that the disciples correctly understand Jesus to be speaking of John the Baptist when he speaks of Elijah.

Given this direct statement by the narrator that the disciples understand (17:13), is the proposed reading of the disciples as essentially misunderstanding Jesus' Messiahship and mission contradicted? Redaction criticism in general has certainly read the text this way. In fact, a number of prominent redaction critics take 17:13 as evidence for the general characterization that, after being taught by Jesus, the disciples understand.[14] Nevertheless, as Trotter so helpfully points out, to say that the disciples understand a specific statement made by Jesus (namely, that they understand his discussion of Elijah to be referring to John the Baptist) does not prove that they understand Jesus' teaching in general or his mission and certainly does not prove that they possess understanding as an abiding character trait.[15]

What should be affirmed is that, although they have so far generally misunderstood Jesus' complete identity and mission (i.e., the nature of his messianic role), they do understand that John the Baptist is the Elijah who was prophesied as coming before the Messiah.[16] In other words, after Jesus' explanation the disciples understand that Jesus is the Messiah as shown in his connection to John as the Elijah-type, the forerunner of the Messiah[17] (just as they have understood him to be the Messiah at 16:16). This does not imply, however, that they understand the *nature of Messiah as the suffering one*

---

[14] Barth speaks of 17:13 substantiating once more the disciples' understanding; Gerhard Barth, "Matthew's Understanding of the Law," in G. Bornkamm, G. Barth, and H. J. Held, *Tradition and Interpretation in Matthew* (Philadelphia: Westminster, 1963) 106. Luz asserts that at 17:13 Matthew makes it clear once more that the disciples come to understand through Jesus' teaching (*Matthäus*, 2:513); cf. also Wilkins, *Concept of Disciple*, 135, 165; and Mark Sheridan, "Disciples and Discipleship in Matthew and Luke," *BTB* (1973) 245. Van Aarde perhaps states it most strongly: Peter's rebuke at 16:21–23 is "neutralized by the disciples' 'insight'" at 17:13; in Andries G. van Aarde, "The Disciples in Matthew's Story," *Hervormde Teologiese Studies Supplement* 5 (1994) 100.

[15] Andrew H. Trotter, "Understanding and Stumbling: A Study of the Disciples' Understanding of Jesus and His Teaching in the Gospel of Matthew" (Ph.D. diss., Cambridge University, 1986) 120, 126.

[16] See Mal 3:1; 4:5–6. Luz understands the eschatological concept of Elijah's coming to be closely connected to the coming of the Messiah, so that if "Elijah has not yet come again, Jesus cannot be Messiah and Son of God" (*Matthäus*, 2:512; my translation). Cf. also Francis W. Beare, *The Gospel according to Matthew: A Commentary* (Oxford: Blackwell, 1981) 366. Davies and Allison (*Matthew,* 2:715) provide a discussion of other proposals regarding the Elijah expectation in first-century Jewish thought.

[17] In his redaction-critical study of John the Baptist, Wink supports this reading: "The identification of John with Elijah is only a consequence of the identification of Jesus as the Messiah;" Walter Wink, *John the Baptist in the Gospel Tradition* (Cambridge: Cambridge University Press, 1968) 32. Cf. also Hagner, *Matthew*, 499–500.

(17:12). In fact, although Jesus has now spoken of his impending suffering twice (16:21; 17:12), there is no indication that as of yet they comprehend this.

MATTHEW 17:14–20

Even though this section begins by focusing on a man coming to Jesus on behalf of his epileptic son, the disciples play a central role in the plot. Moreover, the climax of the story is one of the many *debriefings* that occur throughout 16:21–20:28 between Jesus and the disciples.[18] Thus, the disciples and Jesus are the two primary characters in this pericope.

After Jesus is told by the boy's father that the disciples were unable to cure his son, the theme of faith is introduced in Jesus' response. "You faithless and perverse generation, how much longer must I be with you? How much longer must I put up with you?" (17:17, with the faith theme continued at 17:20). Is Jesus referring to the disciples specifically in his comment concerning the faithless and perverse generation?[19] Since Jesus' words are a direct response to the report concerning the disciples' inability to heal the boy, it is difficult to argue that the disciples are not at least included in the "faithless generation." Given this clear narrative connection, it would seem best to understand the appellation "faithless generation" as including the disciples in the larger group to which Jesus refers.[20] The fact that Jesus will soon identify the disciples as those of "little faith" does not contradict their description as faithless, given the move from Jesus' *general* description of the generation to which he has come and his quite *specific* description of the disciples a little later. In any event, the central faith contrast in this passage is not between those who are faithless and those of "little faith;" it is between a faith (or lack of it) that is unable to heal and true faith that shows itself in healing power.

After his words about this faithless generation, Jesus heals the boy "instantly." The phrase, ἀπὸ τῆς ὥρας ἐκείνης, highlights the contrast

---

[18] See discussion of this structural repetition in the second section of chapter 2. "[Matthew] uses the event as an occasion for Jesus to teach about faith to the disciples…" (Howell, *Inclusive,* 146–47).

[19] The phrase derives from Deut 32:5, where the Septuagint reads γενεὰ σκολιὰ καὶ διεστραμμένη, compared to Matthew's γενεὰ ἄπιστος καὶ διεστραμμένη.

[20] Davies and Allison see it referring to both the disciples and the crowd in the sense that the disciples "have retrogressed to the spiritual level of the multitude" (*Matthew,* 2:724). While Luz points out that the term "generation" (γενεὰ) is nowhere else used to refer to the disciples and so identifies its referent as the crowd mentioned in 17:14 (as indicative of Jesus' Jewish contemporaries), it is unlikely that Jesus is referring to everyone except for the disciples given that the impetus for his statement is related to the disciples specifically (cf. Luz, *Matthäus,* 3:522).

between the ease with which Jesus is able to heal and the inability of the disciples to cure the boy. The disciples then come to Jesus with a question, "Why could we not cast it out?" (17:19). This is the second instance of a question by the disciples that provides Jesus opportunity to teach them further. In this case, their question elicits a teaching on the importance and power of faith. Their question also moves the focus from Jesus and the father/son to Jesus and the disciples.

Jesus points out that his disciples were unable to cure the boy because of their "little faith." The occurrence of ὀλιγοπιστία (or its adjectival cognate, ὀλιγόπιστος) with reference to the disciples is universally recognized as a consistent trait of the Matthean disciples, given its attribution to them and only to them here and at 8:26, 14:31 (to Peter, specifically), 16:8, and a bit more indirectly at 6:30.[21] In this instance, their "little faith" has resulted in an *inability* (οὐκ ἠδυνήθημεν) to heal.[22] In contrast, Jesus speaks of the *ability* they would have had (οὐδὲν ἀδυνατήσει) if they simply had adequate faith or, as Jesus puts it, "faith the size of a mustard seed" (17:20).[23] Thus, one way of denoting their "little faith" at this point in the narrative is as an inadequate faith for healing.

To summarize, 17:14–20 furthers the portrayal of the disciples by showing them via their own actions and Jesus' words as having an inadequate faith (though not completely devoid of faith). Their inability to heal and the way Jesus connects their "little faith" to that inability show the disciples to be falling short of Jesus' expectations for them. This portrayal functions to highlight Jesus' teaching on faith as well as his ability to do what the disciples are unable to do. Coupled with his reference to the faithless generation which he must put up with for a time, the disciples' portrayal as those of "little faith" shows Jesus to be the true model of faith for his disciples. The disciples seem to be emerging not as exemplary for discipleship but as a foil to Jesus' perfect example.

---

[21] Cf. the discussion of "little faith" in ch. 1, pp. 3–6. While the attribution at 6:30 could be addressed to the disciples and the crowds (see 5:1), the discipleship theme in the Sermon on the Mount as a whole points to it as instruction for Jesus' followers more specifically.

[22] "Faith means union with Jesus and a share in his power; lack of faith means lack of power;" John P. Meier, *The Vision of Matthew, Christ, Church, and Morality in the First Gospel* (New York: Paulist Press, 1979) 124.

[23] For a more thorough discussion of the "little faith" characterization of the disciples in Matthew set in the context of other kinds of faith portrayed by Matthew, cf. ch. 4. The definitional term I use there for this mustard-seed faith is "adequate faith."

MATTHEW 17:22–23

Jesus for a second time predicts the suffering, death and resurrection he is soon to experience. This passion prediction is given in direct speech as compared to the indirect speech of the first prediction (16:21). It is also more brief, including the same three components of suffering, death and resurrection but abbreviating the agents of Jesus' suffering from the hands of the elders, chief priests, and scribes to simply human hands. The disciples also respond differently to this passion prediction. Instead of Peter's bold rebuke, here Matthew comments only that the disciples were "greatly distressed" (17:23). Although Matthew's typical means of characterization is indirect,[24] here the reader is given direct information about the disciples by the narrator. Their extreme grief or distress (ἐλυπήθησαν σφόδρα) needs to be assessed in light of their portrayal thus far in 16:21–20:28.

What does this response indicate about the disciples? First, they seem to understand the news that Jesus is to suffer and be killed. Whereas Peter's earlier reaction indicates that he wasn't ready to accept this version of events, the disciples' grief would seem to demonstrate that they comprehend the prediction that Jesus makes concerning his death. Second, it would appear that they are not "hearing" the part where Jesus speaks of resurrection. There is no indication in their response that they comprehend what Jesus means by being raised on the third day. They only get as far as his death.[25] This piece of narration further demonstrates that the disciples do not fully understand the course Jesus has undertaken for himself (or the derivative course he intends for his followers).

MATTHEW 17:24–27[26]

The passage on the temple tax begins with a focus on other characters in addition to the disciples and Jesus. As was the case in 17:14–20, however, the

---

[24] As is the case in ancient characterization in general (cf. discussion in ch. 2).

[25] According to Garland, "they have grasped only half of the statement about Jesus' death and resurrection" (Garland, *Reading Matthew,* 185). Those who read some sort of deficient understanding on the part of the disciples also include Hagner, *Matthew,* 508; and Warren Carter, *Matthew: Storyteller, Interpreter, Evangelist* (Peabody, MA.: Hendrickson, 1996) 250; but contra Barth, "Matthew's Understanding," 106; and Davies and Allison, *Matthew,* 2:735.

[26] Verseput helpfully points out that this incident of temple tax collection and the allusion to the preparation for the pilgrimage feast procession at 17:22 (gathering together: συστρέφεσθαι) tie 17:22–27 together; Donald J. Verseput, "Jesus' Pilgrimage to Jerusalem and Encounter in the Temple: A Geographical Motif in Matthew's Gospel," *NovT* 36 (1994) 109–14.

attention quickly shifts to a dialogue between the disciples (or a representative of them; in this case, Peter) and Jesus. The collectors of the two-drachma tax[27] come to Peter and ask if his teacher pays the tax. Peter affirms that Jesus does pay the tax. The scene then shifts to Peter entering the house where Jesus anticipates a question from Peter (Do you pay the two-drachma tax? or something to that effect) by asking his own question, "From whom do kings of the earth take toll or tribute? From their children or from others?" (17:25). Peter rightly responds, "From others." Jesus then asserts that the children of the kings are free from taxation, clearly implying that this is the situation for himself and also (it would seem) for Peter. They are free from paying the temple tax. Nevertheless, Jesus, to avoid giving offense, tells Peter to go fishing to find a four-drachma coin with which to pay the tax for both of them.[28]

Peter's portrayal in this brief story is not extensive by any means. In fact, his actions are limited to the fact that he "came home;" and his words are so brief as to seem intentionally so (Ναί and Ἀπὸ τῶν ἀλλοτρίων). In addition, there is no direct commentary related to Peter or his characterization. Peter does seem to jump the gun by answering for Jesus without adequate knowledge of his

---

[27] There is question as to what tax is addressed in the pericope. Most scholars agree that it is the temple tax (instituted in Exod 30:11–16, but debated in the first-century as to whether it was compulsory); cf. David Garland, "Matthew's Understanding of the Temple Tax," in *SBLSP* 26 (Atlanta: Scholars Press, 1987) 190–209. Nevertheless, a few argue that it is a Roman tax; e.g., Warren Carter, "Paying the Tax to Rome as Subversive Praxis: Matthew 17:24–27," *JSNT* 76 (1999) 3–31. For a helpful review of the arguments, see Davies and Allison, *Matthew*, 2:738–41. My position is that it refers to the temple tax.

The analysis of first-century historical information to illuminate the text is an appropriate part of the task of narrative criticism. Just as the implied reader envisioned by the text is expected to know the Greek language, the implied reader is also expected to know, for example, who the Pharisees are or what crucifixion is from textual clues as well as from the text's cultural setting. Powell has rightly argued for legitimate areas of expected knowledge for the implied reader of Matthew. These include linguistic competence, universal knowledge, knowledge revealed in other parts of the text, knowledge presupposed by the spatial and social settings of the narrative, and knowledge of other literature cited in the narrative; Mark Allan Powell, "Expected and Unexpected Readings of Matthew: What the Reader Knows," *AsTJ* 48 (1993) 31–51. Contra Edwards, who defines the implied reader as "a non-real reader whose information and attitudes are determined only *by the narrative world* of the story under analysis," although Edwards does allow the implied reader a basic acquaintance with the language used; Richard A. Edwards, *Matthew's Narrative Portrait of Disciples* (Valley Forge: Trinity Press International, 1997) 8.

[28] This the second time in 16:21–20:28 that the word σκανδαλίζομαι, or its cognate σκάνδαλον, is used by Matthew (in Jesus' direct speech; cf. 16:23). See Trotter, "Understanding," for a full discussion of this theme and its relationship to the disciples' understanding in Matthew.

intentions.[29] This may show him to be impulsive.[30] Nevertheless, this minimalist portrayal of Peter, coupled with the fact that the tax collectors drop from the scene before Jesus even enters it, point to the centrality of Jesus and specifically his teaching in this passage.[31]

So while little can be drawn from Peter's portrayal that expands upon his characterization or that of the disciples thus far, the portrayal in 17:24–27 does function in terms of the plot to highlight Jesus' words about the kingdom and its children.[32] The children of the kingdom which Jesus will usher in are free from certain obligations that have typically constrained God's people prior to Jesus' arrival. The theme of freedom is a new piece of the portrait of discipleship first sketched in 16:21–28. While discipleship is typified by self-denial, cross-bearing, and loss of life, it is also characterized by a certain kind of freedom—a freedom that derives from sonship.[33] Nevertheless, Jesus qualifies this freedom, thereby showing that freedom derived from sonship must be constrained in order to avoid giving offense to others.[34] This is the main point of the passage.

To summarize from 16:21–17:27, the disciples have been consistently portrayed thus far as those who, although understanding that Jesus is Messiah (16:16 as the point of departure for 16:21–28; also 17:11–13), struggle to understand the kind of Messiah he is showing himself to be (16:22; 17:22–23). They also are shown to be followers of "little faith" when compared to Jesus and Jesus' expectations for them (17:14–20). Their characterization highlights more clearly for the reader both who Jesus is as Messiah and what he expects of those who follow after him.[35]

---

[29] The narrator's comment that Jesus anticipates Peter with a question of his own, implies that Peter was going to ask the same question of Jesus that the tax-collectors asked of him.

[30] See discussion at 17:4. There is little if any support for the idea that Peter's understanding peaks at 17:24–27 by demonstrating insight into the "son of God" motif as van Aarde argues ("Disciples," 102). Van Aarde's structural proposal creates a need for this to be the case, but his argument is not at all compelling.

[31] Wilkins, *Concept of Disciple*, 200.

[32] References to the kingdom (and related language) become more numerous as one moves through this section of Matthew: 16:28; 17:25–26 (kings and sons); 18:1–14; 18:23; 19:12; 19:14; 19:23–24; 18:28 (thrones); 20:1 and 20:21.

[33] Senior speaks of the implicit "Son of God theology" that connects 17:24–27 to 16:16 and the kingdom theme of chapter 18, with the latter amplifying upon community relationships "based on the love and freedom that existed between God and his children;" Donald Senior, *Matthew*, ANTC (Nashville: Abingdon Press, 1998) 203.

[34] This theme continues in chapter 18 (18:6–9). The teaching of Matt 17:24–27 helps to flesh out what is meant by the self-denial Jesus speaks of at 16:24–25.

[35] Their characterization does not, however, function to highlight the effectiveness of Jesus' teaching (cf. discussion of this redaction-critical conclusion in ch. 1, pp. 13–14).

MATTHEW 18: AN INTRODUCTION TO THE CHAPTER

There is some question as to the exact structure of Matthew 18, which is the fourth of the Matthean discourses. There is a seamlessness to the discourse that derives from the overlapping of terms and ideas between the smaller sections of the discourse (traditionally identified as 1–5, 6–9, 10–14, 15–20, 21–22, and 23–35).[36] Since the goal of this study is to treat the larger units of the Matthean narrative in 16:21–20:28, the focus here will be to identify the major sections of chapter 18. I will argue that the major division in the chapter can be seen between 18:20 and 18:21. I will therefore treat 18:1–20 first, followed by 18:21–35.

Luz gives a number of possible clues to the arrangement of Matthew 18, one of which is the narrative break at 18:21–22.[37] This narrative insertion as well as the chapter's narrative introduction (18:1) provide a way of conceiving its larger structure (and also argue against a complete separation of this chapter as discourse from its surrounding narrative context). These two brief narrative sections (18:1–5 and 18:22–23) both contain a question raised by a/the disciple(s). In both cases, Jesus, in the extended discourses that follow, corrects the underlying premise of each question.[38] In this way, Matthew 18 works far better as narrative than is usually admitted. What have been seen as smaller teaching sections of Jesus actually function quite nicely as Jesus' fairly fluid, discursive responses to two questions raised by his disciples.[39] This also fits

---

Instead, it emphasizes the content of that teaching against the backdrop of their frequent misunderstanding.

[36] Luz, *Matthäus*, 3:6. Luz lists the following catchwords as illustrative of this overlap: παιδίου (18:2–5); ἐν μέσῳ (18:2, 20); ὄνομα (18:5, 20); εἷς τῶν μικρῶν τούτων (18:6, 10, 14); ὁ πατήρ μου ὁ ἐν οὐρανοῖς (18:10, 14; also 19:35); ἐάν (18:12–19; eleven occurrences); ἀφίημι (18:12, 21, 27, 32, 35); ἁμαρτάνω (18:15, 21); and ἀδελφός (18:15, 21, 35).

[37] Ibid., 3:6.

[38] Jesus' point of reference in his corrective teaching is a vision of what the kingdom will be like (note the references to the kingdom that begin the two sections at 18:1, 3, 4, and 18:23).

[39] The more traditional major division of the chapter into 1–14 and 15–35 certainly has evidence to commend it (cf. Davies and Allison for a good defense of this perspective; *Matthew*, 2:750–51). Nevertheless, the thematic (if not catchword) ties between 10–14 and 15–20 make it less than ideal to find the major division at 18:15. 18:10–14 forbids the despising of fellow believers based on God's desire to seek out those who are going astray. 18:15–20 begins with the admonition to confront a fellow believer who has sinned so that that person might be restored to community. While catchwords and terminology are distinct between these two sections, the main points are fairly close: Go after those who are straying with the goal of bringing them back! Cf. Schweizer, who speaks of the joining of the themes

well with the narrative emphasis in 16:21–20:28 upon Jesus' relationship and ideological conflict with his disciples.

MATTHEW 18:1–20

The disciples come to Jesus with a question, which sets the stage for his subsequent teaching: "Who is the greatest in the kingdom of heaven?" (18:1). This is the third question that the disciples ask in this section of Matthew, and it functions like the previous questions to focus attention on Jesus' teaching on a particular subject. In this case, the subject is the true perspective on oneself and one's fellow believers within the Christian community.

Since the initial question is the only part of 18:1–20 that provides information about the disciples' portrayal, it is important to ask what their question says about them. I argue that this question is not an innocent one. Rather, it speaks pointedly to the misperceptions the disciples have about the kingdom.[40] Their concern for "who is the greatest" shows that they view the kingdom in status terms and that they seem quite concerned about their own ranking in it.[41] Their question also shows that they have not appropriated Jesus' earlier teaching on discipleship as self-denial (16:24).[42] Jesus, in his response, corrects their perspective with the truth that the coming kingdom is *not* about

---

of 18:10–14 and 18:15–20 in the literature of Qumran as well; Eduard Schweizer, *The Good News according to Matthew*, trans. David E. Green (Atlanta: John Knox, 1975) 359.

Syreeni argues that the audience shift at 18:21 (from all the disciples to Peter) "may mark a turn in the flow of thought in the community discourse;" Kari Syreeni, "Peter as Character and Symbol in the Gospel of Matthew," in *Characterization in the Gospel: Reconceiving Narrative Criticism*, ed. David Rhoads and Kari Syreeni, JSNTSup 184 (Sheffield: Sheffield Academic Press, 1999) 138. Edwards (*Portrait*, 96–97) understands 18:1–20 to be a major unit within chapter 18. In addition, Kupp identifies "in their midst" (ἐν μέσῳ) at 18:2 and 18:20 as an inclusio; David D. Kupp. *Matthew's Emmanuel: Divine Presence and God's People in the First Gospel*, SNTSMS 90 (Cambridge: Cambridge University Press, 1996) 184.

[40] Senior speaks of the "implicit critique" of the disciples' attitude in 18:1–5 (*Matthew*, 206); cf. also Mark Allan Powell, "Characterization on the Phraseological Plane in the Gospel of Matthew," in *Treasures New and Old: Recent Contributions to Matthean Studies*, SBLSymS 1, ed. David R. Bauer and Mark Allan Powell (Atlanta: Scholars Press, 1996) 169–70. Contra Gundry, who refers to their question at 18:1 as an innocent, even knowing question; Robert H. Gundry, *Matthew: A Commentary on His Handbook for a Mixed Church under Persecution*. 2d ed. (Grand Rapids: Eerdmans, 1994) 359.

[41] Hagner asserts that Jesus' answer shows the disciples to be thinking about greatness "in terms of power, position, and glory..." (*Matthew*, 517).

[42] For Patte, "the theme of self-denial for the sake of others is developed in various ways in 18:1–35;" Daniel Patte, *The Gospel according to Matthew: A Structural Commentary on Matthew's Faith* (Philadelphia: Fortress Press, 1987) 245–46.

preoccupation with status; and he points the way to a proper view of oneself and one's relationship to others in the present, believing community.[43]

Jesus initially brings a child into their circle. "Truly I tell you, unless you change and become like children, you will never enter the kingdom of heaven. Whoever becomes humble like this child is the greatest in the kingdom of heaven" (18:3–4). Jesus is doing something quite unexpected. He is using a child, who in Greco-Roman culture does not attain full human status until adulthood, as an object lesson about kingdom status.[44] Jesus says it is the person who becomes like the child of lowly status (i.e., becomes humble) that is greatest in the kingdom. "The point...is not that children are self-consciously humble but that they are, as part of society at large, without much status and position."[45] The inverse truth of this would seem to be that being concerned about status shows one to be far from the kingdom. In support of this, Jesus does not go on to say that childlikeness is necessary for *kingdom greatness*; rather, he asserts that childlikeness (and its related change of perspective and ambition) is necessary to *kingdom entry* (18:3). His teaching in 18:2–5 directly challenges the disciples' desire for status implicit in their initial question.

---

[43] Although the kingdom is essentially a future reality in Matthew, the values of that kingdom are to be embraced in the present church community. Davies and Allison helpfully point out that it is better to not set the future and present interpretations of the kingdom at odds with each other, since both provide legitimate insights. Regarding 18:1, they note, "Do not the disciples assume that any hierarchy in the future kingdom will be reflected in some way in the structure of the church and that greatness in the kingdom means greatness even now?" (Davies and Allison, *Matthew*, 2:755–56).

[44] The perception of children in Greco-Roman culture was quite negative compared to Western viewpoints. Children were seen as weak and vulnerable, irrational, fearful, and lacking in judgment. This perception was based on the understanding of children as lacking *logos*, which meant that they were not full members of Roman rational society and discourse; see Thomas Wiedemann, *Adults and Children in the Roman Empire* (New Haven: Yale University Press, 1989); cf. also Warren Carter, *Households and Discipleship: A Study of Matthew 19–20*, JSNTSup 103 (Sheffield: JSOT Press, 1994) 99. In Judaism, a male child was not allowed to participate in religious practice until adulthood (Senior, *Matthew*, 217). [For a defense of drawing upon historical and cultural background information within a narrative-critical analysis, cf. n. 27 above.]

[45] Davies and Allison, *Matthew*, 2:757. See also Garland, *Reading Matthew,* 188; Keener, *Matthew*, 284. "[Humility] is not a personal characteristic (certainly not the post-Enlightenment emphasis on the innocence and purity of children) but a social location of powerlessness;" Warren Carter, *Matthew and the Margins: A Sociopolitical and Religious Reading*, The Bible and Liberation Series (Maryknoll, NY: Orbis Books, 2000) 362. For a thorough discussion of this issue, cf. T. Raymond. Hobbs, "Crossing Cultural Bridges: The Biblical World," *McMaster Journal of Theology* 1 (Fall, 1990) 1–21. As Ramshaw points out, the question at 18:1 raises the issue of power (not simply humble attitude) in the Christian community; Elaine J. Ramshaw, "Power and Forgiveness in Matthew 18" *WW* 18 (1998) 403.

All this points to the inappropriate nature of their question. The kingdom (and so the Christian community awaiting its coming) is *not* about keeping track of who's who in ranking.[46] Quite the opposite, it is about embracing humble status and about welcoming children and those like them (18:4–5). It is about *not* being a cause of stumbling to "little ones" (18:6–7) and avoiding stumbling for oneself (18:8–9).[47] Finally, it is about restoring those who are going astray and falling into sin (18:10–14, 15–20). The disciples' question shows a lack of understanding about the true nature of the believing community as Jesus conceives of it. Their focus on status and ranking is directly contrasted with a proper, humble attitude expressed in action for the benefit of others in the community.[48]

The seeking of the straying believer (18:10–14) is closely connected to 18:15–20, where the goal is to win back the brother or sister who has sinned.[49] Each member of the church community has the obligation to work for such restoration (18:15).[50] Beyond this, the seeking of restoration by two or three believers and finally the church as a whole is commanded and is predicated upon the presence of Jesus with them.[51] "For where two or three are gathered in my name, I am there among them" (18:20). Although this verse functions as the culmination of 15–19, it should also be understood as underlying all of the

---

[46] True "disciples do not seek great status or elevation over others," (Carter, *Matthew*, 250). Cf. also Kupp, *Matthew's Emmanuel*, 184.

[47] Note the connection with 17:24–27 regarding not causing offense: σκανδαλίζω or its cognate in 17:27; 18:6, 7 (3 times), 8, and 9.

[48] Matthew consistently uses action verbs to indicate the proper response that Jesus commends in 18:1–20. The focus on humility as a central kingdom quality fits well with the emphasis on discipleship as self-denial at 16:24 and as servanthood at 20:26–27.

[49] The text-critical issue of whether εἰς σέ is original is probably best resolved by its exclusion from 18:15. Positing ἁμαρτήσῃ as original best explains the rise of the other readings based on the aural similarities between the variants; i.e., ἁμαρτήσῃ (the reading supported by the earliest extant manuscripts) gave rise to ἁμάρτῃ εἰς σέ (virtually identical in sound when spoken with fluency) which then produced ἁμαρτήσῃ εἰς σέ through conflation and ἁμάρτῃ through harmonization with Lk 17:3; cf. David Hill, *The Gospel of Matthew*, NCB (London: Marshall, Morgan, and Scott, 1972) 275. This reading would confirm that the situation addressed in 18:15 calls for any community member to seek the restoration of one who has sinned, not only the one sinned against, thus tying 15–20 more closely to 10–14 than to 21–22.

[50] Although some understand the *leadership* of the believing community to be addressed at 18:15–20, there is no explicit mentioning of church leaders in all of chapter 18, as Schweizer observes; Eduard Schweizer, *Matthäus und seine Gemeinde*, Suttgarter Bibelstudien 71 (Stuttgart: Verlag Katholisches Bibelwerk, 1974) 106.

[51] The theme of two or three (seeking restoration) weaves thematically through the rest of the paragraph (note *two/two or three* in vv. 16, 19, 20). As France notes, "The whole focus…is not on the punishment of an offending brother, but on the attempt to 'gain' him;" Richard T. France, *Matthew: Evangelist and Teacher* (Grand Rapids: Zondervan, 1989) 249.

community regulations spelled out in 18:1–19.[52] The theme of Jesus' presence with his people begins and ends Matthew's gospel (1:23; 28:20) and is pivotal at this point in the narrative as well.

To sum up, 18:1–20 continues to show the disciples and Jesus to be involved in an ideological conflict. Matthew portrays the disciples as misunderstanding the nature of true discipleship. This consistent misunderstanding, evidenced in 18:1–20 by their inappropriate question about greatness, highlights Jesus' teaching on what the kingdom will really be about. Nevertheless, after Jesus teaches them, no indication is given that they now understand.[53] In fact, it will become clear at 19:13–15 that the disciples have in no way appropriated Jesus' teaching on children from 18:1–5. This would argue against Wilkins' view that Jesus is shown to be an effective teacher via the disciples' understanding.[54] If the disciples are not shown to understand the true nature of Messiahship or discipleship after Jesus' teaching anymore than they did before it, what is being affirmed through Jesus' teaching in 18:1–20?

What is affirmed at this point in the narrative is that Jesus will be with his disciples as they seek to follow his teachings. It is Jesus' *effective presence* that is affirmed rather than his effective teaching. His teaching may be difficult to understand for the disciples but his promise is that he will be with them and all who attempt to live in community in the way he instructs.[55] Ultimately, it is not the characterization of the disciples as understanding Jesus' teaching that guarantees the fulfillment of his expectations in 18:1–20. Rather, it is the climactic emphasis on the presence of Jesus with the believing community which gives hope that his teachings will indeed be realized.

---

[52] Luz seems to move in this direction when he states, "[Jesus] appears at the center of the chapter as the one who accompanies his community and is present in it…" (*Matthäus*, 3:80; my translation). Hagner states, "The supreme mark of Christ's community is Christ's presence" (*Matthew*, 534). Cf. also Kupp, who speaks of the "presence of Jesus 'in their midst' [as] not just the regulation of disputatious church members…[but as] real empowerment when God's little people gather in Jesus' name" (*Matthew's Emmanuel*, 199).

[53] This is also the case after Jesus' teaching in 16:24–28; 17:20–21; and 17:27. The only place where it is clear that the disciples do understand is after he teaches them concerning John the Baptist. As has been argued in that section, this relates to their understanding of Jesus as Messiah not to their understanding of *the nature* of Messiahship or of discipleship.

[54] Wilkins, *Concept of Disciple*, 166.

[55] As many have noted, there is a widening of the application of the words of Jesus in the Matthean discourses. This is not necessarily a sign of direct transparency but is an expansion to refer to all disciples as well as to the character group of the disciples. The concept of the implied reader is helpful here to designate the textually-constructed reader to whom Jesus' teachings are directed on the discourse level of the narrative (Kingsbury, *Matthew as Story*, 109). See chapter 5 for a discussion of this concept.

MATTHEW 18:21–35

The narrative insertion at 18:21 signals a break in the chapter. Not only does this insertion include another question by (one of) the disciples (thus paralleling 18:1); it also includes the explanation that Peter approaches Jesus to ask this question.[56] This bit of narration signals a slight shift of audience, further emphasizing the break between verses 20 and 21.[57] Nevertheless, there is certainly a connection between 18:15–20 and what follows in 18:23–35. First, the issue of a member sinning is common to both (18:15, 21). Second, the extended discussion of forgiveness in 18:23–35 seems to arise fairly naturally from the discussion of church restoration/discipline in 18:15–20.

The question raised by Peter concerning the number of times he ought to forgive a fellow believer who sins against him seems rather magnanimous initially. As Jesus' response makes clear, however, Peter, in looking for limits to forgiveness, has not gone far enough in his understanding of what true forgiveness entails: "Not seven times, but, I tell you, seventy-seven times." The term ἑβδομηκοντάκις ἑπτά (a *hapax legomenon* in the New Testament) likely refers to 77 times, rather than 70 times 7 (490).[58] As Davies and Allison point out, however, in either case the implication is that forgiveness is not a matter of counting but of forgiving without counting.[59]

Jesus' words concerning the unconventional and lavish nature of forgiveness show Peter's initial question to be basically flawed.[60] If Peter had even an inkling of the kind of forgiveness Jesus expects from his followers, he would not be asking about keeping track of wrongs committed against him. Again,

---

[56] The word προσελθών is better translated as 'approached' rather than 'came,' since there is no indication that Peter has somehow been absent from the first question of chapter 18, given his explicit and prominent presence in 17:24–27. Contra Syreeni who raises the possibility of Peter's absence (*Peter as Character*, 137).

[57] The attention to Peter as question-asker in 18:21–35 does not, however, exclude the presence of the other disciples, since the second-person plural pronouns in 18:35 make it clear that more than Peter are being addressed.

[58] The former reading is supported by the identical rendering in the Septuagint of Gen 4:24, which translates the less ambiguous Hebrew, וְשִׁבְעָה שִׁבְעִים; so Arland J. Hultgren, *The Parables of Jesus: A Commentary,* The Bible in its World (Grand Rapids: Eerdmans, 2000) 22. Garland, commenting on Gen 4:24, points out that "Jesus' response consciously counters the Lamech principle of measureless blood vengeance...Under Lamech there was no limit to hatred and revenge; under Moses it was limited to an eye for an eye, a tooth for a tooth, a life for a life; under Jesus there is no limit to love, forgiveness, and mercy" (*Reading Matthew*, 194).

[59] Davies and Allison, *Matthew*, 2:793.

[60] Although his question could certainly be called reasonable, by asking it "Peter demonstrates that he did not understand Jesus' preceding teaching [about the essential nature of restoration of fellow believers]" (Patte, *Matthew*, 255).

Peter, and the disciples by association, are shown to have an inadequate understanding of kingdom values and their relevance for Christian community. Peter's question not only reveals an inadequate assumption about forgiveness; it also functions to highlight Jesus' teaching on the true nature of forgiveness, begun in 18:22 and continued in the parable he tells in 18:23–35.[61]

The subject of the parable is forgiveness. The story focuses on the servant of a certain king who owed the king a huge, even ridiculous, amount of money.[62] Having been graciously forgiven the entire debt because of the king's compassion, the servant immediately proceeds to find a fellow slave who owes him a miniscule fraction of the amount he has just been forgiven.[63] At a number of points, the details of the story highlight the similarities between the two scenes (e.g., both servants fall down and plead their case; the servants speak their request for patience in almost identical language; and both are under the threat of slavery/prison for their inability to pay), so that the single contrast between forgiveness received for a enormous debt and forgiveness withheld for a rather small debt is more potently communicated. After being informed of the actions of the first servant, the king reinstates the debt and turns the servant over to the torturers for punishment.

The point of the parable is that those who have been forgiven (by God) ought also to forgive one another (cf. 18:33, which is the climax of the parable

---

[61] Some have asserted that the parable is poorly connected to what precedes, since the parable is not an example of the repeated forgiveness called for in 18:21–22; e.g., Bernard Brandon Scott, *Hear Then the Parable*, (Minneapolis: Fortress, 1989) 268; John D. Crossan, *In Parables: The Challenge of the Historical Jesus* (New York: Harper & Row, 1973) 106; Daniel Patte, "Bringing Out of the Gospel-Treasure What is New and What is Old: Two Parables in Matthew 18–23," QR 10 (Fall, 1990) 83. This viewpoint, however, ignores the fact that the parable provides the basis for forgiveness rather than an example of it. The primary character is the unforgiving servant (the only character in all three sections of the parable), and so focuses attention on the irony of one who is forgiven a huge debt but won't forgive a small one. See Davies and Allison for further arguments on this issue (*Matthew*, 2:791–92). As Ringe notes, though the parable does not deal with limitless forgiveness, it does "continue to call the reader toward consideration of transcendent concerns and ultimate values;" Sharon H. Ringe, "Solidarity and Contextuality Readings of Matthew 18:21–35," in *Reading from this Place* 1, ed. Fernando F. Segovia and Mary Ann Tolbert (Minneapolis: Fortress, 1995) 203.

[62] 10,000 talents (μυρίων ταλάντων). Attempts to explain away this amount as Matthean redaction of a much smaller original uttered by Jesus or by claiming that the servant was actually a governor under the king miss the fact that the parable "works" precisely because of the outrageous amount owed and forgiven (Hultgren, *Parables*, 24). For the redactional view, see Martinus C. DeBoer, "Ten Thousand Talents? Matthew's Interpretation and Redaction of the Parable of the Unforgiving Servant (Matt 18:23–35)," *CBQ* 50 (1988) 229.

[63] 100 denarii. The ratio between the two is about 600,000:1 (Hultgren, *Parables*, 27).

proper).[64] In light of the great mercy given by God, it is completely unthinkable to withhold forgiveness from a fellow believer for any sin (or any number of sins). The application of the parable by Jesus is a warning for those who would withhold forgiveness from their Christian brother or sister (18:35). Jesus uses this parable to teach a very different perspective on forgiveness than the one revealed in Peter's question. The expectation of lavish forgiveness toward one another in the Christian community is based on God's prior grace and forgiveness. In the end, this kind of forgiveness is not an option but an expectation of all those who set the kingdom as their priority. It is an expectation like those expectations already spelled out in 18:1–20, rooted in self-denial and predicated on Jesus' continued presence with his community.[65]

MATTHEW 19:1–12

This passage begins with the repetition of the formula that follows each of the five Matthean discourses (Καὶ ἐγένετο ὅτε ἐτέλεσεν ὁ Ἰησοῦς...; cf. 7:28; 11:1; 13:53; 19:1; and 26:1). As such, 19:1 seems to begin a new, major section of Matthew. While the geographical reference at 19:1 coupled with the formulaic introduction does suggest a shift of some sort, the thematic and narrative connections between chapters 18 and 19 point to important continuity between the two as well.[66] The units within 19:1–20:28 continue to focus on what is expected of those who follow Jesus in their community life (building on the themes of chapter 18). In addition, the narrative focus on Jesus' relationship with his disciples and their ideological conflict continues in 19:1–12 and throughout the rest of 19:1–20:28.

This is the only pericope in all of 16:21–20:28 that reintroduces the Pharisees (and the related plot conflict between Jesus and the Jewish leadership). According to 19:3, some Pharisees come to Jesus testing him about his stance on divorce. It is not, however, the conflict between Jesus and the Pharisees that culminates the passage. Instead, as has happened at a number of points so far, the text turns from Jesus' interaction with non-disciples to a

---

[64] Many see 18:33 as the decisive verse of the parable; e.g., Hultgren, *Parables*, 30; Scott, *Hear Then*, 269.

[65] Senior helpfully summarizes Matthew's vision of Christian community from chapter 18 as a "community in which concern for the alienated and marginalized dominates, in which sanctions are applied with utmost care, and in which reconciliation has no limits;" Donald Senior, "Matthew 18:21–35," *Int* 41 (1987) 406–07.

[66] As Bauer helpfully points out, the formula at 19:1 (and in its four other occurrences) is transitional and so connects the previous discourse with what follows (*Structure*, 129).

dialogue between Jesus and the disciples (as in 17:14–20 and 17:24–27).[67] The disciples make a statement, which provides Jesus with the opportunity to teach about expectations for his disciples.[68]

The Pharisees question Jesus about the parameters of lawful divorce, and Jesus refers to the foundational story of God's creation of man and woman (Gen 1:27; 2:24). He concludes, "So they are no longer two, but one flesh. Therefore what God has joined together, let no one separate" (19:6). When the Pharisees cite Mosaic law as a loophole to such strict monogamy, Jesus calls it a concession to their hardness of heart rather than part of the original intention for marriage.[69] He then gives his own teaching on divorce: "And I say to you, whoever divorces his wife, except for unchastity, and marries another commits adultery" (19:9).[70]

At this point in the narrative, the Pharisees drop out of the story completely and are not mentioned again until 22:15. In their place are the disciples who, although not mentioned in 19:1–9, are shown narratively to have been present for the whole conversation. More importantly, their response to Jesus' teaching on divorce turns attention away from the Pharisees as introductory characters to the primary interaction between Jesus and his disciples.[71] Their response to Jesus' teaching on divorce provides further insight into their characterization.

---

[67] This also happens at 19:13–15, "where a situation produced by non-disciples elicit[s] a teaching for disciples;" Paul S. Minear, *Matthew: The Teacher's Gospel* (New York: Pilgrim, 1982) 105.

[68] Jack D. Kingsbury, "The Plot of Matthew's Story," *Int* 46 (1992) 353.

[69] Patte sees this idea of hardness of heart as a theme in 19:1–20:16, related not primarily to a lack of knowledge of God's will but to "the inability to accept or envision the goodness of God" (*Matthew*, 263). The disciples' consistent misunderstanding of Jesus' mission and teaching, as I have argued for it, would certainly imply a consequent lack of acceptance. If the disciples have great difficulty understanding Jesus' perspective, they will certainly demonstrate in various ways that they have not come to accept or appropriate it (e.g., 19:13–15).

[70] There are scores of articles, monographs, and books on the interpretation of this verse. A central issue is whether or not the words, μὴ ἐπὶ πορνείᾳ, provide a true exception and, if so, whether the exception allows for remarriage or only for divorce. The argument is often made that the interpretation of this clause as a legitimate exception does not make sense of the disciples' shocked response at 19:10 (which seems to require an absolute prohibition at 19:9) and therefore is ruled out. This argument is misguided. Even if the exception allows for remarriage, Jesus' teaching on marriage and divorce is still much more stringent than the viewpoint expressed in the Pharisees' question ("for any cause"), which the disciples seem to have appropriated (19:10). Their shock at 19:10 could easily be understood in light of the pronounced contrast between divorce "for any cause" and divorce only in the case of unchastity.

[71] Luz speaks of this scene in which the Pharisees participate becoming the occasion for "disciple instruction" ("*Jüngerbelehrung*"); *Matthäus*, 3:87.

The disciples respond to Jesus' teaching on divorce by declaring, "If such is the case of a man with his wife, it is better not to marry" (19:10). What does their statement imply about them? While at first glance their inference may seem to be an adequate reflection of the seriousness of Jesus' teaching on marriage, Davies and Allison point out that the proper response to Jesus' exaltation of life-long marriage is certainly not an exaltation of the unmarried state.[72] Their response, in fact, shows that they do not truly understand the nature of marriage as intended from the beginning by God. Rather, it seems to reflect a much more lenient perspective on divorce similar to the viewpoint of 19:3.

To understand the disciples' statement concerning the teaching on marriage and divorce it is important to examine Jesus' response to them beginning at 19:11: "Not everyone can accept this teaching, but only those to whom it is given." Does Jesus essentially agree or disagree with their assessment that it is better not to marry given the strictures Jesus imposes? The answer to this question lies in part in the identification of the antecedent to "this teaching" (τὸν λόγον τοῦτον in 19:11), which is most likely their statement at 19:10.[73] If Jesus is referring to their stated preference for singleness given the difficulty of monogamy, 19:11–12 is not simply a clarification but is an implicit correction of their statement at 19:10. Their statement that it is better to remain unmarried in response to the finality of marriage amounts to saying that the difficulty of life-long marriage can be avoided by remaining single (which by implication is the easier course). Jesus provides a critique of their point of view by implying that their assumption (to be unmarried is 'easier' than being married for life) is inaccurate.[74] He corrects their misconception. Being a eunuch for the kingdom is not the easier course. It is the right and good course for those to whom it is given (and therefore should be accepted by those who can do so—19:12). But it

---

[72] Davies and Allison, *Matthew*, 3:19.

[73] Versus his teaching at 19:9 (the more distant and therefore a less likely antecedent) or 19:12 (since demonstrative pronouns are less likely to anticipate than to refer back). So Davies and Allison, *Matthew*, 3:20; Senior, *Matthew*, 215; Hagner, *Matthew*, 550; and Craig L. Blomberg, "Marriage, Divorce, Remarriage, and Celibacy: An Exegesis of Matthew 19:3–12," *TJ* 11 (1990) 184.

[74] "V. 12 is not an endorsement of v. 10 but a qualification of it" (Davies and Allison, *Matthew*, 3:21). Patte speaks of the disciples drawing a wrong implication from Jesus' teaching on marriage. "By concluding that it is better not to marry, they show that they cannot conceive of marriage without the possibility of divorce" (*Matthew*, 266). Cf. also Blomberg ("Marriage, Divorce," 184) and Carter (*Matthew and the Margins*, 382), who contend that the disciples misunderstand at 19:10.

is not for all, and so is not the easy way out for those who find Jesus' teaching on marriage and divorce to be too difficult.[75]

The disciples' statement at 19:10 has provided Jesus with an opportunity to teach about the kingdom once again. His message in 19:11–12 is that there are some who embrace the unmarried state for the sake of the kingdom (διὰ τὴν βασιλείαν), having been given this gift by God.[76] Jesus calls those who are able to embrace this to do so, even while acknowledging that not all do embrace it.[77] In the end, Jesus affirms the godly ideal for both marriage and singleness in this passage: life-long marriage as one flesh according to the original intention of God and singleness for the sake of the kingdom according to the power of God.[78]

The effect of these pronouncements on status issues is important. While the call to life-long marriage is a high expectation, it is also an implicit affirmation of the worth and importance of women in the kingdom scheme.[79] The viewpoint related by the Pharisees (and possibly held by the disciples) seems to indicate that divorce was or at least should be a more readily available option for men (thereby devaluing women). Jesus demonstrates that in God's perspective women are to be valued in life-long marriage relationships, and divorce allowed only in the most serious of circumstances.[80] In addition, the value of those who respond to Jesus' call to remain unmarried ("eunuchs for the sake of the kingdom") is in contrast to prevailing cultural views.[81] "Jesus' blessing of that

---

[75] Garland puts it this way: "the reasons for renunciation of marriage [for the kingdom] have nothing to do with the desire to avoid getting a lemon (the disciples' worry)..." (*Reading Matthew*, 199).

[76] Some who view the exception clause as only pertaining to the first part of Jesus' saying in 19:9 argue that the "eunuchs for the kingdom" are those that have divorced according to the allowance of the exception clause but remain unmarried thereafter in obedience to Jesus' saying; e.g., Carter, *Households*, 71; Gundry, *Matthew*, 382–83; Paul E. Dinter, "Disabled for the Kingdom: Celibacy, Scripture and Tradition," *Commonweal* 117 (1990) 571. My reading follows Hagner, Patte, and others who identify these eunuchs as those who have renounced marriage for the kingdom (Hagner, *Matthew*, 550; Patte, *Matthew*, 267; Garland, *Reading Matthew*, 199–200).

[77] The verb χωρέω brackets this teaching at the beginning of 19:11 and the end of 19:12.

[78] The implication of God's power arises from the (divine) passive δέδοται in 19:11 along with ὁ δυνάμενος in 19:12.

[79] Senior, *Matthew*, 217; Blomberg, "Marriage, Divorce," 173; Carter, *Households*, 71: In contrast to "the Pharisees' inquiry about unrestricted male power...Jesus...restrict[s] the use of male power in divorce to one cause, the wife's unfaithfulness." Keener asserts that "Jesus' male contemporaries valued the great and powerful; Jesus summoned status-seeking men to love their wives..." (Keener, *Matthew*, 294).

[80] The clearly stated addressee of Jesus' instruction at 19:9 is men rather than women.

[81] Rabbinic tradition reflects a prevalent viewpoint that an unmarried person is of less value than married people. "Any man who has no wife is no proper man" (*b. Yebam. 63a*). In

choice [to forego marriage] once again goes against the grain of societal norms."[82] Jesus continues to counter expectations that the disciples have concerning the kingdom, at this point particularly their perceptions of greatness and status. Those who are viewed as less important in first-century society will be granted unusual status in the kingdom.

MATTHEW 19:13–15

This brief scene illuminates the characterization of the disciples, although the reader is given only a few-word description of their activity. When little children are brought to Jesus for prayer and blessing, Matthew indicates that the disciples "spoke sternly to those who brought them" (19:13). Jesus, in response to the disciples' action, reformulates a previous teaching about children (and childlikeness): "Let the little children come to me, and do not stop them; for it is to such as these that the kingdom of heaven belongs" (19:14; cf. 18:2–4). Jesus then lays hands on the children as those who brought them had desired.

The disciples' stern rebuke to those who brought the children shows that the disciples consider children to be a waste of Jesus' time and efforts. This does not fit Jesus' own perspective on children expressed in his response to their rebuke here as well as his earlier words on the subject (see 18:1–5). In fact, given Jesus' recent teaching on the importance of children and those like them, the disciples by their actions at 19:13 show that they have not truly understood what Jesus taught at 18:2–5 about status renunciation for the kingdom. Jesus' earlier comment that welcoming children amounts to welcoming Jesus himself (18:5) becomes a glaring indictment of the disciples, who would turn children away rather than welcome them. The irony is palpable at this point in the narrative. The disciples, who seem to believe that the kingdom belongs to them given their close association with Jesus, are being told that the kingdom belongs to those like the ones they are attempting to keep from Jesus' presence.

Thus, Matthew shows the disciples to misunderstand again the nature of the kingdom. They would send away children whom Jesus desires to welcome and bless. They would do this even after hearing Jesus' teaching about the importance of children and the necessity of childlikeness for entering the kingdom.[83] The disciples have not truly understood or appropriated Jesus'

---

this regard, Kodell surmises that "'[e]unuch' could well have been a derogatory term directed at...[Jesus'] unmarried followers;" Jerome Kodell, "Celibacy Logion in Mt 19:12," *BTB* 8 (1978) 19.

[82] Garland, *Reading Matthew*, 200.

[83] Carter (*Households*, 90–91) speaks of the "double affirmation" of this passage. At the literal level, the importance of children is being affirmed; at the metaphorical level, children

perspective on status in the kingdom.[84] Consequently, they do not provide an example of true kingdom perspective and action but act as a foil to Jesus' perfect example.[85]

MATTHEW 19:16–26

This passage begins with a young man asking Jesus, "Teacher, what good deed must I do to have eternal life?" (19:16; note identification as a young man in 19:20). The dialogue continues between these two through 19:22. As we have seen throughout 16:21–20:28, however, the passage ends with the focus returning to the disciples and Jesus with emphasis on Jesus teaching his disciples about the kingdom.

Jesus answers the man's question with a question of his own, "Why do you ask me about what is good? There is only one who is good." This initial hesitation to answer the man's question directly should raise doubts for the reader about the legitimacy of the question.[86] Jesus subverts the implication that good deeds are the foundation of eternal life, and instead emphasizes the "one who is good," suggesting that it is not a good deed but a good God that is the basis for eternal life (this is confirmed by 19:26).[87] Nevertheless, Jesus does answer his question after having qualified it. "If you wish to enter into life, keep the commandments." There is a relationship between eternal life and

---

are a model for discipleship (cf. τοιούτων in 19:14). Davies and Allison affirm the point that the passage is about both those who are child-like and about children who are without societal status; *Matthew*, 3:35–36.

[84] Kingsbury speaks of the disciples' "status-consciousness" at 19:13–15 (*Matthew as Story,* 80).

[85] As in 17:14–20. "Jesus becomes the model to be imitated;" Davies and Allison, *Matthew*, 2:760.

[86] In narrative-critical perspective, the evaluative point of view of any particular character in a gospel is judged to be true or untrue by a comparison with the reliable points of view of God, Jesus, and the narrator; cf. Mark, Allan Powell, *What is Narrative Criticism?* GBS (Minneapolis: Fortress, 1990) 54. This should caution the reader about implicitly trusting the questions or statements of the young man (or any other character that is not shown to be completely reliable by the narrator). Carter (*Households,* 124); Patte (*Matthew*, 276); Bruner, and Schottroff express doubt as to the legitimacy of the question; cf. Frederick D. Bruner, *Matthew: A Commentary* (Dallas: Word, 1990) 699; Luise Schottroff, "Human Solidarity and the Goodness of God: The Parable of the Workers in the Vineyard," in *God of the Lowly: Socio-Historical Interpretations of the Bible*, ed. W. Schottroff and W. Stegemann (Maryknoll, NY: Orbis Books, 1984) 139.

[87] "What the questioner seeks can be found only in relation to God" (Carter, *Households*, 119). Carter also speaks of the attention being upon the "limits of [human] actions in contrast to God's actions (19:26)" (119, n. 4).

keeping the commandments. Their exact relationship, however, will need to be assessed as the narrative progresses.

In response to Jesus' exhortation to keep the commandments, the man asks, "Which ones?" Jesus obliges him with a selection of the commandments from Exodus 20:12–17 (Deut 5:16–21) along with the command to love one's neighbor (Lev 19:18).[88] The young man says that he has kept *all* these (emphatic position in the Greek). Yet he still senses something missing ("…what do I still lack?").

Jesus provides the answer. Selling his possessions, giving the money to the poor, and following Jesus will give the man the completion he lacks.[89] Here, Jesus moves beyond the commandments he has cited to a particular command for this particular man that will cost him everything he holds dear (his many possessions). Then Jesus calls the man to follow him. It seems that the man's original question was flawed; eternal life is not only tied to keeping the commandments. It now revolves around Jesus and his expectations (which are based upon but are more stringent than the Torah as it has been understood; cf. the Antitheses of the Sermon on the Mount). It is about following Jesus at the highest of costs (and Jesus seems to have known just what the highest cost was for this young man). The young man is unable to do this, "for he had many possessions" (19:22).

The story and its point about eternal life do not end at 19:22, however.[90] Although the man leaves the scene, Jesus and his disciples come to center stage in one of their many debriefings. Commenting on his interaction with the rich young man, Jesus tells his disciples that it is virtually impossible for a rich person to enter the kingdom of God (19:24).[91] Matthew tells the reader that the

---

[88] It may be telling that the commandments that are omitted are those that relate to a person's relationship with God (the prohibition against idolatry included) as well as the prohibition against coveting. These seem to be the very commands the young man has the greatest difficulty keeping (see 19:22). So Jesus' answer allows the man to respond that he has kept "all these."

[89] The words, ὑστερέω and τελείος, belong to a similar semantic field as antonyms. Aristotle provides a lengthy definition of τελείος, in which the focus is upon completion, that is, having no lack or deficit (ἐλλιπής) in the area being discussed (*Metaph.*, 5,16). Davies and Allison affirm that the sense of completeness fits the Matthean usage best (cf. Matt 5:48; at 19:21 thus in reference to complete obedience); *Matthew*, 3:48.

[90] The passage is easily misread when it is seen as ending at 19:22, with the young man's departure.

[91] The difficulty of the rich entering the kingdom in the first statement is intensified to a virtual impossibility by the figure of the camel going through the eye of a needle in the second (contra Hagner, *Matthew*, 561). This is confirmed by the response of the disciples, which is astonishment that anyone at all can be saved. The point of the metaphor is to strike down all solely human attempts to enter the kingdom; cf. Augustine Stock, *The Method and Message of Matthew* (Collegeville, MN: The Liturgical Press, 1994) 306.

disciples were greatly astounded when they heard this, asking, "Then who can be saved?" By this question, the disciples are reflecting a cultural understanding of wealth as God's blessing upon those who have it.[92] If the rich, who show by their wealth that they have been blessed by God (in God's good graces, as it were), cannot be saved, then the poor certainly don't have much chance for salvation.

Jesus' final words provide the key to the entire passage. He responds to the disciples' question not by contradicting their view of wealth and the wealthy directly but by capitalizing on the scope of their question to address the issue of salvation for any and all. Jesus' answer is that for humanity salvation is impossible, "but for God all things [including salvation] are possible" (19:26). The power for salvation is from God and not from human beings. This final statement in a very real sense both subverts and answers the initial question posed by the young man. It is not a good deed accomplished by human means that brings eternal life; instead, it is the power of God enabling one to follow Jesus and to obey the commandments wholeheartedly that saves.[93]

In terms of characterization, the disciples are described by Matthew as "greatly astonished" by Jesus' words about the impossibility of the rich entering the kingdom (19:25). Coupled with their question about who can be saved (if even the rich cannot), their response indicates that they believe that the rich are shown by their material blessings to be spiritually blessed as well. The disciples show that they believe the rich to be of greater religious status, since their question assumes the greater likelihood of the wealthy receiving salvation.

Jesus once again corrects the inadequate understanding of the disciples through his teaching. The rich do not have an added advantage for salvation as the disciples assume. In fact, their wealth might very well be a hindrance to following Jesus and so entering the kingdom (19:22–24). Instead, Jesus shows that even those who might appear to be of greater stature and blessing in religious terms are still in need of God's power to be saved (19:26). Jesus' teaching has the effect of equalizing status in terms of kingdom entry. The rich are shown to be at a disadvantage when it comes to entering the kingdom. But those who are not wealthy are also disadvantaged, since Jesus states that for humans salvation is impossible. The answer lies not in human ability or status but in God's ability to bring salvation (19:26).

This theme of status weaves through 19:1–12, where the status of women and the unmarried is elevated; through 19:13–15, where children are not only

---

[92] Davies and Allison speak of the common assumption that wealth was a sign of divine favor (*Matthew*, 3:53). See also Hagner, *Matthew,* 561; Robert H. Mounce, *Matthew*, NIBCNT (Peabody, MA: Hendrickson, 1991) 492.

[93] Senior talks about the radical commitment to Jesus as being both "a call and a grace" (Senior, *Matthew,* 221).

affirmed as important in the kingdom but as exemplary for kingdom entry (cf. also 18:1–5); and through 19:16–26, where the wealthy are no longer the religious elite but are equalized in terms of status by Jesus' saying at 19:26. In addition, Matthew's Jesus shows kingdom entry to be based on the power of God (19:26) and childlike humility (18:1–5; 19:13–15).

MATTHEW 19:27–20:16

While it is common to divide this section of Matthew into two parts, Jesus' response to the question by Peter in 19:27 clearly includes the parable of 20:1–15, given the repetition of the saying about the first and the last. The sayings bracket the parable (19:30; 20:16) and is integrally tied to the first part of Jesus' answer in 19:28–29.[94] 19:27–20:16 actually works very well as one story unit dealing with the topic of reward in the kingdom.

As we have seen at 16:22 and 18:21, Peter again speaks on behalf of the disciples: "Look, *we* [emphatic position] have left everything and followed you. What then will we have?" (19:27). This question derives from the previous passage in which the rich young man does not follow Jesus but instead returns to his possessions. The disciples have done the opposite, and so Peter asks about their reward for leaving all to follow Jesus. While Peter's question follows naturally from 19:16–26, it does not necessarily reflect well on Peter or the disciples in general. Rather, it shows the disciples to be focused once more on their own concerns related to the kingdom ("What then will *we* have?") rather than an attitude of self-denial (16:24) or a caring-for-another orientation (ch. 18). This is evident from the implicit critique of the original question at the climactic point of his teaching (19:30–20:16).[95]

The effect of Peter's question is once again to provide Jesus an opportunity to instruct the disciples. Jesus' reply comes in three parts. First, Jesus assures the disciples that they will judge Israel in the regeneration (19:28). While it is common to view this judging activity as a unique *leadership* role, there is no

---

[94] I.e., no one breaks the passage after 19:29; yet there is no compelling reason to separate the two virtually identical sayings in 19:30 and 20:16 by dividing the passage after 19:30. Although he divides this part of Matthew into 19:16–30 and 20:1–16, Luz acknowledges the bridging function ("*Übergangsfunktion*") that 19:27–30 has in relation to 20:1–16 (*Matthäus*, 3:119).

[95] Davies and Allison understand 20:1–16 to be a caution to the rewards mentioned in 19:27–29 (*Matthew*, 3:53). Barth argues for understanding the question at 19:27 negatively, given the subsequent "sharp warning" of 20:1–16 ("Matthew's Understanding," 120). For Edwards (*Portrait*, 90), Peter shows through his question that he "does not understand the implications of Jesus' recent emphasis on death as a possible result of following the Son of Man." Contra Luz who views it as a blameless question (*Matthäus*, 3:28).

compelling reason to do so. Luz asserts that it is "unequivocally false" ("*eindeutig falsch*") to define κρίνω as "rule" ("*herrschen*"). In addition, he shows that the reference to thrones is best understood contextually as related to judging rather than ruling (cf. 25:31).[96] It seems best, therefore, to understand the reference to the disciples judging Israel in relation to other statements in Matthew that seem to indicate that Jesus' followers are the new, eschatological community (e.g., 21:43; also 8:11–12).

Jesus then speaks of the reward of eternal life and abundance given to all who have left home, family, and lands to follow him ("for my name's sake," 19:29). The application of reward is broadened to all of Jesus' followers rather than a special group of them.[97] In addition, the promise of receiving a hundredfold does not seem to be a separate reward from receiving eternal life itself or, at least, the focus is on eternal life as the reward.[98] Consequently, the first part of Jesus' answer is that those who leave all other allegiances to follow him will be rewarded with abundance, namely, with eternal life. The notion of a

---

[96] Luz, *Matthäus*, 3:129. Contra Hagner, *Matthew*, 565; and Minear, *Matthew*, 107. In a different vein, Carter argues that "the disciples here are representatives of all disciples and the image is one of their vindication in judgment." Carter bases his conclusion on the lack of Matthean support that the disciples will judge/rule the church or Israel (*Households*, 125–26, n. 5).

[97] This does not apply only to those who have given up all possessions, since only two of the seven items listed concern possessions (households and farms). The emphasis of the saying is upon having left *family* to follow Jesus. This promise, therefore, should be understood as referring to all of Jesus' followers, since discipleship for Matthew necessitates shifting allegiance from family to Jesus (Matt 10:35–39; 12:46–50; also 6:24 in reference to giving up allegiance to money). Cf. Kingsbury's discussion of this saying and its paradigmatic function; Jack Dean Kingsbury, "The Verb *akolouthein* ("To Follow") as an Index of Matthew's View of His Community," *JBL* 97 (1978) 72–73.

[98] Kingsbury, *Matthew as Story*, 142; and Hultgren, *Parables*, 41. The reference to receiving a hundredfold may simply be in synonymous parallelism to eternal life, given the highly stylized properties of 19:29 and the clear poetic quality of 19:30. In addition, the figurative nature of the "hundred-fold" language argues for its poetic and hyperbolic quality (since it makes no sense to speak literally of one-hundred times recompense of one's family; cf. Mounce, *Matthew*, 496). For other Matthean reward passages that exhibit this same poetic quality, cf. 10:40–42 and 6:1–18.

There is no distinct content given to the concept of reward elsewhere in Matthew's gospel and thus no distinction between separate rewards for different groups of believers. Instead, the primary distinction is either between earthly reward (focused on honor and recognition from people) which is transient and heavenly reward which is permanent (6:1–18) or between receiving the (heavenly) reward and losing it (e.g., 10:40–42). In either case, the focus is on God's recompense for deeds done (see 16:27) with either a heavenly reward or no heavenly reward.

distinct, special reward for certain disciples is qualified by the final, climactic part of Jesus' teaching in 19:30–20:16.[99]

The final part of the answer is rather cryptic. Jesus qualifies his previous answer (and so Peter's question) by the saying, "But many who are first will be last, and the last will be first" (19:30).[100] Jesus' saying about the first and the last seems to address the issue of presumption. Almost as soon as he speaks of the reward for following him, he qualifies it with a warning. Any presumed status related to what he has just said is not a part of the deal. In context, the first referred to in this saying are those who have been first to follow Jesus in discipleship (including the twelve). The warning of 19:30 is that these followers should not presume that they will be first in the kingdom in terms of status. To understand the exact nature of the saying, it is crucial to understand the parable inserted between the two parallels sayings (which act together as an inclusio to the parable).[101]

The focus of the parable of the vineyard is on a landowner who hires laborers throughout the day to work in his vineyard. The first-hour workers toil the entire day, while the eleventh-hour workers put in only one hour's labor. When it is time to pay, the landowner pays the eleventh-hour workers a day's wage, the same amount promised to the first-hour workers. So when the first-hour workers come to be paid, they expect to receive more than a day's wage. In fact, they are angry to receive just what they had been promised. They grumble at the landowner, saying, "These last worked only one hour, and you have made them equal to us who have borne the burden of the day and the scorching heat" (20:12). Their basic complaint is the supposed injustice of the landowner's payment. The climax of the story is the landowner's response to the first-hour workers, in which he denies any injustice on his part: "I am doing

---

[99] Luz argues that Matthew does not accent the distinctiveness of the reward for the twelve. Instead Luz views 19:28 and 19:29 together: "...the seating of the twelve on the thrones is for [Matthew] a special form of the 'hundred-fold' which is promised to all" (*Matthäus,* 3:129; my translation).

[100] The δέ is disjunctive rather than conjunctive, given the contrasting content in 19:28–29 and 19:30–20:16. Contra Schottroff, who understands 19:30 not as a warning to the disciples (and thus a contrast to 19:28–29) but as a warning to those who would be like the rich man of 19:16–22 ("Human Solidarity," 141); also Michael L. Barré, "The Workers in the Vineyard," *Bible Today* 24 (1986) 177, who understands "the last" to refer to the disciples.

[101] Gundry and Patte both speak of the parable interpreting the saying(s) (Gundry, *Matthew,* 395; Patte, *Matthew,* 273). Contra Harrington, who speaks of the connection between the parable and saying at 20:16 as "somewhat weak;" Daniel J. Harrington, *The Gospel of Matthew,* SP (Collegeville, MN: Liturgical Press, 1991) 283. This takes the highly stylized language of reversal at 20:16 (and 19:30) too literally; cf. the discussion of the relationship between the sayings and the parable in Petri Luomanen, *Entering the Kingdom of Heaven: A Study on the Structure of Matthew's View of Salvation* (Tübingen: Mohr Siebeck, 1998) 149–50.

you no wrong; did you not agree with me for the usual daily wage?" (20:13). He goes on to claim his prerogative in dispensing wages as he sees fit (as long as he meets his commitments): "Am I not allowed to do what I choose with what belongs to me? Or are you envious because I am generous?" (20:15).

The affront felt by the first workers is that "you have made them equal to us." The scandal of the parable is the apparent injustice of the equity between the first and last workers. Likewise, the scandal of the kingdom is the equal treatment of the first to sign on and the last to do so. The answer given by the landowner focuses on both his justice and his generosity. He was perfectly just to the first workers and wonderfully generous to the last. His contention is that no one can fault him in either case because it is his money to give as he pleases. The point of the parable is that God's generosity is the basis for the equality that is characteristic of the kingdom.[102]

If the point of the parable is focused on the (disturbing) equality of the kingdom, then the two parallel sayings which bracket the parable must be understood in this light. The point of 19:30 and 20:16 is not that there is a *status inversion* that occurs in the kingdom. Rather, there is an *equalization of status* in the kingdom that is unexpected and possibly offensive, and those who refuse to embrace this truth are warned that they may be last (thus losing their reward).[103] This idea is confirmed by the previous passages. The enhancement of the status of women and the unmarried in 19:1–12, children in 19:13–15, and the poor in 19:16–26 is not about a reversal of status. In other words, women, eunuchs, children, and the poor are not now elevated to the highest status in the kingdom. Rather, there is an equalization of the value and status of all kingdom persons. This is made explicit by Jesus' statement about kingdom entry not being a matter of human ability (or status) but made possible by God (19:26).

This leads to a further qualification. In response to the disciples' earlier question concerning greatness in the kingdom, Jesus pointed to children who by their humble status show the way into the kingdom. This could certainly be construed as an inversion of status in the kingdom, whereby those who are seeking greatness (namely the disciples via their question) are shown to be lower in status than the child Jesus puts before them (by virtue of the child's humility). That, however, would be granting legitimacy to the assumption

---

[102] "The parable...show[s] that no one will have seniority in the kingdom. All will be treated equally...when the rewards are bestowed" (Garland, *Reading Matthew*, 205). Cf. also Schweizer, *Matthew,* 394; and Schottroff, who speaks of the parable's dual focus on God's goodness and consequent human solidarity ("Human Solidarity," 138).

[103] Carter, Households, 160. (Carter defines "being last" as being condemned.) For Elliott, the parable is thus "a warning to the community against competition for favor and status;" John H. Elliott, "Matthew 20:1–15: A Parable of Invidious Comparison and Evil Eye Accusation," BTB 22 (1992) 62.

behind the question that the kingdom is about greatness. Jesus' response seems to indicate the opposite. The kingdom is about humility, that is, an intentional focus away from self and status altogether. To take Jesus' expectation of humility as a way to measure greatness would be highly ironic. Instead, Jesus is teaching about an equalization of status, so that the kingdom is no longer perceived to be about greatness and status, but about God's gracious activity in and to all who follow Jesus and his teachings.[104]

MATTHEW 20:17–19

The third passion prediction of Jesus occurs in this pericope near the end of Matt 16:21–20:28. As Jesus approaches Jerusalem, Matthew narrates that Jesus takes the twelve aside to speak to them about his coming betrayal, death, and resurrection. As in 16:21, the chief priests and scribes are mentioned. In addition, in this prediction alone, Jesus mentions that he will be handed over to the Gentiles to be mocked, flogged and crucified.[105] This particular passion prediction does not include a response by the disciples. Contrary to the first two predictions (cf. 16:21–22; 17:22–23), the reader is given no indication at 20:17–19 that the disciples do or do not understand what Jesus as Messiah is going to experience. Examining the differences between the three passion predictions, it could be argued that the disciples come to accept Jesus' prediction of his coming death and resurrection. The reactions move from outright denial by Peter (16:22) to grief by the disciples (17:23) to (possibly) implicit acceptance via their silence at 20:19. However, the placement of "[t]his third...passion prediction...exactly *between* Jesus' warning parable against spiritual pride and Jesus' warning encounter with spiritual ambition," argues against such acceptance of Jesus' mission on the disciples' part.[106]

---

[104] "[The divine grace] destroys all human reckoning and therefore all Christian presumption" (Davies and Allison, *Matthew*, 3:76). Hultgren, *Parables*, 43: The parable presents a "way of thinking [which] goes deeper into the gospel of God...God's way with us is to make no distinctions."

[105] Note that the Gentiles are mentioned again in 20:25, where Jesus refers to their use of absolute authority in ruling. The joining of both Jewish and Gentile leadership in the betrayal and crucifixion of Jesus in this passion prediction (20:17–19) provides a point of contrast to how believers are to function in the kingdom (19:27–20:16 and 20:20–28).

[106] Bruner, *Matthew*, 728. "The tragic solemnity of 20:17–19 is a perfect foil for 20:20...[with the disciples] preoccupied with their self-centered hopes..." (Davies and Allison, *Matthew*, 3:82).

MATTHEW 20:20–28

Matt 20:20–28 concludes this section of Matthew in which the focus has been upon Jesus with his disciples.[107] Throughout this section, the disciples have been engaged in an ideological conflict with Jesus over the nature of the coming kingdom, including both the nature of Messiah and the nature of discipleship. Matt 20:20–28 highlights this conflict, showing the disciples once again to misunderstand the kind of kingdom that lies ahead.

James and John (described only as the "sons of Zebedee;" cf. 4:21) accompany their mother to ask a favor of Jesus. Their mother requests that her sons sit on Jesus' right and left sides in his kingdom. Jesus replies, "You [second person plural verb in Greek] do not know what you are asking. Are you able to drink the cup that I am about to drink?" (20:22). His statement that they do not know what they are asking implies that these two disciples have not really understood the prediction Jesus has just made about his coming death. Their response to his question about drinking the same cup Jesus is about to drink confirms this. They reply, "We are able."[108] They seem to understand the kingdom only in glorious terms. They are less able to envision the cup of his death to which Jesus has now referred on three occasions, otherwise they would not so readily agree to drink from it. Jesus confirms that they will drink from the cup of suffering and death but denies their request as out of his hands.[109]

When the other disciples hear of this bold request, they become angry with James and John. A rivalry seems to be brewing.[110] The focus of the initial request as well as the ensuing rivalry is once more about status in the kingdom. The disciples, here represented by James and John, are interested in their particular status in the coming kingdom. They are asking for the second and third positions! Preoccupation with status again characterizes the disciples.[111] They show that they have misunderstood the central themes of the kingdom that Jesus has been teaching them throughout this section of Matthew.

---

[107] Davies and Allison agree that this passage concludes this larger section of Matthew (*Matthew*, 3:1).

[108] Note the ironic contrast between Jesus' earlier words about the inability (ἀδύνατος) of human beings to enter the kingdom (19:26) and the confident declaration of ability (δύναμαι) to share Jesus' fate by James and John.

[109] For examples of "cup" referring to God's wrath, cf. Jer 25:15; 49:12.

[110] Most scholars agree that the rest of the disciples are angry because they also aspire to these same positions; e.g., Kingsbury, *Matthew as Story*, 142; Garland, *Reading Matthew*, 208; Hagner, *Matthew*, 581; Senior, *Matthew*, 225.

[111] Hagner, *Matthew*, 578. Kingsbury speaks here of the disciples' desire for power and privilege (*Matthew as Story*, 80).

The disciples' misunderstanding once again functions to occasion Jesus' teaching on discipleship: "You know that the rulers of the Gentiles lord it over them, and their great ones are tyrants over them. It will not be so among you; but whoever wishes to be great among you must be your servant, and whoever wishes to be first among you must be your slave" (20:25–27). Jesus speaks again to the issue of status in the kingdom. As opposed to the role of absolute master, which characterizes Gentile rulers, Jesus' disciples are to be characterized by service with no regard for position.[112] Matthew, in using κατακυριεύω and δοῦλος, evokes the language of masters and slaves. In contrast to Gentile leaders who play the master in their use of absolute power,[113] followers of Jesus are to serve one another as slaves would.[114] The contrast, however, is not only between Gentile (human) rule and godly servanthood. The narrative also contrasts the disciples' presumption of and desire for status with that of a servant/slave, who does not have any privileged rank or status.[115] In this way, the request for James and John at 20:21 informs the interpretation of the negative example of the Gentile rulers at 20:25.

This is supported by the reoccurrence of two important words from the previous narrative context that have been used to speak to the improper status-focus of the disciples. The disciples' concern over *greatness* in the kingdom elicited Jesus' teaching on humility using a child of lowly status (18:1–5). Now

---

[112] There is debate whether the two verbs in 20:25 generally have negative connotations (κατακυριεύω as "lording over" and κατεξουσιάζω as "tyrannizing," respectively, as in NRSV) or more neutral meanings referring to the exercise of authority. (Cf. Luz, *Matthäus*, 3:163, where he states that the question of whether the two verbs have a negative or neutral sense must remain open.) Clark argues vigorously for the latter in the case of (κατα) κυριεύω; and his argument is cited by Carter and Davies/Allison as compelling; Kenneth W. Clark, *The Gentile Bias and Other Essays* (Leiden: Brill, 1980) 207–12. Nevertheless, Clark does not deal with the only other New Testament occurrences of κατακυριεύω outside of Matt 20:25 and its synoptic parallel in Mark, namely Acts 19:16 and I Peter 5:3. Both occurrences support a meaning of "complete control" or "mastery" for κατακυριεύω. This concurs with Matthew's usage in which the element of "mastery" ("exercising lordship") is drawn upon to contrast with the proper attitude of slave/servant in 20:26–27. So, while these two words may not have the oppressive connotations that are evident in the NRSV, they do not simply mean to "exercise authority." Instead, given the parallelism of 20:25 as well as the slave/master imagery evoked in 20:25–27, these words refer to "exercising lordship" or "acting as master over" others.

[113] "In the heathen world, the great ones were those who could best bend the wills of others to conform to their own" (Garland, *Reading Matthew*, 208).

[114] Hultgren provides a helpful discussion of δοῦλος. In contrast to the modern conception of a servant, the first-century slave was owned by another person and so was under that person's domination (*Parables*, 473–76).

[115] Meier defines "slave" in the social context as "the non-person who has no rights or existence of his own, who exists solely for others;" John P. Meier, *Matthew*, New Testament Message 3 (Wilmington: Glazier, 1980) 228.

at 20:26, being *great* is tied to being a servant, also of lowly status. At 19:30 and 20:16, Jesus has warned the disciples that presumption about one's position and reward in the kingdom will lead to the *first* becoming last. Now at 20:27, he ties being *first* to becoming a slave to others. These two words in this section of Matthew are used to show that desire for status and position does not fit true discipleship.[116] In fact, these verses reinterpret greatness and "firstness" to such an extent that all sense of rank is removed from them. Thus Luz rightly asserts that 20:26–27 is not about "a new way to greatness." Rather, there is no 'being-great" and no "being-the-first" in the Christian community.[117]

Jesus provides the ultimate example of his expectation that his followers will be servants (without status-focus) in his own mission to serve his people: "just as the Son of Man came not to be served but to serve, and to give his life a ransom for many" (20:28). This final verse echoes the three passion predictions that Jesus has made in 16:21–20:28. Thus, 16:21 and 20:28 form an inclusio to this entire section, focusing attention on the kind of Messiah Jesus comes to be, a Messiah who will suffer and die.[118] Jesus shows himself to be the true, servant Messiah.

SUMMARY

In 16:21–20:28, the disciples are characterized as being in an ideological conflict with Jesus. Jesus in 16:21 turns his attention to his disciples and demonstrates for them the nature of his Messianic role as well as their role as his followers. The coming kingdom that he envisions is counter to the expectations of the disciples, shown repeatedly by their consistent misunderstanding of both Jesus' role and their discipleship. Throughout this section of Matthew, the disciples give no indication that they come to understand better the kind of Messiah Jesus is and the kind of disciples they are called to be. They also are shown to be disciples of inadequate faith when it comes to fulfilling the tasks of ministry.

---

[116] As Coninck rightly notes, Jesus inverts the world's scheme where "'first'…is associated with power, and 'great' with domination" (my translation); Frederic Coninck, "Le royaume de Dieu comme critique des royaumes des homes," *FoiVie* 85 (1986) 60.

[117] Luz, *Matthäus,* 3:164, 163 ("*kein 'Gross-Sein' und kein 'Der-Erste-Sein'*"). Contra Patte who asserts that Jesus does not object to the desire for greatness (*Matthew,* 282–83).

[118] Those who speak of 20:28 as a climax or recapitulation to the entire section begun at 16:21 include Senior, *Matthew,* 226; and Bauer, *Structure,* 98. In this final passage, Matthew ties in some of the major themes from earlier parts of 16:21–20:28. As already mentioned, greatness (18:1–5; 20:26) and being first (19:27–20:16; 20:27) are thematic. In addition, the initial call to a discipleship defined by cross-bearing and self-denial (16:24–26) finds a sense of completion in the call to servanthood in this passage.

This rather grim (and non-progressive) portrayal of the disciples does not highlight the effectiveness of Jesus' teaching.[119] Rather, their characterization functions on the plot level to highlight the unexpected nature of Jesus' teaching. The disciples' often-inept questions focus the reader's attention on what Jesus has to say, thereby shaping the reader's perspective on the kingdom and discipleship.[120] In addition, on the plot level, the disciples' lack of understanding, while not significantly endangering the mission of Jesus,[121] does seem to endanger his legacy. Jesus' vision for discipleship is meant to be enacted by his disciples as well as taught to future disciples (cf. 28:19–20). The ability of the disciples to do this is brought into question by their frequent misunderstanding of Jesus' vision. There is hope for Jesus' legacy, however, a hope which is intimated in Matthew 16:21–20:28 in at least three ways. First, the disciples continue to follow Jesus in spite of their failings.[122] They may be imperfect and uncomprehending disciples, but they are disciples nonetheless.[123] Second, the Matthean reader, in direct contrast to the disciples, understands Jesus' teaching. In fact, the disciples function as a foil for the reader, encouraging the reader in understanding (cf. chapter 5). Finally, the very presence of Jesus is promised to his future community as they seek to live out the values of God's kingdom (18:20).[124]

In summary, the kingdom Jesus describes and embodies in 16:21–20:28 will be entered by those who, by God's power, have become humble and have followed Jesus (18:3; 19:26). True discipleship focuses on self-denial and servanthood rather than on striving for status and position within the Christian community (16:24–25; 20:26–27). Living in this community is characterized by freedom constrained by care for others, the welcoming of children, and the pursuit and forgiveness of straying ones based on God's own example (ch. 18). It is also about valuing the marginalized, including women, the unmarried, children, and the poor, as Jesus does (ch. 19). This kind of discipleship within community does not make sense from a human perspective but only from God's perspective (16:23). Ultimately, such a way of life is based on Jesus

---

[119] As some have claimed regarding the disciples' portrayal when read in a more positive light; e.g., Wilkins, *Concept of Disciples,* 166.

[120] The impact of the disciples' portrayal on the reader will be addressed in chapter 5.

[121] Kingsbury rightly notes that in general the disciples do not greatly influence the plot of Matthew (*Matthew as Story*, 13).

[122] Frank, Matera, "The Plot of Matthew's Gospel" *CBQ* 49 (1987) 245.

[123] As Kingsbury observes (*Matthew as Story*, 131), Matthew highlights the disciples as those "with Jesus" (μετά + genitive).

[124] "[One thing which] qualifies the disciples for teaching is the continuing presence of Jesus among them;" Mark Allan Powell, *God With Us: A Pastoral Theology of Matthew's Gospel* (Minneapolis: Fortress Press, 1995) 83.

himself: his presence with his community and his example as a suffering and serving kind of Messiah as he gives his life a ransom for many.

CHAPTER 4

CONTEXTUAL ANALYSIS OF THE DISCIPLES' PORTRAYAL

The goal of this chapter is to analyze the narrative of Matthew that surrounds 16:21–20:28, in order to show the connection between the reading proposed in the previous chapter and the disciples' portrayal in the rest of the gospel. As was the case in chapter 3, the characterization of the disciples with regard to *their understanding* will be highlighted in particular. The two primary sections of this chapter will include analysis of the disciples' portrayal in Matthew 1:1–16:20 followed by their portrayal in 20:29–28:20.

CONTOURS OF THE DISCIPLES' PORTRAYAL IN 16:21–20:28

Before moving to the portrayal of the disciples in the rest of Matthew's gospel, it is helpful to summarize the analysis of 16:21–20:28 by highlighting four structural and thematic issues, namely, (1) the structural function of the passion predictions; (2) the role of the disciples' questions; (3) the theme of discipleship as servanthood against the backdrop of the disciples' less than ideal narrative portrayal, and (4) the place of the discourse of chapter 18 within the narrative.

The importance of the three passions predictions in this part of Matthew has been widely noted. The passion predictions tie 16:21–20:28 together both thematically and structurally. The theme of Jesus' impending death introduced in the first passion prediction (16:21) is not only reiterated in the second and third passion predictions; it also reappears in the final, climactic passage of the entire section (20:28: "...to give his life a ransom for many..."). In addition, the death of Jesus is paradigmatic for the kind of discipleship Jesus envisions for his followers (cf. 16:24–26).[1] Structurally, the passion predictions begin and conclude this section of Matthew (16:21; 20:17–19).[2]

The disciples' responses to the three passion predictions give the first indication that they do not understand or accept Jesus' messianic mission to suffer and die. Peter's rebuke (16:22), the disciples' grief (17:23), and their concern over their ranking in the kingdom (20:20–28) show them to be at odds with God's perspective (16:23). This contrary perspective (or ideological conflict) is further substantiated by the frequent questions posed by the disciples to Jesus.

The disciples' questions to Jesus and evocative statements in response to his teaching are important to the flow of the narrative in 16:21–20:28. First, these questions and responses show that the disciples do not understand the nature of Jesus' mission as Messiah or his intention for them as his disciples. In fact, their words show that the disciples are in an ideological conflict with God's perspective which is underscored in Jesus' teachings.

"Who is the greatest in the kingdom of heaven? (18:1).

"Lord, if another member of the church sins against me, how often should I forgive? As many as seven times?" (18:21).

"If such is the case of a man with his wife, it is better not to marry" (19:10).

"Then who can be saved?" (19:25).

"What then will we have?" (19:27).

"Declare that these two sons of mine will sit, one at your right hand and one at your left, in your kingdom" (20:21). [Cf. also questions at 17:10, 19.]

These questions and reactions also provide Matthew's Jesus with an opportunity to teach his disciples, shaping the reader's understanding of the kingdom and its community. In this way, the disciples function to elicit and emphasize Jesus' teaching.[3]

---

[1] Luz speaks of the passion predictions having "a central theological function, because it is the *story* of Jesus, especially the story of his passion and death, which is impressed upon the life of the community;" Ulrich Luz, *Das Evangelium Nach Matthäus*, EKKNT (Zurich: Benziger/ Neukirchener, 1985–1997) 2:484 (my translation). Cf. also Augustine Stock, *The Method and Message of Matthew* (Collegeville, MN: The Liturgical Press, 1994) 270.

[2] This is especially true when 20:20–28 is read as a kind of response by the disciples to Jesus' third prediction. Davies and Allison seem to view 20:20–28 in this light when they note that "following Jesus' announcement of pain and suffering [at 20:17–19] we do not next read that his disciples showed concern for him—only that some people were preoccupied with their self-centred hopes;" William D. Davies and Dale C. Allison, *A Critical and Exegetical Commentary on the Gospel according to St. Matthew* ICC (Edinburgh: T&T Clark, 1988–97) 3:82.

[3] Best notes that "[i]t was customary in material from [the period in which the Gospels were written] which concerns a teacher and disciples for the disciples to ask questions and to perform actions which elicit instruction from the teacher;" Ernest Best, *Disciples and*

In fact, the disciples and their perspective provide the backdrop against which the theme of *discipleship as servanthood* stands in bold relief. Jesus' teachings and activity are highlighted against that backdrop. The central intention for discipleship which emerges in his teaching is self-denying servanthood (cf. 16:24–26 and 20:26–27, effectively bracketing together the entire section). This self-denying servanthood is more closely defined, particularly in chapter 18, as gracious activity on behalf of others in the Christian community. In chapters 19–20, it is defined by a rejection of status-focused attitudes and activity.

This leads to the relationship between chapter 18 and its surrounding context, as well as to the purpose of chapters 19–20 in Matthew's gospel. The community discourse of chapter 18 should be read in continuity with the narrative that surrounds it. Not only are there narrative elements within the chapter (18:1; 18:21) that tie it to the broader narrative context focused on the disciples; there are also numerous thematic connections between chapter 18 and 16:21–20:28.[4] To treat chapter 18 in relative isolation from its narrative context misses its significant continuity with 16:21–20:28.

Finally, the difficulty of determining the purpose of Matthew 19–20 has been frequently acknowledged within Matthean scholarship. According to Luz, there is no overarching theme for these chapters other than the general characteristic of disciple-instruction (*Jüngerbelehrung*).[5] Carter, whose *Households and Discipleship* focuses on the purpose of Matt 19–20, speaks of "the need to identify the coherence of chs. 19–20 and to establish their contribution to the gospel's presentation of discipleship."[6] Carter's proposal of

---

Discipleship: Studies in the Gospel according to Mark (Edinburgh: T&T Clark, 1986) 108. Cf. also an analysis of Greco-Roman literature related to disciples and teachers in Whitney T. Shiner, *Follow Me! Disciples in Markan Rhetoric*, SBLDS 145 (Atlanta: Scholars Press, 1995). In addition, Dodd speaks of the form-critical category of apophthegmata, in which the questioner "may be a...foil or lay figure, with the sole function of eliciting the authoritative pronouncement of Jesus;" Charles H. Dodd, "The Dialogue Form in the Gospels," *BJRL* 37 (1954–1955) 60.

[4] Cf. ch. 2, p. 45, for related discussion. Connecting themes include: the identification of true discipleship with denial/servanthood/humility (16:24; 18:4; 20:26); the stumbling block theme (16:23; 17:27: 18:5, 7); the unexpected teaching of Jesus regarding status within the kingdom (18:1–5; 19:13–15; 19:24–25; 19:30; 20:16); the presence of kingdom parables (18:23; 20:1); the importance of Peter's role (16:22; 17:24–27; 18:21; 19:27); discussions concerning kingdom entry (18:3; 19:16–26); and teachings on children (18:1–5; 19:13–15).

[5] Luz, *Matthäus*, 3:87.

[6] Warren Carter, *Households and Discipleship: A Study of Matthew 19–20*, JSNTSup 103 (Sheffield: JSOT Press, 1994) 29. Crosby, like Carter, understands this section of Matthew (specifically, for Crosby, 19:3–20:16) to be an expression of ancient household codes; Michael H. Crosby, *House of Disciples: Church, Economics, and Justice in Matthew* (Maryknoll, NY: Orbis Books, 1988) 119–25.

19–20 as a subversion of the four standard subjects of Greco-Roman household codes (*Haustafeln*) rightly emphasizes the issue of status that Matthew raises in 19–20. Nevertheless, his specific thesis is less than convincing, given its tendency to downplay the narrative aspects of 19–20[7] as well as its inability to account adequately for 20:1–16 (the parable of the workers in the vineyard) and 20:29–34 (the healing of the two blind men) in the household code scheme.[8]

The argument of this work is that chapters 19–20 function within the larger framework of 16:21–20:28 to illuminate Matthean discipleship (not unlike Carter's broader proposal). Further, discipleship, in chapters 19–20, is defined by a rejection of the presumption of status within the kingdom (somewhat akin but not precisely equivalent to Carter's conclusion of "anti-structural existence"). This discipleship is illuminated through the contrast between the perspective of the disciples and Jesus' perspective (rather than Carter's proposed contrast between traditional household codes and Jesus' teaching).

In conclusion, in Matthew 16:21–20:28, the central theme of Matthean discipleship is illuminated through the weaving of narrative with discourse. The three passion predictions of Jesus, as well as the disciples' questions and reactions, provide the narrative framework for Jesus' words on the nature of ideal discipleship. The disciples' frequent misunderstandings about discipleship provide a foil for ideal discipleship, which is revealed by Jesus' words and deeds. Ideal discipleship does not focus and presume upon one's own status (the disciples' point of view). Rather, ideal discipleship is about giving up desire for status entirely to focus one's attention on others in gracious service.

THE DISCIPLES' PORTRAYAL IN MATTHEW 1:1–16:20

From their introduction into the narrative at 4:18, the disciples are characterized in a consistent though multifaceted manner by Matthew. Their portrayal in 4:17–16:20[9] can be analyzed in terms of three major categories: the role of the disciples in relation to Jesus and his ministry; the "little faith" of the disciples; and the level of understanding exhibited by the disciples. These three categories are fluidly interwoven throughout 4:17–16:20 and so must be

---

[7] Treating 19–20 as essentially a household code tends to focus attention away from the narrative quality of these chapters, downplaying the sustained interaction between Jesus and his disciples and their conflicting points of view regarding the kingdom community.

[8] Luz, *Matthäus,* 3:87. Luz also points out that "possessions" (one of the four household codes analyzed by Carter) is not actually a *Haustafel* theme (3:87, n. 2). Davies and Allison, on the other hand, find Carter's proposal "very helpful and largely convincing" (*Matthew,* 3:2, n. 3).

[9] This is Kingsbury's second division of the gospel, focusing on the structural markers at 4:17 and 16:21.

understood in relation to each other. Therefore, I will first analyze each of these categories individually, followed by a summary of their relationship to each other.

The Disciples as Jesus' Helpers

The role of the disciples in relation to Jesus and his ministry is introduced in Matt 4:18–22. We first meet the disciples by means of this call narrative.[10] Simon (Peter), Andrew, James and John are called by Jesus to leave their vocation as fishermen to follow Jesus. Jesus then promises that he will make them fishers of people. The four men immediately leave their livelihood to follow Jesus (cf. also 9:9 for a similar call to and response from Matthew, the tax-collector). From this point on, Matthew defines the disciples in part through their role of *being with Jesus*. They are to be with him, i.e., to follow him. Kingsbury discusses this aspect of the role of the disciples, noting that, other than the twelve disciples (in part or whole), only Mary, Jesus' mother (2:11), and tax collectors and sinners (9:11) are described as being "with Jesus" (μετά + reference to Jesus). "In Matthew's story, then, Jesus grants the privilege of his company almost without exception only to his own."[11]

In addition to being with Jesus, being part of the character group of the disciples is also defined by helping Jesus in his ministry.[12] The call narrative sets the tone for this aspect of being a disciple through Jesus' commission to be "fishers of people." The continuity between this commission and Jesus' ministry is emphasized in context by the summary statement at 4:23–25. Jesus teaches, proclaims the kingdom, and heals. His ministry is directed toward people, and he casts his net widely with the result that "great crowds" followed him from a wide, geographic area (4:25).[13] In a similar way, the disciples are to be fishers of people.

Specifics of this adjunct ministry are spelled out at 10:1–4, 7, where Jesus gives the twelve disciples authority to cast out unclean spirits, heal sickness,

---

[10] "Discipleship begins with the call of Jesus which…separates disciples from nondisciples;" Warren Carter, *Matthew: Storyteller, Interpreter, Evangelist* (Peabody, MA: Hendrickson, 1996) 244.

[11] Jack D. Kingsbury, *Matthew as Story*, 2d ed. (Philadelphia: Fortress Press, 1988) 131. Cf. also Terence L. Donaldson, "Guiding Readers—Making Disciples: Discipleship in Matthew's Narrative Strategy," in *Patterns of Discipleship in the New Testament*, ed. R. Longenecker (Grand Rapids: Eerdmans, 1996) 32.

[12] Cf. Andries G van Aarde, "The Disciples in Matthew's Story," *Hervormde Teologiese Studies Supplement* 5 (1994) 87: "…the role of the disciples consists of that of *helpers* of Jesus." Cf. also Donaldson, "Making Disciples," 35.

[13] Notice the frequent use of the words, πᾶς and ὅλος, in this summary (five times in 4:23–24).

and proclaim the good news of the kingdom.[14] These very activities, along with teaching, have characterized Jesus' ministry thus far in Matthew. Now the disciples are given the authority to join Jesus in part of his ministry.[15] It is at this point in the narrative that Matthew delineates the twelve disciples by name (with only five having been explicitly called in the preceding narrative). Up to this point in the narrative, the disciples have been portrayed in a quite positive manner.[16] In fact, their role so far has encouraged the reader to identify with the disciples as those who respond to Jesus' call and are with him in his ministry.[17]

The final two passages that give further attention to the role of the disciples in Jesus' ministry are the feedings of the 5000 and the 4000 (14:13–21 and 15:32–39, respectively). The primary activity of the disciples in both stories is their assistance in distributing food to the crowds (14:19; 15:36; with the wording being very similar in both stories). They function as helpers, as intermediaries to the crowds. Nevertheless, Jesus intends for their role in these feedings to be more significant. At 14:16, before Jesus himself multiplies the food, he instructs *his disciples* to feed the crowds: "[Y]ou give them something to eat." It would seem that Jesus expects the disciples to draw on the authority given at 10:1 to provide food in a miraculous way for thousands of people. But the disciples in their response demonstrate that they are unable to conceive of this kind of role for themselves: "We have nothing here but five loaves and two fish" (14:17). As Weaver aptly notes, "they respond not with the self-assurance

---

[14] Edwards speaks of these verses as a "call" to accept authority from Jesus, thus linking 10:1–4 with 4:18–22; Richard A. Edwards, "Uncertain Faith: Matthew's Portrait of the Disciples," in *Discipleship in the New Testament*, ed. F. Segovia (Philadelphia: Fortress, 1985) 54.

[15] The task of teaching is conspicuously absent from the commission of the disciples here. This task is not given to the disciples until the very end of the gospel (28:18–20). In addition, unlike Mark, the disciples are never actually shown as embarking on the mission delineated in ch. 10. Weaver argues that the commission of ch. 10 (10:5–6) (1) is not fulfilled by the twelve disciples within the confines of Matthew's story; and (2) is transformed into a universal commission at 28:18–20; Dorothy Jean Weaver, *Matthew's Missionary Discourse: A Literary Critical Analysis,* JSNTSup 38 (Sheffield: JSOT Press, 1990) 151–53. Donaldson captures the irony: "though [the disciples] have been called to fish for people, to bring in the harvest, and to gather the flock, in the rest of the story they do precious little fishing, harvesting, or shepherding" ("Making Disciples," 36).

[16] The one exception to this is the attribution to them of "little faith" at 6:30. Cf. discussion on pp. 103–04 of this chapter.

[17] Cf. Donald A. Hagner, *Matthew*, WBC (Dallas: Word Books, 1993) 78; Davies and Allison, *Matthew*, 1:406. Both speak of the disciples at 4:18–22 as an example or a model for readers. Tannehill, in his study of the Marcan disciples, speaks of readers identifying with the disciples because the latter "share this essential quality [of positive response to Jesus with] the readers' self-understanding;" Robert C. Tannehill, "The Disciples in Mark: The Function of a Narrative Role," *JR* 57 (1977) 393–94.

of those who know they have the 'authority' to carry out such 'deeds of power' but rather with the incredulity of those faced with an impossible task."[18] So Jesus miraculously provides food instead.

The same tenor is present in the account of the feeding of the 4000. Jesus has compassion on the crowds, not wanting to send them away hungry. The disciples ask, "Where are we to get enough bread in the desert to feed so great a crowd?" Their response indicates that they perceive Jesus to be asking *them* to be part of the solution to the problem. It also indicates that, although they have recently seen just what Jesus can do with a little bread, they do not trust him in this new situation to do the same. As Verseput concludes, "the feeding [of the 4000] emphasizes again the immeasurable fullness of Jesus' ἐξουσία superimposed upon the backdrop of the disciples' continued dullness…The deliberate parallels between this episode and the first feeding account render the disciples' continued lack of insight into the mighty power of Jesus all the more incomprehensible for the reader…, impressing upon him the utter foolishness of their 'little faith'."[19]

In Matt 4:17–16:20, the portrayal of the disciples as those who follow Jesus and act as his helpers in ministry weaves through the narrative. This part of their portrayal has both positive and negative aspects. The disciples do leave their former lives to follow Jesus, and they are present with him in his ministry. Nevertheless, in their role as helpers to Jesus they fall short of his intentions for them. They do not embrace the significant ministry they are given authority to perform, and thus their helper function is far more limited than what is expected of them.[20]

The Disciples as Those of "Little Faith"

A consistent and explicit theme in the Matthean portrayal of the disciples is their "little faith." The word ὀλιγόπιστος or its cognate noun is used five times in Matthew and only in reference to the disciples. This characterization is universally acknowledged in Matthean scholarship. The little-faith concept, however, has not always been well-defined. Defining what is meant by "little faith" will require an analysis of Matthew's concept of faith in general as well as a narrative analysis of characters exhibiting a range of faith responses, including commendable faith, adequate faith, "little faith," and unbelief.

---

[18] Weaver, *Missionary Discourse*, 134.

[19] Donald J. Verseput, "The Faith of the Reader and the Narrative of Matthew 13:53–16:20," *JSNT* 46 (1992) 18–19.

[20] Cf. van Aarde ("Disciples," 88) who speaks of the disciples being "inclined to deny their *helper function*." According to Donaldson ("Making Disciples," 36), "when [the disciples] do appear in ministry situations with the crowds, they are ineffectual."

In general, the concept of faith in Matthew is related to Jesus' authority and the source of that authority (as from God). Those who are commended for faith exhibit a faith in the power of Jesus, usually in connection with healing for themselves or someone important to them (e.g., 8:9–10; 9:1–8; 9:21–22; 9:28). In addition, when the disciples are referred to as those of "little faith," the context usually indicates that they are not exhibiting adequate trust in Jesus' power (e.g., 8:23–27; 14:29–32). When Jesus teaches the disciples about faith, he teaches that an adequate faith will result in powerful, miraculous activity (17:19–20; 21:20–22). Thus, faith in Matthew is, in part, a trust in the authority of Jesus.[21]

Matthew's concept of "little faith" is illuminated by observing that which is contrasted to it. First, "little faith" is not unbelief (ἀπιστία and its adjectival cognate, ἄπιστος). Those characterized by unbelief in Matthew include Jesus' hometown, who cannot see beyond his familial identity and so take offense at (versus, trust in) his teaching and miraculous powers. The end result is that Jesus "did not do many deeds of power there, because of their unbelief (ἀπιστία)" (13:58). The only other place in Matthew where the term, ἀπιστία/ος, is used, is at 17:17, where Jesus refers to the present generation as unbelieving and perverse. This is a general reference to the unbelief that Jesus has been encountering in his ministry (as well as an indictment of the disciples for falling into the mindset of this generation; cf. 17:14–20). Finally, the Jewish leaders as a character group are portrayed as lacking faith in Jesus and his authority.[22] The Jewish leaders are accused by Jesus of not believing in John the Baptist who pointed the way toward Jesus himself (21:32). Even more to the point, the Pharisees accuse Jesus on two occasions of having an authority derived from the ruler of demons rather than from God (9:34; 12:24).[23] Their accusation demonstrates that they do not believe Jesus' authority is from God. Lack of faith in the divine source of Jesus' authority is central to the concept of unbelief in Matthew.

"Little faith" is not a complete lack of faith, therefore, but is rather a faith that proves to be inadequate on the whole.[24] This is seen by a second

---

[21] Verseput, "Faith of the Reader," 22–23.

[22] Although the specific term, ἀπιστία, is not used of their stance toward Jesus, they are consistently *shown* to lack faith in the true source of Jesus' authority.

[23] For a social scientific analysis of this conflict between the Pharisees and Jesus in Matthew, especially as it relates to defamation and deviant labeling, cf. Bruce J. Malina and Jerome H. Neyrey, *Calling Jesus Names: The Social Value of Labels in Matthew* (Sonoma, CA: Polebridge Press, 1988).

[24] "In Matthew, ὀλιγόπιστος…does not imply an absence of faith but a broken or insufficient faith" (Davies and Allison, *Matthew,* 1:656). As Doyle puts it, "[t]here is faith there, but in continuing need for growing;" B. Rod Doyle, "Disciples as Sages and Scribes in Matthew's Gospel," *Word in Life* 32 (1984) 6.

comparison. While "little faith" in Matthew is not the equivalent of unbelief, it is also not the same as adequate faith. On two occasions, Jesus explicitly teaches his disciples about faith. In the first instance, Jesus contrasts their "little faith" with the faith of a mustard seed, which though small is enough to move mountains (17:20). This could then be termed "adequate faith." At 21:21, this same kind of mountain-moving faith is defined as a faith without doubting or wavering (διακρίνομαι).[25] Faith is exemplified by various characters in the first gospel, a number of whom are commended by Jesus for their faith. Interestingly enough, those who demonstrate commendable faith are not from the character group of the disciples but are from among the supplicants, i.e., minor characters who come to Jesus seeking his help. Seekers that are praised for their faith in Matthew include a Roman centurion (8:5–13) and a Canaanite woman (15:21–28). Other supplicants are granted what they ask because of their faith (paralytic's friends—9:1–8; hemorrhaging woman—9:20–22; and two blind men—9:27–31). Commendable faith, in each of these cases, is complete trust in Jesus' power to heal.[26]

Given that "little faith" in Matthew is not unbelief nor is it adequate or commendable faith, a contextual analysis of the five instances of this term will illuminate what "little faith" actually is. In 6:25–34, "little faith" is linked to anxiety for daily needs. The Sermon on the Mount, of which 6:25–34 is a part, is directed primarily to the disciples with the crowds also in view as part of the audience (cf. 5:1; 7:28).[27] At 6:25–34, Jesus commands that his followers not be anxious for their sustenance. His argument is based on their worth in the eyes of their heavenly Father. The centerpiece of his argument is a *qal wahomer* argument, in which Jesus argues from lesser to greater: If God feeds the birds, will he not also feed you, since you are worth more than birds? If God clothes the lilies, will he not also clothe you?

This argument ends with a surprising appellation: Jesus calls his audience "you of little faith" (6:30). In spite of the ubiquitous use of the second person pronoun throughout chapters 5–7, this is one of the few explicit statements of characterization of the disciples (Jesus' audience) in the Sermon on the Mount. What Jesus has been teaching throughout most of chapters 5–7 has to do with the attitude and behavior of an "ideal disciple" (i.e., what Jesus expects of his

---

[25] BDAG, 231.

[26] With an eye to recognizing Jesus' identity. Note the frequent ascription to Jesus of authoritative titles by these seekers: "Son of David" (9:27; 15:22); "Lord" (8:5; 15:27).

[27] The "you" of the sermon is clearly directed at those who follow Jesus, i.e., his disciples (e.g., 5:11; 5:17–20; 7:22); cf. Donald J. Verseput, "The Davidic Messiah and Matthew's Jewish Christianity," *SBLSP* (1995) 111.

disciples).[28] At 6:30, however, we get a brief glimpse of what the disciples (as character group) *actually are*, namely, those of "little faith."[29] The implication is that his disciples do not fully trust in the goodness of God who knows their needs and cares for them (6:26, 32).[30] The result is anxiety about their needs. "Little faith" is thus illuminated by its close association with anxiety.

In 8:23–27, "little faith" is connected to timidity. The disciples and Jesus are in a boat, when a storm arises. The disciples awaken Jesus and implore him, "Lord, save us! We are perishing!" Jesus asks, "Why are you timid, you of little faith?" (8:26; my translation). Then he calms the sea. The word translated as timid is δειλός whose only New Testament occurrence is here. It refers to being cowardly or timid.[31] The implication is that, if the disciples had enough faith in Jesus' power (adequate faith versus "little faith"), they would not be cowardly but would have confidence in Jesus to care for them.

The next time the disciples are referred to as those of "little faith" is during another sea narrative. In 14:22–33, the story of Jesus walking on the water is told. Peter, who requests that he might join Jesus, becomes afraid and begins to sink. Jesus takes hold of Peter to keep him from sinking and responds, "You of little faith, why did you hesitate?" (my translation). "Little faith" is here identified with both fear (φοβέομαι at 14:30) and hesitation (διστάζω at 14:31).[32] Peter does leave the boat and come toward Jesus on the water; he is not without faith in the power of Jesus. But he wavers or hesitates out of fear, showing himself to be one of "little faith" in relation to Jesus' power.[33]

Although not explicitly connected, faith and understanding are implicitly linked in the passages discussed thus far. The insufficient trust in God's inclination and ability to care for basic needs is, at least in part, a deficiency in

---

[28] The terminology, "ideal disciple," is introduced by Patte to distinguish the ideal disciple envisioned in Jesus' teaching from the portrayal of the "actual disciples;" Daniel Patte, *The Gospel according to Matthew: A Structural Commentary on Matthew's Faith* (Philadelphia: Fortress Press, 1987) 136, n. 16.

[29] The other explicit description of the audience in the Sermon on the Mount is "you are the salt of the earth/light of the world" at 5:13–14. The appellation at 7:5 ("you hypocrite") and description at 7:11 ("if you then, who are evil") could also be construed as characterizing the audience (i.e., Jesus' disciples), but the first is conditional upon a certain kind of behavior (described in 7:3–4) and the second seems to be universal (cf. contrast with God in the latter part of the verse). Neither then is actually a specific characterization of the disciples.

[30] Hagner, *Matthew*, 165.

[31] BDAG, 215.

[32] The frequent translation of διστάζω as "doubt" is not to be preferred. Cf. discussion of 28:17 on pp. 116–17 of this chapter.

[33] The disciples are also described by Matthew as "worshiping" (προσκυνέω) Jesus at 14:33. The same combination of worship and hesitation by the disciples (προσκυνέω and διστάζω) reappears at 28:17.

understanding, since Jesus counteracts the propensity toward anxiety by trying to convince his disciples of the *knowledge* that God considers them very valuable and knows their needs (6:26, 32). The disciples' timidity at 8:26, focused on their insufficient faith in Jesus' power to protect them from perishing, is rooted in their inadequate understanding of the extent of Jesus' authority (over even nature). And at 14:31 Peter, as representative of the disciples, hesitates rather than trusts in Jesus' power to sustain him on the water, again showing an inadequate understanding of the extent of Jesus' authority and its application to his own situation.

In 16:5–12 the connection between "little faith" and understanding is made explicit. Following the request by the Pharisees and Sadducees for a sign from heaven to substantiate Jesus' activity and authority (cf. 12:38–45),[34] he says, "Watch out, and beware of the yeast of the Pharisees and Sadducees" (16:6). The disciples, thinking that Jesus is speaking literally, conclude that Jesus is referring to the fact that they have neglected to bring bread. Jesus corrects their mistaken interpretation: "You of little faith, why are you talking about having no bread? Do you still not perceive?" (16:8–9). He then indicts them for not understanding (νοέω) the miraculous feedings of the 5000 and 4000.[35]

At 16:8–9, "little faith" is directly tied to a lack of understanding.[36] What the disciples misunderstand is not merely Jesus' enigmatic saying.[37] As Verseput argues, "such an interpretation would greatly weaken the climactic nature of the question in v. 11a..., which expresses incredulity at the very possibility of misunderstanding Jesus' words."[38] Rather, the disciples do not understand Jesus' warning as well as the truth that, even though they had forgotten to bring physical bread, this would not be problematic for Jesus. His ability to provide for their daily bread is not bound by whether they have remembered to bring

---

[34] "They "demand a sign from heaven to validate the divine origin of his ministry" (Verseput, "Faith of the Reader," 19).

[35] A vivid distinction between νοέω and συνίημι is not warranted (as is sometimes implied in redaction-critical work). Both of these terms refer to understanding or comprehension, so that the use of the negation of νοέω with reference to the disciples connotes a lack of understanding just as much as if the negation of συνίημι was used.

[36] According to Garland, the disciples' "little faith" is the result of a lack of understanding; David Garland, *Reading Matthew: A Literary and Theological Commentary on the First Gospel* (New York: Crossroad, 1993) 167. So also Alexander Sand, *Das Evangelium nach Matthäus*, Regensburger Neues Testament (Regensburg: Pustet, 1986) 322.

[37] Contra Barth, who asserts that "in Matthew the main point is not that the disciples had failed to recognise the ἐξουσία of Jesus [as in Mark] but that for a time they had not understood an enigmatic saying;" Gerhard Barth, "Matthew's Understanding of the Law," in G. Bornkamm, G. Barth, and H. J. Held, *Tradition and Interpretation in Matthew* (Philadelphia: Westminster, 1963) 114.

[38] Verseput, "Faith of the Reader," 20, n. 2.

bread with them. That is why Jesus reminds them of the two previous displays of his power in the feeding miracles (16:9–10). And this is why they are once more guilty of "little faith." They do not adequately understand the extent of Jesus' authority.[39] In this instance, they fail to understand and so trust in the extent of Jesus' ability to provide their daily food.[40]

The final occurrence of ὀλιγόπιστος/ια in Matthew's gospel is at 17:20 in Jesus' response to his disciples, after they are unable to heal a boy with a demon.[41] When the disciples ask why they were not able to cast it out, Jesus responds, "Because of your little faith. For truly I tell you, if you have faith the size of a mustard seed, you will say to this mountain, 'Move from here to there,' and it will move; and nothing will be impossible for you." Here "little faith" is linked to an inability to carry out a task the disciples have been given the power to do. At 10:1 Jesus had given the disciples authority to cast out unclean spirits. At 17:20 they are shown to have inadequate faith to appropriate the authority already granted to them by Jesus. Once more, the disciples are shown to be of "little faith" in relation to Jesus' authority—this time in relation to the extension of his authority to their own role in his ministry.[42]

To summarize, the disciples are characterized by "little faith" in Matthew's gospel. Matthew defines this "little faith" narratively as an inadequate faith in the *extent of Jesus' authority*.[43] The disciples do not trust that Jesus' authority is great enough to save them when they are in grave physical danger (8:26; 14:31). Neither do they trust that his authority extends to miraculous provision for everyday needs (16:8; with 14:13–21 and 15:32–39; cf. also 6:30).[44] Finally, the disciples do not adequately trust that Jesus' authority extends to their role in

---

[39] "As Jesus' adversaries have failed to grasp the heavenly source of his authority, so the disciples fail to comprehend its extent" (Verseput, "Faith of the Reader," 20).

[40] This hearkens back to 6:30, in which "little faith" is related to anxiety about *daily needs of food and clothing*. "[T]he disciples have done more than just misunderstand Jesus' saying...they have also...come to wonder about their provisions" (Davies and Allison, *Matthew*, 2:590). Cf. also Zumstein, who connects 16:8 and 6:30 in terms of yielding to worry; Jean Zumstein, *La condition du croyant dans l'Evangile selon Matthieu*, OBO 16 (Göttingen: Vandenhoeck & Ruprecht, 1977) 239.

[41] Cf. discussion of this passage in chapter 3.

[42] The disciples' "little faith" also highlights Jesus' own ability to do what they were not able to, showing Jesus to be the true *model of faith* for his disciples.

[43] "'Little faith' is "the unjustified incapacity of the disciple to grasp and rely upon Jesus' inexhaustible power" (Verseput, "Faith of the Reader," 23). For Ogawa, "faith consists in the steadfast trust in Jesus that he can help;" Akira Ogawa, "Action-Motivating Faith: The Understanding of 'Faith' in the Gospel of Matthew," AJBI 19 (1993) 72.

[44] Gnilka combines these categories and speaks of their deficient faith when they are in "existential danger" ("*existentiellen Gefährdungen*"), citing 6:30; 14:31; and 16:8; Joachim Gnilka, *Das Matthäusevangelium*, HTKNT (Freiburg: Herder, 1986) 2:108.

his ministry (17:20), although he has clearly granted such authority to them (10:1). In addition, Matthew closely connects the "little faith" of the disciples with anxiety (6:30); fear and timidity (8:26); hesitation (14:31); inadequate understanding (16:8); and an inability to complete the miraculous tasks to which the disciples are called (17:20; cf. also14:13–21 and 15:32–39).

The Disciples as Prone to Misunderstanding

Unlike Matthew's explicit characterization of the disciples as those of "little faith," the disciples' level of understanding is primarily communicated *indirectly* in the narrative. In fact, if only direct characterization is taken into account, it would be easy to conclude that the Matthean disciples are portrayed as possessing understanding (cf. 16:12 and 17:13).[45] But the words and actions of the disciples as well as the words and actions of Jesus toward the disciples are a crucial part of their portrayal. This indirect characterization shows the disciples to be prone to misunderstanding. Specifically, in 4:17–16:20, while the Matthean disciples do understand the identity of Jesus as Messiah, Son of God, they do not comprehend the extent of his authority as it relates to their own experiences. In addition, they frequently lack an adequate understanding of Jesus' teaching in the many parables he speaks.

The first act of the disciples (the four introduced at 4:18–22) is to follow Jesus. Jesus calls them, and they follow immediately (4:20, 22). Although there is no explicit evidence of what the disciples understand about Jesus at this early moment, that they do follow him certainly implies they consider him to be worthy of having disciples. Although one could guess that they view him as a rabbi or a prophet, or possibly even as the Messiah, their understanding of who Jesus is at this point is unclear. Matthew simply does not give enough information about the disciples to make this determination.[46]

The very first words of disciples in the gospel are "Lord, save us! We are perishing!" (8:25), spoken to Jesus during the storm at sea. The designation of Jesus as "Lord" hints that the disciples have an inkling of Jesus' true identity,

---

[45] This is why, in part, redaction-critical studies have concluded that the disciples possess understanding. These verses, however, are quite limited in the scope of what the disciples come to understand. In 16:12, they come to understand the meaning of one of Jesus' sayings. In 17:13, they come to understand that Jesus refers to John the Baptist in his discussion of the Elijah who precedes the Messiah. These verses do not provide adequate evidence that the Matthean disciples possess understanding as a general characteristic.

[46] This does not imply, however, that the disciples do not recognize him to be Messiah, only that the reader does not yet know who the disciples understand Jesus to be.

since this title is not attributed to Jesus by unbelievers in Matthew's gospel.[47] The rhetorical question at 8:27 ("What sort of man is this, that even the winds and the sea obey him?") need not imply that the disciples do not understand who Jesus is.[48] In fact, as a rhetorical question, their response is less a call for information than an exclamation of the uniqueness of Jesus shown in his authority over the sea.[49] Still, at this point in the narrative, it is not yet clear whether the disciples accurately comprehend Jesus' identity as Messiah.

At 14:22–32 it becomes quite clear to the reader that the disciples understand Jesus to be in a unique relationship to God the Father. After Jesus rescues Peter and the wind stops, the disciples worship Jesus, saying, "Truly you are the Son of God." The title, "Son of God," indicates the intimate relationship that Jesus has with the Father.[50] This title is also closely connected to messianic identity at 16:13–20, where the disciples confess Jesus to be "the Messiah, the Son of the living God" (16:16).[51] "Matthew can summate the two confessions [Messiah, and Son of God] under the single term, χριστός [at 16:20], because of the supportive role played by the filial relationship to the Father."[52] By 16:20, it is completely clear to the reader that the disciples have understood Jesus' identity as Messiah.

Thus, I would argue that there is no discernable progression in the disciples' understanding of Jesus' identity in 4:17–16:20. Rather, they are portrayed as understanding his identity as Messiah. What does progress is the *reader's perception* of the disciples' understanding, with more explicit indication of their understanding being provided as the narrative proceeds. So, while it does

---

[47] "Mt...reserves διδάσκαλε for the Pharisees, Judas Iscariot and the uncommitted. Elsewhere he has κύριε" (W. Foerster, "κύριος," *TDNT* 3:1093).

[48] "Some interpreters have...been tempted by the enticing parallel between 8:27 and 14:33 to suppose that the disciples actually progress in their grasp of Jesus' identity, but surely this reads too much into the astonished reaction of 8:27..." (Verseput, "Faith of the Reader," 11).

[49] It may be significant in this regard that Matthew has substituted Ποταπός ἐστιν οὗτος ("What sort of man is this?") for Mark's Τίς...οὗτός ἐστιν ("Who...is this?" 4:41). In any event, the attribution of the question at 8:27 to some group other than the disciples (cf. Luz, *Matthäus*, 2:27–28) is not convincing and is certainly unnecessary if the question is understood as a rhetorical exclamation. Cf. also Hagner (*Matthew*, 222), who states that the disciples "knew beyond a shadow of a doubt that Jesus was an extraordinary person with incomparable power and authority."

[50] Donald J. Verseput, "The 'Son of God' Title in Matthew's Gospel," *NTS* 33 (1987) 539.

[51] Peter is representative of all the disciples in this story, since the *disciples* answer Jesus' initial question at 16:13, and Jesus orders the *disciples* not to tell anyone of Peter's confession at 16:20. Cf. Jack D. Kingsbury, "The Figure of Peter in Matthew's Gospel as a Theological Problem," *JBL* 98 (1979) 74–75.

[52] Verseput ("Son of God," 544) goes on: "The Davidic category is of primary concern to Matthew, since it propels the narrative from the birth to the crucifixion. At the same time it exists in inextricable relation to the divine Sonship..." (544).

become clearer to the reader as the narrative progresses that the disciples understand Jesus to be the Messiah, the disciples are not portrayed as progressing from a point at which they do not believe Jesus to be Messiah to a point at which they do. Rather, they are portrayed as having received the knowledge of Jesus as Messiah via revelation from God (16:17); it might even be supposed that this is the case from the beginning of their association with Jesus.

Although understanding the important truth that Jesus is the Messiah, the disciples do not understand the extent of Jesus' authority (and, by extension, the appropriation of that authority in their role as his helpers). This is most clearly seen in the intersection of the disciples' portrayal as those who lack both understanding and adequate faith at 16:1–12. Part of their "little faith," which has already been defined as an inadequate faith in the extent of Jesus' authority, has to do with a lack of understanding of that authority.[53] The disciples think Jesus' warning to beware of the yeast of the Pharisees and Sadducees has to do with his concern for their lack of physical bread. Jesus finds fault with their misperception, because it implies that Jesus does not have the power to remedy their bread-less situation. This on the heels of two miracles through which Jesus provides bread for thousands of people! The disciples clearly are deficient in their understanding of the extent of Jesus' power.[54]

Finally, the disciples do not appear to understand Jesus' teaching in a consistent or adequate fashion. In chapter 13 the disciples need Jesus' interpretation to understand the parables that he speaks to the crowds.[55] In fact, Jesus' affirmation that the disciples are given knowledge of the "secrets of the kingdom" not given to others (13:11) is closely tied to receiving Jesus' interpretation of the parables. In Jesus' teaching, the idea that knowledge of kingdom secrets is withheld from non-disciples is logically connected to the fact that Jesus speaks to non-disciples in parables *without interpretation* (13:11, 13). Thus, the special knowledge given to the disciples in chapter 13 is precisely the interpretation of his parables that Jesus provides for them, rather

---

[53] Cf. previous discussion on the relationship between "little faith" and understanding.

[54] The statement at 16:12 that they then understood the referent of Jesus' saying is important. It means that the disciples fall short of understanding what Jesus clearly expects them to grasp. Only after Jesus' explanation do they comprehend his meaning. No indication, however, is given that they have come to understand and trust the extent of Jesus' authority, which is the greater problem at 16:5–12.

[55] Note, for example, their request for interpretation at 13:36 as well as Jesus' interpretation of the parable of the dragnet at 13:49–50.

than some sort of *guarantee* that they will completely understand after hearing his interpretation.[56]

Nevertheless, at the end of the parables discourse in chapter 13, the disciples explicitly affirm that they understand "all of these things [the parables]" (13:51). Since Jesus does not question their response, the assumption of the reader at 13:51 would be that the disciples have understood his parables when given explanation by Jesus.[57] Yet this assumption is called into question at 15:15–20.[58] In 15:1–14, Jesus challenges the authority of the "tradition of the elders" that the Pharisees uphold. Calling the crowds, Jesus makes this statement: "it is not what goes into the mouth that defiles a person, but it is what comes out of the mouth that defiles" (15:11). Peter requests that Jesus explain this "parable" to the disciples (15:15, referring back to the maxim at 15:11). Jesus responds, "Are you also still without understanding?" and then goes on to give an interpretation of the parable. Clearly Jesus expects that the disciples should have understood these sorts of parables by now. (Jesus' question and its inclusion of ἀκμήν strongly implies this expectation.)[59] So, while the disciples have claimed to understand Jesus' parables after hearing his interpretation (13:51), it becomes clear at 15:16 that they have not

---

[56] It is precisely in this way that they are clearly distinguished from the crowds, to whom Jesus speaks in parables *without interpretation* (13:10–17, 18).

[57] Orton, for example, speaks of their understanding being "emphatically announced" at 13:51, thereby indicating that he trust the disciples' word to provide Matthew's (and Jesus') perspective; David E. Orton, *The Understanding Scribe: Matthew and the Apocalyptic Ideal*, JSNTSup 25 (Sheffield: Sheffield Academic Press, 1989) 141. Narrative criticism, however, has provided a greater awareness of issues related to point of view. The disciples in Matthew are not consistently endowed with the reliable point of view shared by Jesus and the narrator. Rather, their point of view is often limited or skewed, so that the reader learns to judge what they say and do in the light the perspective espoused by Jesus (and Matthew). This means that their confident word at 13:51 that they do understood needs to be seen in light of the words of Jesus toward them in the broader context. Cf. Kingsbury, *Matthew as Story*, 34–35; Mark Allan Powell, *What is Narrative Criticism?* GBS (Minneapolis: Fortress, 1990) 25.

[58] "Although the disciples answer in the affirmative that they have understood, in subsequent scenes the depth of their perception will be called into question (cf. 15:15–16; 16:9);" Larry Chouinard, *Matthew*, The College Press NIV Commentary (Joplin, MO: College Press, 1997) 254. Carter speaks of the disciples' confidence at 13:51 being misplaced when viewed from their activity in the following three chapters (*Matthew*, 248). Cf. also Hagner (*Matthew*, 401).

[59] The identification of Jesus' saying as a parable (παραβολή) at 15:15 connects this passage with chapter 13 and the issues of understanding raised there. So Lamar Cope, *Matthew: A Scribe Trained for the Kingdom of Heaven*, CBQMS 5 (Washington: Catholic Biblical Association, 1976) 58.

demonstrated the level of understanding related to his teaching that Jesus expects.[60]

Summary of the Disciples' Role, "Little Faith," and Understanding

The intersection of these three areas provides a complete portrait of the disciples in 4:17–16:20. On the positive side, the disciples are legitimate followers of Jesus; they recognize and worship him as Messiah; and they have been assigned an important role in his ministry. Nevertheless, the disciples consistently lack faith in and therefore are shown to misunderstand: (1) the extent of Jesus' authority as it relates to miraculous provision and deliverance for them (8:26; 14:31; 16:6) and (2) the extent of Jesus' authority as it extends to their own part in his ministry (e.g., their expected participation in the feedings, as well as in the healing at 17:20).[61] In addition, the disciples frequently demonstrate an inadequate understanding of Jesus' teaching communicated through his parables. This foreshadows their misunderstanding of Jesus' teaching on the kingdom in 16:21–20:28.[62] It is because of their misunderstanding and "little faith" that they often fall short of Jesus' expectations for them in their role as his followers.

This portrait contradicts Barth's often-accepted conclusion that Matthew has removed the noetic element from his concept of faith. For Barth, "[t]he intellectual element...is excluded from the πίστις—concept of Matthew."[63] In contrast, the narrative reading of this chapter indicates that faith and understanding are integrally connected in the Matthean story. Part of the problem of "little faith" is a lack of understanding (made explicit at 16:5–12). Verseput affirms this connection when he states that "little faith" is the incapacity to "grasp and rely upon Jesus' inexhaustible power." True faith, in

---

[60] Readers are led to trust the words of Jesus more than that of the disciples when these appear to be in conflict. Such is the case, I would argue, at 13:51 and 15:16 (cf. n. 57). "We are expected to judge the words and actions of [other characters] in light of the words and actions of Jesus" (Tannehill, "Disciples in Mark," 391); cf. also David B. Howell, *Matthew's Inclusive Story: A Study in the Narrative Rhetoric of the First Gospel*, JSNTSup 42 (Sheffield: JSOT Press, 1990) 203. In addition, 15:12–20 does not conclude with a statement that the disciples come to understand Jesus' teaching. Thus, the final word on whether the disciples' understand Jesus' parables is more negative than positive.

[61] Bauer identifies the disciples' two main difficulties in 4:17–16:20 as lack of understanding and weakness of faith; David R. Bauer, "The Major Characters of Matthew's Story: Their Function and Significance," *Int* 46 (1992) 362.

[62] With the emphasis in 16:21–20:28 on their misunderstanding of Jesus' mission as well as the nature of discipleship.

[63] Barth, "Matthew's Understanding," 113–14. Cf. my earlier discussion in ch. 1, pp. 3–4.

turn, is engendered in part by a *"cognitive awareness* of Jesus' limitless authority."[64]

THE DISCIPLES' PORTRAYAL IN MATTHEW 20:29–28:20

In Matt 20:29–28:20 the disciples are less visible overall than in 16:21–20:28. Nevertheless, their portrayal in this final section of Matthew is consistent with what we have seen in the rest of the gospel. The disciples are prone to misunderstand, and they do not progress toward greater faith or understanding.

The role of the disciples as Jesus' helpers continues to be important in Matt 20:29–28:20 (as in 4:17–16:20). In fact, at two points in the narrative, the reader is explicitly told that the disciples complete the tasks given to them by Jesus. At 21:1–11 two of the disciples bring a donkey and colt to Jesus "as Jesus had directed them" (21:6) in preparation for his entry into Jerusalem. At 26:17–19 the disciples again follow Jesus' instructions in preparation for their Passover observance.

In spite of these brief indications that the disciples are fulfilling their role as Jesus' helpers, their portrayal in the surrounding context provides an implicit critique of this assumption. As Donaldson points out, the disciples provide only the most mundane kind of assistance to Jesus.[65] When all is said and done, the disciples fall short of the more significant role that they are expected to play in Jesus' ministry and mission. Three passages in chapters 21–26 show this to be the case.[66]

At 21:18–22 the disciples "are amazed" at the withering of the fig tree after Jesus curses it. They respond, "How did the fig tree wither at once?" (21:20). Jesus' answer centers on the need for faith and mirrors the earlier teaching at 17:20 in response to the disciples' "little faith."[67] The disciples' "little faith," which has been portrayed as an inadequate faith in the extent of Jesus' power, is still operative at 21:18–22. The disciples are amazed that Jesus' words can have the powerful effect that they do. Jesus' answer shows that their problem continues to be an inadequate faith. Jesus once again affirms not only that he is

---

[64] Verseput, "Faith of the Reader," 23. Cf. his discussion of Barth's viewpoint on pp. 4–5 of the same article. Cf. also Ogawa, "Action-Motivating Faith," 84.

[65] Donaldson, "Making Disciples," 38.

[66] The only other places the disciples are part of the narrative action are at 23:1 and 24:1—as audience to Jesus' teaching/discourses.

[67] "Truly I tell you, if you have faith and do not doubt, not only will you do what has been done to the fig tree, but even if you say to this mountain, 'Be lifted up and thrown into the sea,' it will be done" (21:21). Cf. to 17:20: "For truly I tell you, if you have faith the size of a mustard seed, you will say to this mountain, 'Move from here to there,' and it will move; and nothing will be impossible for you."

able to do what they cannot conceive,[68] but also that *they* would be able to do all things if only they had adequate faith. Thus, even though the term ὀλιγόπιστος is not used in this context, Matthew's obvious allusion to 17:20 (where this concept is addressed) indicates that the disciples continue to be those of "little faith," falling short of the role they might have fulfilled if they only had enough faith.

At 26:6–13 (the anointing of Jesus by the woman at Bethany) the disciples are angry (ἀγανακτέω[69]) that such costly ointment is wasted by the woman. Their anger and Jesus' stunning affirmation of the woman's action[70] demonstrate that they have not adequately understood either the significance of her action or the soon-to-be-culminated mission of Jesus. According to Jesus, the woman has prepared him for burial (26:12).[71] It seems that she has understood the significance of this time in Jesus' ministry, with his death close at hand.[72] "[S]he alone understands that the *kairos* has come."[73] The disciples, on the other hand, do not comprehend the significance or the timing of this act. They are instead preoccupied with more temporal concerns. They, who have been the recipients of four passion predictions (16:21; 17:22–23; 20:17–19; 26:1–2), miss the opportunity to be a part of preparing for Jesus' burial. Instead, a nameless woman prepares Jesus' body for burial and becomes memorialized for all time in doing so.[74] The disciples fall short of the role they might have

---

[68] Their amazement signals to the reader that the disciples lack sufficient understanding of Jesus' power. As we have already seen, understanding and faith are linked by Matthew (cf. discussion of 16:5–12 on pp. 105–06).

[69] This is the same word found at 20:24, where the disciples are angry at James' and John's request for second and third positions in the kingdom.

[70] "Truly I tell you, wherever this good news is proclaimed in the whole world, what she has done will be told in remembrance of her" (26:13).

[71] Wainwright observes that the role of anointing belonged to prophets and priests, so that the woman is characterized as a prophet in the narrative; Elaine Mary Wainwright, "Tradition Makers/Tradition Shapers: Women of the Matthean Tradition," *WW* 18 (1998) 385.

[72] "Though Jesus reminds [the disciples] that he must die (26:2), they resist the woman who recognizes his divinely authorized role in anointing him for burial" (Carter, *Matthew,* 253). Cf. also Donald Senior, *The Passion of Jesus in the Gospel of Matthew* (Wilmington, DE: Michael Glazier, 1985) 175.

[73] Senior, *Passion of Jesus,* 54. Cf. also Elaine Mary Wainwright, "Tradition Makers/Tradition Shapers: Women of the Matthean Tradition" *WW* 18 (1998) 385.

[74] Davies and Allison speak of Jesus' words of commendation toward her as an indirect reproach to the disciples (*Matthew,* 3:447). Mattila contrasts the woman with the disciples, those "chosen insiders who fail to understand;" Talvikki Mattila, "Naming the Nameless: Gender and Discipleship in Matthew's Passion Narrative," in *Characterization in the Gospel: Reconceiving Narrative Criticism,* ed. D. Rhoads and K. Syreeni, JSNTSup 184 (Sheffield:

fulfilled if only they had understood that the time of Jesus' death was upon them.[75]

At 26:36–46 (Jesus in Gethsemane) the disciples are not able to keep watch and pray with/for Jesus as he requests. Instead, they fall asleep. According to Jesus, their "spirit indeed is willing, but the flesh is weak" (26:41). Their actions imply that the disciples continue to lack understanding that the time for the fulfillment of Jesus' mission has arrived.[76] They continue to fall short of the role that they are called to have at the climax of Jesus' mission, here specifically, the role of watching and praying. In Matt 21–26, although they complete the tasks given by Jesus for his entry into Jerusalem and for Passover, the disciples do not fulfill the more significant role of preparing for Jesus' death.

When the time for Jesus' arrest and crucifixion arrives, the disciples respond by abandoning Jesus to his fate.[77] Although they have promised to be faithful to Jesus (26:31–35), all of them flee upon Jesus' arrest (26:56).[78] Peter does follow Jesus at a distance, when Jesus is brought before Caiaphas. But, as Jesus has predicted (26:34), Peter denies that he ever knew his master (26:69–75). So in the end, all the disciples abandon Jesus at his passion.[79] "One of them betrayed

---

Sheffield Academic Press, 1999) 162. Cf. also Ronald F. Thiemann, "The Unnamed Woman at Bethany," *ThTo* 44 (1987) 179–88.

The fact that the final passion prediction occurs immediately before this story makes the disciples' lack of understanding all the more ironic.

[75] Donaldson, "Making Disciples," 38.

[76] In her discussion of 26:1–56, Weaver argues that there is no evidence that the disciples have yet to understand Jesus' mission (*Missionary Discourse*, 148). Senior notes that the disciples' weakness of the flesh fits well with their "little faith" designation; Donald Senior, *Matthew*, ANTC (Nashville: Abingdon Press, 1998) 305.

[77] The portrayal of Judas as the one who betrays Jesus is clearly not representative of the other disciples. The uniqueness of his characterization is foreshadowed at 10:4, where he is referred to as "the one who betrayed [Jesus]." His reintroduction at 26:14–16 portrays him as acting on his own rather than in concert with the rest of the disciples. He is clearly characterized individually from this point on, rather than as a representative of the other eleven disciples (cf. 26:23–25, 47–50; 27:3–5).

[78] In his discussion of the denial scene and elsewhere, Trotter connects the disciples' stumbling (σκανδαλίζειν at 26:31) with their lack of understanding: "Jesus is not only the reason for their stumbling but their stumbling consists in misunderstanding and denying him" ("Understanding," 230).

[79] Although Peter's denial is an example of a special characterization of an individual disciple, it also fits the larger pattern of the disciples' characterization as those who abandon Jesus in his final hour. Thus, while the reader has a more detailed picture of Peter after his denial, it is not a picture that is in contrast to the other disciples. Cf. Burnett for a helpful discussion of the issue of Peter's characterization in relation to the other disciples; Fred W. Burnett, "Characterization and Reader Construction," *Semeia* 63 (1993) 20–23. Syreeni, like Burnett, asserts that Peter in the denial scene comes close to full characterhood; Kari Syreeni,

him, another denied him, the rest forsook him and fled. If they had indeed comprehended, they ought to have reacted differently."[80]

This abandonment results in the absence of the eleven disciples from the narrative between 27:1 and 28:16. During Jesus' interrogation before Pilate, his crucifixion and burial, the disciples as character group are absent from the narrative. This absence is significant for their characterization. The disciples, who have been defined in part as those who are "with Jesus," have now deserted him.[81] They have fallen short in their most important role as his disciples.

In their place, those who remain with Jesus through this time, though not a part of the disciples as character group, are shown to be loyal followers/disciples by their presence. The women who had followed Jesus from Galilee and had provided for him (including "Mary Magdalene, and Mary the mother of James and Joseph, and the mother of the sons of Zebedee") remain near him at his crucifixion (27:55–56). Joseph of Arimathea, who had become a disciple of Jesus,[82] takes Jesus' body and places it in his own tomb (27:57–60). Mary Magdalene and "the other Mary" stay near the tomb after Jesus' burial (27:61) and return after the Sabbath to the grave (28:1). In fact, they are the first witnesses to the resurrection (28:9–10). By their presence with Jesus, these characters demonstrate their allegiance to him.[83] In contrast, the disciples as character group once again provide the foil for ideal discipleship, this time by their abandonment of Jesus in his final hours.[84]

Matthew's final word on the disciples is an important aspect of the ending of his gospel.[85] The eleven disciples go to Galilee as Jesus has directed them to do

---

"Peter as Character and Symbol in the Gospel of Matthew," in *Characterization in the Gospel: Reconceiving Narrative Criticism*, ed. David Rhoads and Kari Syreeni, JSNTSup 184 (Sheffield: Sheffield Academic Press, 1999) 145.

[80] Bertram L. Melbourne, *Slow to Understand: The Disciples in Synoptic Perspective* (Lanham, MD: University Press of America, 1988) 72.

[81] For Kingsbury's concept of being "with Jesus," cf. p. 99 of this chapter.

[82] The verbal form μαθητεύω is used in reference to Joseph, rather than the noun μαθητής. This shows Joseph to be outside the *character group* of the disciples, although he is still *a disciple* within Matthew's scheme. [Cf. my related discussion in ch. 2, p. 41.] Doyle points out the significance of this description of Joseph in this particular place in Matthew following the flight and denial of the (named) disciples; "Rod B. Doyle, "Disciples in Matthew: A Challenge for the Church Today," *East Asian Pastoral Review* 29 (1992) 323.

[83] "What is important from the narrative's point of view is that they are *there*, present" (Mattila, "Naming the Nameless," 166). Kopas speaks of the women at the cross having learned their lessons of discipleship well, shown by their faithfulness to the end; Jane Kopas, "Jesus and Women in Matthew," *ThTo* 47 (1990) 20.

[84] Cf. ch. 5 for a more complete discussion of Matthean discipleship.

[85] "[I]t remains striking that the last thing said of the disciples in Matthew's story is that they doubted Jesus;" David D. Kupp, *Matthew's Emmanuel: Divine Presence and God's*

through the women (28:10, 16) to reunite with Jesus. The implicit message at this point is that the disciples continue to *be* disciples (i.e., they are "with him" and intended to be his helpers, as 28:18–20 makes clear).[86] Matthew's final characterization of the disciples follows: "When they saw him, they worshiped him; but they hesitated" (28:17; my translation). After this provocative description of the eleven, Jesus commissions his disciples to go and make disciples of all nations, promising his presence with him as they do so. Matthew's gospel ends with this commission and promise.

There has been much debate over the exact meaning of Matthew's final words about the disciples. There are two primary issues. First, does διστάζω mean "doubt," as it has traditionally been translated (KJV, RSV, NIV, NKJV, NRSV)? Second, who is it that "doubts?" All of the eleven disciples? Some of the eleven? Or a group other than the eleven disciples? The two issues are closely interwoven, given the seeming incongruence of characterizing the disciples as both worshipping and doubting simultaneously.

The meaning of διστάζω is complicated by its scant usage in the New Testament, limited to two occurrences, both in Matthew (14:31; 28:17). In both occurrences, it is used to describe the disciples in part or whole (ascribed to Peter at 14:31). According to BDAG, it can be defined, "to be uncertain, to have second thoughts about a matter." BDAG lists two English equivalents, (1) doubt or waver; and (2) hesitate, and includes Matt 28:17 as a possibility under both.[87]

What can be ascertained about διστάζω from Matthew's usage is that it does not connote the complete absence of faith, since at 14:31 it is directly associated with and so defined by "little faith" (i.e., an inadequate faith rather than no faith). Thus, the argument that the disciples cannot both "worship" (προσκυνέω) and "doubt" (διστάζω), because the terms are mutually exclusive, is faulty.[88] In fact, at 14:28–33, Peter is described by both διστάζω and προσκυνέω (14:31 and 14:33, respectively). Thus, "hesitate" or "waver" is a better English equivalent for διστάζω than "doubt," since doubt in English

---

People in the First Gospel, SNTSMS 90 (Cambridge: Cambridge University Press, 1996) 207.

[86] "Their desertion does not seem to have affected their status at all" (Donaldson, "Making Disciples," 40). Cf. also Edwards, "Uncertain Faith," 59.

[87] BDAG, 252.

[88] Carson seems to favor this position when he states that "doubt about who Jesus is or about the reality of his resurrection doesn't seem appropriate for true worship;" D. A. Carson, *Matthew,* The Expositor's Bible Commentary 8 (Grand Rapids: Zondervan, 1984) 593.

can be understood as diametrically opposed to faith, rather than as a sign of the presence of faith, however inadequate.[89]

The second issue, which is related to the exact subject of the verb διστάζω turns on the translation of the οἱ δέ immediately preceding the verb. Although οἱ δέ typically signals a change of subject,[90] there is no individual/group other than the eleven disciples in context to which the οἱ can refer.[91] Given this constraint, οἱ δέ either refers to the eleven disciples or some part of that group. The latter conclusion is preferred in the majority of English translations, which read, "but some doubted" (e.g., KJV, NRSV, NIV, and NKJV; cf. NASB: "but some were doubtful").[92] This reading has in its favor the change of subject that characterizes οἱ δέ (even if it is not a completely different subject but only a subgroup of the subject of the preceding verb προσκυνέω).[93] Nevertheless, there may be cases in which οἱ δέ does not necessitate a subject change (cf. 26:67) but connects two verbs with the same subject.[94] As Hagner has pointed out, the question of whether the text should be rendered as "they doubted" or

---

[89] Ellis defines διστάζω as divided in conviction rather than as unbelief; I. P. Ellis, "But Some Doubted," *NTS* 14 (1968) 576. Hagner speaks of the disciples' "indecision" and "hesitation" at 28:17 (*Matthew,* 885); cf. also Davies and Allison, *Matthew*, 3:682.

[90] Daniel B. Wallace, *Greek Grammar Beyond the Basics: An Exegetical Syntax of the New Testament* (Grand Rapids: Zondervan, 1996) 211–12. Cf. also the exchange between Grayston and McKay in *JSNT* related to the translation of οἱ δέ; K. Grayston, "The Translation of Matthew 28:17," *JSNT* 21 (1984) 105–09; K. L. McKay, "The Use of *hoi de* in Matthew 28:17: A Response to K. Grayson," *JSNT* 24 (1985) 71–72.

In Matthew, all examples of οἱ δε except for 26:67 and 28:17 clearly indicate a change of subject. None of the former, however, are examples of the partitive usage of οἱ δέ. Only 26:67 and 28:17 are possible examples of the partitive usage, and whether they are in fact used that way is precisely the question being discussed.

[91] Contra W. C. Allen, *Gospel according to St. Matthew,* ICC (Edinburgh: T&T Clark, 1907) 305. Cf. also Goulder, who states that "[t]he Twelve...now have faith in full, they worshipped: others of the brethren...were weaker;" Michael D. Goulder, *Midrash and Lection in Matthew* (London: SPCK, 1974) 343.

[92] Also Davies and Allison, *Matthew*, 3:681–82; Gnilka, *Matthäus*, 506; Daniel J. Harrington, *The Gospel of Matthew*, SP (Collegeville, MN: Liturgical Press, 1991) 414.

[93] This is referred to as the partitive usage. Van der Horst, who indicates that the "change of subject may be complete or partial," draws upon examples from Greco-Roman literature to demonstrate that the partitive usage is well known; P. W. van der Horst, "Once More: The Translation of οἱ δέ in Matthew 28:17," *JSNT* 27 (1986) 27–30.

[94] Those who read 28:17 as "but *they* doubted/wavered," include Hagner, *Matthew,* 884–85; Sand, *Matthäus,* 594–95; Kupp, *Matthew's Emmanuel*, 207; Douglas Hare, *Matthew,* Interpretation (Louisville: John Knox Press, 1993) 332–33; and Walter Grundmann, *Das Evangelium nach Matthäus*, THKNT I (Berlin: Evangelische Verlagsanstalt, 1968) 516: "All see him, all pay homage to him, and all doubt" (my translation).

"some doubted" cannot be determined with certainty solely on the basis of grammatical considerations.[95]

This does not, however, cause as significant a problem for determining the disciples' portrayal as has been suggested. If it is true that the characterization of an individual or subgroup of the disciples functions as representative of the whole (as I have argued in chapter 2), then either reading characterizes the disciples as hesitant even as they worship. They are not full of faith, even after the resurrection.[96] Consequently, even the reading in which *some* hesitate endows the disciples in general with this same characteristic.[97] This is substantiated by the usage of these two verbs at 14:31–33, where the disciples are characterized by both worship and hesitation (the latter via Peter, their representative).[98] The result is that the disciples are implicitly characterized by "little faith" at 28:17 as they have been explicitly portrayed elsewhere in Matthew's gospel. The direct association of "little faith" with hesitation at 14:31[99] argues for the same association at 28:17, where hesitation is again attributed to the disciples, implying that they continue to be characterized by "little faith."[100]

In summary, the disciples fall short of the significant role they are expected to have in Matt 20:29–28:20, that of anticipating and preparing for Jesus' death. They demonstrate by their actions and responses that they inadequately understand the impending culmination of Jesus' mission to suffer and die. They desert Jesus as he is arrested and crucified, putting their very identity as disciples (i.e., those who are "with Jesus") at risk. And even when they are reunited with Jesus after his resurrection, the portrayal of the disciples as those of little (i.e., inadequate) faith is reaffirmed, for in their worship of him they still hesitate or waver.[101]

---

[95] Hagner, *Matthew*, 884.

[96] According to Gundry, in Matthew doubt is not removed by the appearance of Jesus. Robert H. Gundry, *Matthew: A Commentary on His Handbook for a Mixed Church under Persecution*, 2d ed. (Grand Rapids: Eerdmans, 1994) 594.

[97] Patte (*Matthew*, 398) argues the same point from a different angle. "Even if one chooses the translation that suggests that only some of the disciples doubted, it remains that Jesus gives the responsibility and authority to make disciples of all the nations to all the disciples, including those who doubted." Cf. also Kupp, *Matthew's Emmanuel*, 207.

[98] As well as fear, which is attributed explicitly to the disciples as a whole (14:26) and Peter specifically (14:30).

[99] "You of little faith why did you hesitate [διστάζω]?" (my translation).

[100] Kingsbury makes this connection explicit: "...they [the disciples]...still fall victim to 'little faith' (28:17)" (*Matthew as Story*, 17). Cf. also Kupp, *Matthew's Immanuel*, 207; John P. Meier, *Matthew*, New Testament Message 3 (Wilmington: Glazier, 1980) 369.

[101] The function of this consistent and rather negative portrayal of the disciples will be closely examined in chapter 5. Suffice it to note here that the hope for the continuation of

SUMMARY: THE PORTRAYAL OF THE MATTHEAN DISCIPLES

In Matthew, the disciples are consistently portrayed as misunderstanding Jesus' mission and message, as exhibiting inadequate faith, and as falling short of the significant role intended for them as Jesus' disciples.

The Matthean disciples do understand who Jesus is. They confess him to be Messiah/Son of God (14:33; 16:16; cf. 17:13). Matthew also affirms that the disciples come to understand some of Jesus' sayings, when given further explanation by Jesus himself (16:12; 17:13). Nevertheless, the disciples significantly misunderstand Jesus' teachings related to his mission as Messiah to suffer and to die (e.g., 16:21–23) as well as their intended role as his followers (e.g., 16:24–28; 20:20–28). In addition, they do not fully understand or accept Jesus' perspective on the kingdom and the community that awaits its consummation (e.g., 18:1–5; cf. 19:13–15). Finally, the disciples do not comprehend and so lack faith in the *extent* of Jesus' authority (16:5–12).

For Matthew, the "little faith" of the disciples is an insufficient trust that Jesus' authority extends to the provision of their own safety and care (8:26; 14:32; 6:30; 16:8), as well as to their role as Jesus' ministry helpers (17:20; cf. the delegation of authority to them at 10:1). Their "little faith" is evidenced by anxiety for daily needs (6:30); fear and timidity (8:26); hesitation (14:31); and inadequate understanding (16:8). They still exhibit this "little faith" after the resurrection, when they both hesitate and worship in response to the risen Christ.

In their propensity to misunderstand and by their inadequate faith, the disciples fall short of their intended role as Jesus' disciples. While fulfilling some of the tasks Jesus instructs them to carry out (e.g., distributing bread at the feedings, preparing for his entry into Jerusalem and the Passover meal), the disciples do not embrace their more significant role as those who are to mediate the authority of Jesus in miraculous works (14:16–17) and healing (17:14–20) and who should be the ones to prepare and accompany Jesus to the cross (26:6–13; 26:36–46; as well as their flight at Jesus' arrest). Their slowness to understand and hesitancy to trust impede the fulfillment of this greater role.

Finally, it has been demonstrated by this character analysis that the disciples do not progress is their understanding (or move toward greater faith) as the

Jesus' mission and for the fulfillment of the disciples' commission does not lie in the exemplary nature of their faith or understanding (since neither are exemplary!). The ending of Matthew makes it clear that the hope for this fulfillment rests in the continuing presence of Jesus with his community (28:18–20).

narrative comes to a conclusion.[102] Instead, the disciples are consistently portrayed as prone to misunderstand and as wavering in their faith. It is true that the disciples' portrayal is only gradually revealed to the reader as the story unfolds. This does not mean, however, that the disciples go through any significant change from the beginning of Matthew's story to the end. Their desertion and Matthew's final description of them as hesitating before the resurrected Jesus confirms that they have not grown in understanding or faith.[103] It only remains to examine how this fairly consistent and rather negative portrayal functions on various levels of Matthew's narrative. This will be the task of the next chapter.

---

[102] As Powell asserts, "[n]othing has changed" at the end of the gospel in terms the conflict between Jesus and his disciples; Mark Allan Powell, "The Plot and Subplots of Matthew's Gospel," NTS 32 (1992) 198.

[103] Contra Kingsbury, Matthew as Story, 145; Richard A. Edwards, "Reading Matthew: The Gospel as Narrative," List 24 (1989) 255–56; Terence J. Keegan, "The Reader of Matthew's Gospel," in Interpreting the Bible: A Popular Introduction to Biblical Hermeneutics (New York: Paulist Press, 1985) 126; and others. See ch. 1, p. 24, for a survey of perspectives on this issue. Verseput ("Faith of the Reader," 11) speaks of the disciples as "largely static figures...evidenc[ing] no linear development over time from a condition of fundamental incomprehension or unbelief, through uncertainty, to full faith or full understanding." This fits with the tendencies of ancient narrative toward static characterization rather than personality development (cf. discussion in ch. 2).

CHAPTER 5

THE FUNCTION OF THE DISCIPLES IN MATTHEW

The portrayal of the disciples as those who lack adequate faith, frequently lack understanding, and do not progress in their faith or understanding affects the reading of Matthew on a number of levels. As was the case in chapter 1, Syreeni's three-tiered model of understanding the Gospels will be used to clarify the issues related to the function of the Matthean disciples. The three worlds that Syreeni identifies are the textual world, the concrete world, and symbolic world of Matthew's gospel.[1]

THE FUNCTION OF THE DISCIPLES IN MATTHEW'S TEXTUAL WORLD

The textual world of Matthew actually involves two narrative levels. These two levels are delineated in narrative criticism as the story and the discourse levels. The story level has to do with the characters, events, and setting of the story. On the discourse level, the implied author communicates with the implied reader via the way that the story is told.[2] Both the story and discourse levels can be examined to determine the function of the Matthean disciples' portrayal.

---

[1] Kari Syreeni, "Separation and Identity: Aspects of the Symbolic World of Matt 6:1–18," *NTS* 40 (1994) 523; cf. also Kari Syreeni, "Peter as Character and Symbol in the Gospel of Matthew," in *Characterization in the Gospel: Reconceiving Narrative Criticism*, ed. David Rhoads and Kari Syreeni, JSNTSup 184 (Sheffield: Sheffield Academic Press, 1999) 112–16.

[2] For a more complete description of these two levels of the narrative, cf. ch. 1, p. 35. The discourse level of Chatman's scheme actually intersects with both the textual and symbolic worlds of Syreeni's model. Syreeni understands the narrator and the narratee to be included with the story's characters in the textual world, while the implied author and reader inhabit the narrative's symbolic world. The present discussion makes no distinction between the

The Function of the Disciples at the Story Level

The disciples (as prone to misunderstand) function on the story level to highlight Jesus' teaching about the kingdom. As it has been argued in the preceding chapters, the Matthean disciples are frequently shown to misunderstand the nature of Jesus' mission, the extent of his authority, and the role Jesus intends them to have as his disciples. Their often misguided questions and reactions function as a kind of foil to Jesus' teaching, providing a backdrop against which that teaching is set in bold relief.

This conclusion contrasts, to some extent, with the common redaction-critical viewpoint that the disciples' portrayal highlights Jesus as effective teacher. Given that redaction critics typically sketched a portrait of the disciples as possessing understanding, at least after being taught by Jesus, their deduction that Jesus is shown to be an effective teacher was justified. If, however, the disciples are not portrayed as those who adequately understand, then Matthew cannot be emphasizing the *effective* teaching of Jesus. Rather, what is emphasized is the *content* of Jesus' teaching as well as the extent of his authority against the backdrop of the disciples' misunderstanding (i.e., via their ideological conflict).[3]

In addition to highlighting Jesus' teaching and authority, the disciples' portrayal as those who often lack understanding functions to highlight Jesus' *effective presence.*[4] If the disciples are characterized as misunderstanding much of Jesus' teaching, as I have argued, the accurate transmission of Jesus' teaching is at risk, since the commission of 28:18–20 clearly assigns *the disciples* the task of "teaching [future disciples] to obey everything that [Jesus has] commanded" (28:20).[5] But it is precisely at this point that Jesus promises

---

narratee and the implied reader in its examination of how this textually-defined entity (implied reader/narratee) interacts with the character group of the disciples. Consequently, I will discuss how the disciples as character group function in relation to the textually-defined hearer/reader under the heading of Matthew's textual world. Matthew's symbolic world will be reserved for the discussion of the values associated with Matthean discipleship, i.e., *how* the implied author uses the disciples as part of a larger composite to convey *what* discipleship is.

[3] Verseput, in his study of the disciples in Matthew 13:53–16:20, concludes that the disciples' "little faith" (which includes their lack of understanding) is "a foil to impress upon the reader the greatness of Jesus' awesome power;" Donald J. Verseput, "The Faith of the Reader and the Narrative of Matthew 13:53–16:20," *JSNT* 46 (1992) 23. The disciples' misunderstanding in 16:21–20:28 functions to highlight Jesus' teaching about his mission and discipleship.

[4] Cf. discussion of this idea at 18:20 in ch. 3.

[5] Redaction critics have often argued that the disciples do understand precisely because they must be able to carry out their teaching role in the great commission. For example,

his presence to his disciples: "And remember, I am with you always, to the end of the age." As at 18:20, Jesus at the very end of Matthew's gospel ensures that his legacy will be preserved, not by means of the exemplary understanding of the disciples, but through the guarantee of his presence with those who are his disciples until the end of the age. In this way, the disciples' lack of understanding functions to emphasize Jesus' effective presence, which is the final assurance that his teaching will be both preserved and spread to all the nations.[6]

The Function of the Disciples at the Discourse Level

Narrative perspectives emphasize the way the story is told as the means of communication between the implied author and the implied reader. Given the varied ways that the implied reader has been defined by narrative and reader-response criticisms, it is necessary first of all to define what I mean by the 'implied reader' before it is possible to describe the effect of the disciples' portrayal upon the implied reader.

Definition of the Implied Reader

The implied reader will be defined as the persona constructed from the narrative text that responds appropriately to the text's rhetorical devices and thus fulfills the goals of the text.[7] This definition draws upon definitions by

---

Hartin states, "[the disciples] could only effectively carry out this [teaching] role by first understanding Jesus' teaching;" Patrick J. Hartin, "Disciples as Authorities within Matthew's Christian-Jewish Community," *Neot* 32 (1998) 395. As Overman asks, "How can these disciples teach if they never quite understood Jesus?" J. Andrew Overman, *Matthew's Gospel and Formative Judaism: The Social World of the Matthean Community* (Minneapolis: Fortress, 1990) 129.

[6] Cf. ch. 3, p. 92. There I indicate that the hope for Jesus' legacy is also ensured by the implied reader's understanding and knowledge, which is superior to that of the disciples. "[T]he invitation and demands of discipleship are extended beyond the characters in the story to the implied reader...[who] is challenged with the disciples in the Great Commission to be obedient to Jesus' teaching;" David B. Howell, *Matthew's Inclusive Story: A Study in the Narrative Rhetoric of the First Gospel.* JSNTSup 42 (Sheffield: JSOT Press, 1990) 251.

[7] The devices and goals of the text might just as readily be called the devices and goals of the implied author (also a textual construct). The text is the focus within this definition, since reference to the real author's goals or intentions is often confused with a psychological and extra-textual entity rather than the intentions of the author as revealed in the text itself. Cf. Fowl for a helpful distinction between a "communicative intention" (*what* an author is trying to say) and a "motive" (*why* it is being said), with the former rather than the latter being the (or at least one) goal of interpretation. Stephen E. Fowl, "The Role of Authorial Intention in

Fowler (who speaks of the reader or persona the text invites us to be);[8] Staley (who speaks of the one affected by the text's strategies and moved toward the implied author's goals);[9] as well as numerous narrative critics who emphasis the textual nature of the implied reader.[10]

The emphasis on the implied reader as a textual entity is not uniformly agreed upon by narrative critics. Iser, for example, speaks of the implied reader as an incorporation of two activities: "the prestructuring of the potential meaning by the text, and the reader's actualization of this potential through the reading process."[11] Howell in his work on Matthew draws upon Iser's definition of the implied reader as both a textual and reader construct and defines the implied reader as the textual structure to be realized as well as the structured act of realization.[12] Part of the rationale for seeing the implied reader as both a textual and reader construct rather than simply the former is the presence of 'gaps' within narrative texts. For Iser, the answers that are missing from the text (i.e., its gaps) promote the reader's active participation in the realization of the meaning of the text.[13]

Nevertheless, other narrative critics see the gaps of the text as part of its overall shaping of the implied reader. Booth contends that "[w]hat the author felt no need to mention tells us who he thinks we'll be—or hopes we'll be"

---

the Theological Interpretation of Scripture," in *Between Two Horizons: Spanning New Testament Studies and Systematic Theology*, ed. Joel B. Green and Max Turner (Grand Rapids: Eerdmans, 2000) 74.

[8] Robert M. Fowler, "Who is 'the Reader' in Reader Response Criticism?" *Semeia* 31 (1985) 10.

[9] Jeffrey Lloyd Staley, *The Print's First Kiss: A Rhetorical Investigation of the Implied Reader in the Fourth Gospel*, SBLDS 82 (Atlanta: Scholars Press, 1988) 33.

[10] For example, Wayne C. Booth, *The Rhetoric of Fiction*, 2d ed. (Chicago: University of Chicago Press, 1983) 138; and Seymour Chatman, *Story and Discourse: Narrative Structure in Fiction and Film* (Ithaca: Cornell University Press, 1978) 150; as well as Mark Allan Powell, *What is Narrative Criticism?* GBS (Minneapolis: Fortress, 1990) 19–20; Richard A. Edwards, *Matthew's Narrative Portrait of Disciples* (Valley Forge: Trinity Press International, 1997) 9 [his "text-connoted reader"]; and Jack D. Kingsbury, *Matthew as Story*, 2d ed. (Philadelphia: Fortress Press, 1988) 38. Booth and Chatman are literary critics while Powell, Edwards, and Kingsbury are biblical scholars who have applied narrative criticism to Matthew's gospel.

[11] Wolfgang Iser, *The Implied Reader* (Baltimore: The Johns Hopkins University Press, 1974) xii.

[12] Howell, *Inclusive*, 210. Cf. also Fowler ("Reader," 15) and Anderson for examples of definitions which, while primarily focusing on the textual nature of the implied reader, also emphasis the role of the real reader in its construction; Janice Capel Anderson, *Matthew's Narrative Web*, JSNTSup 91 (Sheffield: JSOT Press, 1994) 28, 31–32.

[13] Iser, *Implied Reader*, 34–5. Cf. also Anderson's reliance on Iser's concept of indeterminate gaps in her work on Matthew (*Narrative Web,* 33).

(i.e., what he hopes for the implied reader).[14] Kingsbury, citing Iser, speaks of the gaps in the narrative that the reader must "fill in" but makes it clear that the text itself provides the clues for filling in those gaps.[15] Rhoads, Dewey, and Michie also understand the filling in of gaps to be implied for readers from the text itself.[16] Therefore, while taking seriously the caution that the particular backgrounds and preunderstandings of real readers will inevitably impact their construction of the implied reader (including this real reader's construction), my definition affirms there is a textually-derived implied reader who responds appropriately to the text's goals and this implied reader is a valid aim of narrative criticism. As Powell affirms, "the goal of reading the text 'as the implied reader' may be somewhat unattainable, but it remains a worthy goal nevertheless."[17]

There are a few distinctions that will help to further define the implied reader assumed in this chapter. First, within narrative and reader-response criticisms, the implied reader is at times distinguished from the 'ideal reader.' The ideal reader according to Rhoads, Michie, and Dewey is "the imaginary reader with all the ideal responses *implied by* the narrative itself."[18] Kingsbury, on the other hand, has essentially this same definition for the *implied* reader: "an imaginary person who respond[s] to the text at every point with whatever emotion, understanding, or knowledge the text ideally calls for."[19] Since my own definition does "idealize" the implied reader as the one who fulfills the goals of the text, I see no great practical difference between these two constructs. As Howell points out, it is "unnecessary to assume that qualities attributed to the ideal reader are not already contained in the concept of an implied reader."[20]

Second, the implied reader is defined by some as a first-time reader. This is Edwards' conception of his "text-connoted reader." For Edwards, this reader is informed only by what has already occurred in the narrative and not by what takes place later in the story.[21] This is also characteristic of the implied reader in

---

[14] Booth, *Rhetoric,* 423.

[15] Jack Dean Kingsbury, "The Rhetoric of Comprehension in the Gospel of Matthew," *NTS* 41 (1995) 361.

[16] David Rhoads, Joanna Dewey, and Donald Michie, *Mark as Story: An Introduction to the Narrative of a Gospel*, 2d ed. (Minneapolis: Fortress, 1999) 138.

[17] Powell, *Narrative Criticism*, 21. Powell understands the implied reader to be a textual construct.

[18] Rhoads, Dewey, and Michie, *Mark as Story* (2d. ed.) 138.

[19] Kingsbury, *Matthew as Story*, 38.

[20] Howell, *Inclusive*, 210. Cf. also Fowler's discussion of these terms ("Reader," 15).

[21] Edwards, *Portrait*, 10.

much reader-response criticism.[22] Nevertheless, not all narrative critics equate a narrative-critical reading with a first-time reading. Burnett, for example, argues against a purely sequential reading (i.e., first-time reading). "The reader does not just construct a character by reading sequentially…the reader constructs a *paradigm* of traits *at the story level* from indicators that are strewn along the textual continuum."[23] Powell also asserts that the implied reader is not necessarily the first-time reader: "In some instances the narrative text apparently assumes the reader will come to an understanding only after multiple readings."[24] Finally, Stanton offers a critique of this kind of reader, calling it "an exercise of doubtful value," citing probable characteristics of a first-century Matthean audience to make his critique.[25]

Powell expands his discussion of this issue in an article on the implied reader of Matthew.[26] While acknowledging that the issue of whether the implied reader is a first-time reader has not yet been resolved in narrative criticism, Powell claims that the issue may not be as significant as it first appears. Powell's reasoning for this claim is that the real reader, in order to identify with the *characters* of the story, must have the ability to adopt the viewpoint of one who does not know the story's ending (i.e., must take the perspective of a first-time reader in some fashion).[27] Powell also points out that suspense is *not* a

---

[22] For example, Anderson refers to the first-time reader in Janice Capel Anderson, "Matthew: Sermon and Story," in *Treasures New and Old: Recent Contributions to Matthean Studies*, SBLSymS 1, ed. David R. Bauer and Mark Allan Powell (Atlanta: Scholars Press, 1996) 247.

[23] Fred W. Burnett, "Characterization and Reader Construction," *Semeia* 63 (1993) 23, n. 11. Tannehill defines his work on Luke-Acts as narrative commentary rather than an expanded reading; in other words, his work "represents part of what might be said after reading a second, third, or fourth time. It is not confined to what is happening when reading for the first time, with much of the text still unknown;" Robert C. Tannehill, *The Narrative Unity of Luke-Acts: A Literary Interpretation* I (Philadelphia: Fortress, 1986) 6.

[24] Powell, *Narrative Criticism*, 20; cf. also Syreeni, "Peter as Character," 121, n. 39. Staley seems to confirm this viewpoint when he states that "a narrative text's manipulation of temporality…gives rise to the rhetorical devices of surprise and suspense, and these qualities do not disappear with a second reading. They are merely confirmed and become less evocative as the overall design becomes more apparent" ("Reader," 34).

[25] Hearers of Matthew "are unlikely to have become acquainted with Matthew by means of an oral performance of the whole gospel. They are much more likely to have heard shorter sections…[F]or most of the first recipients, Matthew's gospel was an extended commentary on what the original readers and listeners already knew;" Graham N. Stanton, *A Gospel for a New People: Studies in Matthew* (Louisville: Westminster/John Knox Press, 1992) 76.

[26] Mark Allan Powell, "Expected and Unexpected Readings of Matthew: What the Reader Knows," *AsTJ* 48 (1993) 31–51.

[27] Powell, "What the Reader Knows," 35.

major motif in Matthew and thus a first-time reading is not essential to an understanding of the plot of Matthew.[28] This perspective will be the one assumed for my own concept of the implied reader. The implied reader is not limited to a first-time reader, although the temporal nature of the narrative plays an important role in the interpretation of Matthew particularly as it has to do with the issue of characterization (since *the characters* obviously "experience" the story in a completely linear fashion).

Third, in Chatman's model that has influenced much biblical narrative criticism, the implied reader is distinguished from the narratee (the one who is on the receiving end of the narration). Most narrative critics, however, affirm that in Matthew there is no distinction between the narratee and the implied reader. Chatman's distinction between the two is meant to assist in the analysis of literary works in which a narratee is more noticeable *and* is distanced from the implied reader in some way.[29] Fowler, drawing on Chatman's work, sees the usefulness of the term 'narratee' as distinct from the implied reader only when the implied reader is expected to distance himself from a gullible narratee.[30] Since this is not the case in Matthew, and since Matthew's 'narratee' is essentially a stand-in for the implied reader,[31] 'implied reader' will be used without reference to the narratee in the present discussion.

Finally, what knowledge can be assumed for the implied reader of Matthew's gospel? Edwards asserts that the text-connoted reader cannot fill in gaps in the story with historical or cultural information from outside of the narrative.[32] Powell, on the other hand, defends the view that the implied reader's knowledge is derived from both within and outside of the narrative.[33] For Powell, the implied reader knows everything that the gospel (or implied

---

[28] For example, to answer whether the implied reader understands 9:15 as foreshadowing Jesus' death when his death is not explicitly mentioned until later, Powell states that in either case it will soon become clear (at 16:21). The question is not *whether* 9:15 foreshadows for the implied reader the death of Jesus but only *when* the implied reader realizes that it is a foreshadowing ("What the Reader Knows," 35).

[29] Chatman (*Story and Discourse*, 150–51) gives the example of Conrad's *Heart of Darkness*. For an interpreter who does distinguish between the Matthean narratee and implied reader, cf. Terence J. Keegan, "The Reader of Matthew's Gospel," in *Interpreting the Bible: A Popular Introduction to Biblical Hermeneutics* (New York: Paulist Press, 1985) 111–13. I find Keegan's distinction unhelpful and his argument for it quite unpersuasive.

[30] Fowler, "Reader," 11.

[31] Kingsbury, *Matthew as Story*, 38.

[32] Edwards, *Portrait*, 10. Cf. also Staley ("Print's First Kiss," 35–36) for a similar way of conceiving what the implied reader knows.

[33] Booth also lends support to the idea that the implied reader knows certain (historical) facts that lie outside of the narrative (*Rhetoric*, 423).

author) expects him to know.[34] This includes linguistic competence (in the case of Matthew, Greek competence), universal knowledge (such as, the recognition of the miraculous nature of certain events described in Matthew's story), knowledge presupposed by the spatial, temporal, and social setting of the narrative (including geography, history, social and cultural realities, such as, coinage, and symbolic language, such as, "brood of vipers"), as well as knowledge of other literature that is cited either by reference or allusion within the narrative (e.g., the Hebrew Scriptures).[35] Powell's perspective on this issue makes more sense than Edwards' view, given the importance of certain extra-textual knowledge for rightly understanding Matthew, which is what the implied reader is expected to do.[36]

To summarize, the definition of the implied reader that I will be assuming for the rest of this discussion is the persona constructed from the narrative text that responds appropriately to the text's rhetorical devices and thus fulfills the goals of the text. It is a textual construct and is essentially the same as the ideal reader of various narrative perspectives. It is not limited to a first-time reader and is indistinguishable from the narratee of Matthew. Finally, the implied reader has knowledge of what is revealed within Matthew as well as some specific knowledge derived from outside of Matthew's narrative, including historical and cultural information necessary for understanding the gospel.

Effect of the Disciples' Portrayal upon the Implied Reader

The discourse level of the textual world consists of the communication between the implied author and the implied reader of Matthew's gospel. According to narrative theory, the implied author (a textual construct that comes to be discerned from the narrative itself) shapes the implied reader through the rhetoric of the narration, including how the various characters are portrayed.[37] Thus, the way Matthew's implied author characterizes the disciples directly impacts the creation of a reader who fulfills the goals of the text. In other words, understanding the impact of the disciples upon the implied reader is one step toward illuminating the goals of the implied author.

---

[34] Powell, "What the Reader Knows," 32.

[35] Powell's criteria for determining what the implied reader knows include (1) recurrence, (2) thematic coherence, and (3) availability.

[36] For example, knowing that a denarius is essentially a day's wage is important for understanding that the landowner of 20:1–15 is acting fairly to the first-hour workers.

[37] As Tannehill asserts, "…the author's shaping of the disciples' role…[is] indirect communication with the reader;" Robert C Tannehill, "The Disciples in Mark: The Function of a Narrative Role," *JR* 57 (1977) 405, also 389.

Initially, the implied reader is encouraged to identify with the disciples. As Howell states, "positive characterizations and responses will attract the implied reader, create sympathy for those characters, and encourage identification between the two."[38] The reader will particularly identify with the disciples at first because (1) their initial portrayal is quite positive (cf. 4:18–22 where the four fisherman leave everything to follow); and (2) "a reader will identify most easily and immediately with characters who seem to share the reader's situation."[39] For Matthew's reader, the disciples' positive response to Jesus engenders identification because the reader has been predisposed by the preceding narrative to respond positively to Jesus.[40]

Nevertheless, the reader is soon confronted with a number of negative characterizations of the disciples (e.g., their "little faith"). The effect of this negative portrayal upon the implied reader is two-fold. First, their negative portrayal causes the reader to distance herself from the character group of the disciples, i.e., to choose not to identify with the disciples at that particular point.[41] This first effect draws the reader to evaluate the inappropriate values or behavior of the disciples in light of the reliable perspectives of the narrator and of Jesus.[42] Second, the disciples' negative portrayal works as a pedagogical tool to steer the implied reader toward values or behavior in contrast to that of the disciples.[43] The positive contrast to the disciples' attitudes or actions might be

---

[38] Howell, *Inclusive*, 208. Cf. also David R. Bauer, "The Major Characters of Matthew's Story: Their Function and Significance," *Int* 46 (1992) 363.

[39] Tannehill, "The Disciples in Mark," 392. Wilkins affirms that in Matthew, "...although Jesus is the ultimate model of the norms and values commended by the implied reader, the experience of the implied and actual readers is closer to that of those who are with Jesus (the disciples...)" Michael J. Wilkins, "Named and Unnamed Disciples in Matthew: A Literary/Theological Study," in *1991 SBLSP* (Atlanta: Scholars Press, 1991) 439.

[40] Tannehill argues this for Mark as well: "The implied author of Mark shapes a story which encourages the reader to associate himself with the disciples" ("The Disciples in Mark," 394).

[41] For example, Verseput states that, when the disciples are portrayed as those of "little faith," "the reader is called upon to distance himself from [the disciples'] deplorable behavior" ("Faith of the Reader," 12). For a literary analysis of the reader's relationship to characters of a story, cf. Steven Mailloux, "Learning to Read: Interpretation and Reader-Response Criticism," *Studies in Literary Imagination* 12 (1979) 103–05.

[42] "[The implied audience is] ultimately called upon to stand with Jesus and the narrator and judge events and characters according to the ideological point of view of the implied author" (Howell, *Inclusive*, 208). Cf. also Tannehill, "The Disciples in Mark," 393; Jack Dean Kingsbury, "The Figure of Jesus in Matthew's Story: A Literary-Critical Probe," *JSNT* 21 (1984) 50.

[43] "[A]lthough there can be little doubt that the implied reader is encouraged by Matthew to identify readily with the disciples, he is nonetheless occasionally required to evaluate their

provided to the reader by the words/actions of Jesus or the words/actions of another character group. In any event, the reader is drawn to embrace the positive values or behavior affirmed by the implied author via the rhetoric of his narration.[44]

In this way, the disciples' negative portrayal works as a foil in the narrative, challenging the reader to follow Jesus more faithfully than the disciples do. One way to conceive of the disciples' function at the discourse level, then, is as *an incentive to the implied reader toward ideal discipleship.* Ideal discipleship might be defined as the Matthean ideal for discipleship envisioned in Jesus' teaching and exemplified by various characters in Matthew's gospel who in some way fulfill that vision.[45] In one sense, the implied reader becomes that ideal disciple, since the implied reader as a textual construct is defined as the reader who fulfills the goals of the text.[46] For example, while the disciples frequently misunderstand Jesus' teaching regarding his mission and their own discipleship, the implied reader, who has information and teaching from the

---

shortcomings, *learning from their mistakes*" (Verseput, "Faith of the Reader," 12, n. 4, emphasis mine).

[44] "When a character gives utterance to an ideological stance...[it may be that he/she] represents Matthew's ideology indirectly by representing a false or defective ideological stance criticized and modified by Matthew in the story itself" (Syreeni, "Peter as Character," 118). Verseput fleshes this out in his discussion of the "little faith" of the Matthean disciples. "It is the faith *of the reader* which ultimately consumes the Evangelist's attention as he relentlessly manipulates his narrative to expose [the] 'little faith' [of the disciples]" (Verseput, "Faith of the Reader," 23). Cf. also David D. Kupp, *Matthew's Emmanuel: Divine Presence and God's People in the First Gospel.* SNTSMS 90 (Cambridge: Cambridge University Press, 1996) 242. Even though closely related to the consideration of the relationship of the disciples to the implied reader, the contribution of the disciples' portrayal to Matthew's ideology of discipleship will be discussed under the heading of Matthew's symbolic world later in the chapter.

[45] Here I draw upon Patte's helpful distinction between "ideal disciples" (as described in Jesus' teaching) and "actual disciples" (the twelve as they are actually portrayed in the narrative); Daniel Patte, *The Gospel according to Matthew: A Structural Commentary on Matthew's Faith* (Philadelphia: Fortress Press, 1987) 136, n. 16. Although Matthew does not explicitly distinguish between two types of disciples (Howell's critique of Patte; *Inclusive*, 234), Matthean discipleship can be understood in terms of his ideal for discipleship (i.e., the ideal disciple). This ideal can and should be distinguished from the actual characterization of the twelve disciples, which as we have noted frequently falls short of the ideal disciple Matthew envisions throughout his narrative. Patte seems to limit this concept to the ideal disciple of Jesus' teaching. I would broaden the concept to include the ideal disciple envisioned by Matthew via both Jesus' teaching and the narration of characters who embody some aspect of Matthean discipleship.

[46] Howell, while arguing against Patte's particular use the term "ideal disciple" affirms this basic idea: "The 'ideal disciple' should...be seen as a version of the implied reader" (Howell, *Inclusive*, 234–35).

implied author which is not available to the disciples as characters, *does understand* and so fulfills Matthew's goal in this regard.[47]

The use of the disciples' negative portrayal as a foil for the implied reader is all the more effective, given the initial and significant identification between the two. The movement from identification to dissociation is a powerful pedagogical tool used by Matthew to inculcate discipleship in the implied reader. In fact, this movement does not happen once but many times throughout the narrative, as the reader identifies here and distances himself at other points from the disciples.[48]

If the effect of the disciples' negative portrayal is to provide a potent contrast and incentive to ideal discipleship, is there any sense of identification that arises from their negative portrayal? Best, in his analysis of the Marcan disciples, has stated that the failure of the disciples would give his readers hope when they themselves failed.[49] Is this true of the Matthean portrait of the disciples as well? It is highly unlikely that the very points at which the reader is prone to distance herself from the disciples would also be the occasions for hope and encouragement via a sense of identification with the disciples' failures. Nevertheless, the implied author seems to provide reason for the implied reader to identify with the disciples, even when they fail, *by means of Jesus' response to them*. In other words, the implied reader might be said to identify with the disciples, even at points of negative portrayal, if Matthew's Jesus treats the disciples in a positive fashion. More precisely, the implied reader will derive hope from Jesus' gracious words toward his fallible followers.[50]

---

[47] Howell, *Inclusive*, 232.

[48] The reader will, for example, identify with the confession of Jesus' identity at 16:16 but then will distance himself from Peter's rebuke of Jesus at 16:22. Tannehill, analyzing the Marcan disciples, contends that "something of the initial identification remains" ("The Disciples in Mark." 393). I would argue that in Matthew the initial identification is reaffirmed at various points where the disciples are portrayed more positively. Cf. also Edwards, who speaks of the "both/and" technique of the narrator regarding the disciples' fluctuating portrayal; Richard A. Edwards, "Uncertain Faith: Matthew's Portrait of the Disciples," in *Discipleship in the New Testament*, ed. Fernando F. Segovia (Philadelphia: Fortress, 1985) 52.

[49] Ernest Best, *Disciples and Discipleship: Studies in the Gospel according to Mark* (Edinburgh: T&T Clark, 1986) 114. Garland seems to imply such an identification in Matthew, when he states at 28:17 that "the fluctuation between worship and indecision is every disciple's struggle;" David Garland, *Reading Matthew: A Literary and Theological Commentary on the First Gospel* (New York: Crossroad, 1993) 266.

[50] According to Wilkins, "[t]he stumbling disciples provide an example for the readers of how Jesus would work with them" ("Named and Unnamed Disciples," 439).

For example, in spite of the disciples' rather selfish question at 19:27 ("...what then will there be for us?"), Jesus' response includes not only a warning but also a promise. The promise of eternal life for the disciples encourages the reader to find hope as well, even while distancing himself from the selfish concerns of the disciples. The hope is derived then from Jesus' response to the disciples rather than from their negative portrayal. A significant illustration of this same kind of "identification" occurs at 28:10. The disciples have abandoned Jesus at his arrest and trial at 26:56–75. Now, the resurrected Jesus instructs the women to tell his "brothers" to meet him in Galilee. In spite of their failure and abandonment, Jesus speaks of the disciples positively, continuing to view them as his family (cf. 12:46–50). Jesus' positive response not only reinstates the disciples but also encourages the reader to hope and rely upon Jesus' gracious response.

Powell, in his study of how Matthean characters are portrayed via their words (i.e., on the phraseological plane), comes to a similar conclusion.

> Matthew supplements the mostly negative portrait of the disciples offered through their own speech with a much more positive portrait offered through the speech of Jesus. By doing this, he indicates that the positive aspects of the disciples' characterization derive from Jesus and can only be realized through him...The reader ultimately views these disciples as characters with tremendous potential...not derive[d] from any qualities the disciples evince on their own, but from what Jesus sees in them and is able to impart to them.[51]

If we may speak of the implied reader deriving hope from the disciples' negative portrayal, it is not because of a sense of identification with them but because of Jesus' gracious attitude toward them.[52] Thus, while the implied reader will disassociate herself from the inadequate behavior of the disciples,

---

[51] Mark Allan Powell, "Characterization on the Phraseological Plane in the Gospel of Matthew," in *Treasures New and Old: Recent Contributions to Matthean Studies*, SBLSymS 1, ed. David R. Bauer and Mark Allan Powell (Atlanta: Scholars Press, 1996) 171.

[52] Part of what Jesus speaks about his disciples has to do with their future role as disciples. This tends to be much more positive than their actual behavior within the temporal boundaries of Matthew's story (e.g., 16:18–19; 19:28). Donaldson refers to these statements by Jesus as "indications...of a significant role for the disciples in the future—in that state of affairs that will emerge on the far side of the cross;" Terence L. Donaldson, "Guiding Readers—Making Disciples: Discipleship in Matthew's Narrative Strategy," in *Patterns of Discipleship in the New Testament*, ed. R. Longenecker (Grand Rapids: Eerdmans, 1996) 39. Bauer considers this future role an important component in Matthew presentation of the disciples ("Major Characters," 363).

she will identify with any positive treatment that Jesus shows towards them, deriving hope from this gracious treatment.[53]

In conclusion, the implied reader will both identify with the more positive aspects of the disciples' portrayal and distance himself from their negative characterization. Both positive and negative aspects of the disciples' portrayal, therefore, function as an incentive for the implied reader toward the Matthean ideal of discipleship. In addition, the implied reader derives hope and encouragement from Jesus' gracious treatment of the disciples in spite of their failures and faults.

THE FUNCTION OF THE DISCIPLES IN MATTHEW'S CONCRETE WORLD

A second category Syreeni proposes is the concrete world of a gospel. By this he refers to the extra-textual (real) world of the evangelist's community. Another way of understanding this concept is as the referential aspect of the text. The issue for this study is how, if at all, the character group of the disciples functions in Matthew's concrete world.

It has become axiomatic in redactional studies to speak of the disciples as transparent for the Matthean community.[54] For example, Luz concludes that "[t]he disciples of Jesus are transparent for the present situation. Behind them stands Matthew's community."[55] As a result, redaction critics who stress that Matthew's disciples adequately understand also contend that this understanding points to the disciples as transparent for Matthew's actual readers (i.e., his community).

There are a number of problems with this one-to-one correspondence between the disciples and the real author's community. First, Johnson has persuasively argued that greater caution in general must be exercised in drawing connections between the textual and concrete worlds of a gospel.[56] He warns that, even in epistle interpretation, one must be careful to avoid mirror reading, showing that at least the same level of caution should be used in study of a gospel. Johnson also argues that the determination of a crisis in the evangelist's audience for every theological emphasis or concern "reduces [the

---

[53] "The consideration that Jesus refuses to abandon the disciples to their failure…gives hope to readers that the exalted Christ will likewise assist them in their own struggles" (Bauer, "Major Characters," 363).

[54] Cf. discussion in ch. 1, pp. 14–16.

[55] Ulrich Luz, "The Disciples in the Gospel according to Matthew," in *The Interpretation of Matthew*, ed. Graham Stanton, 2d ed. (Edinburgh: T&T Clark, 1995) 128.

[56] Luke Timothy Johnson, "On Finding the Lukan Community: A Cautious Cautionary Essay" in *SBLSP 1979* (Missoula, MT: Scholars Press, 1979) 87–100.

Gospels] to the level of cryptograms, and the evangelists to the level of tractarians."[57] Johnson concludes by asserting that "[w]ithout the clear and unequivocal indication by the author in his text, we cannot establish the connection between the presence of a particular motif and the stance of the readers."[58]

Johnson's critique revolves around the issue of the nature of the Gospels. Are the Gospels meant to provide insight into the historical situation out of which they were written?[59] Another way to phrase the issue is: Is the first gospel communication *about* Matthew's audience or communication *to* Matthew's audience (or if some combination of the two, which emphasis is primary)? The view that the disciples are transparent for the Matthean church assumes the former. I want to argue for the latter. What the gospel of Matthew does best in its portrayal of the disciples is not provide historical information about the community from which the gospel arose (although it may offer a glimpse of this third *Sitz im Leben* when all is said and done). Rather, Matthew's characterization of the disciples is best read as part of the communication to his audience of a particular ideological viewpoint on discipleship. In other words, what Matthew offers is a *portrait* of discipleship rather than a *window* into the community behind the gospel.[60]

Second, the observation by narrative critics that the implied reader will be led to distance himself from the disciples when they are portrayed negatively argues against a simple one-to-one correspondence between the disciples as

---

[57] Johnson, "On Finding the Lukan Community," 90.

[58] Ibid., 91. Johnson helpfully points out that "individual elements within [a Gospel's] structure have as their *primary* meaning a literary function" and that a motif could just as readily be attributed to theological purposes as polemical ones (92).

[59] I am not addressing the larger issue of the referential function of Matthew. The narrative clearly refers to all sorts of extra-textual entities we know to be realities in the first-century— King Herod, the denarius, and the Jewish temple to name a few. A substantial knowledge of these realities can only aid in the study of Matthew. The issue I am raising here is whether and how well Matthew functions to illuminate the third *Sitz im Leben*, i.e., the social setting from which Matthew writes his gospel.

[60] Here I borrow and modify Powell's terminology (derived from Krieger). According to Powell, historical criticism views the text as a window to historical information; while literary criticism regards the text as a mirror (*Narrative Criticism*, 8). I prefer the term *portrait* rather than mirror, because it emphasizes that the focus of study is on the text itself (mirror implies that the interpreter studies only herself in the interpretive process) and that Matthew is a literary work with artistic merit as well as theological import. Modifying the image slightly, Duling speaks of the text as a "foggy or steamy window," indicating the more nuanced perspective of recent social-scientific criticism regarding the issue of transparency; Dennis C. Duling, "'Egalitarian' Ideology, Leadership, and Factional Conflict within the Matthean Group," *BTB* 27 (1997) 125.

character group and the intended readers of the gospel.[61] Instead, the audience (whether the concrete audience or the one implied in the text) will have a more complex and ambivalent relationship to the character group of the disciples, so that the disciples could not be transparent for the Matthean community. "The necessity for distinguishing the implied reader from the disciples as character group becomes visible in the conflicting character traits with which the disciples are portrayed."[62]

Finally, as Kingsbury has argued, many reconstructions of Matthew's concrete world are based on a fairly fragmented reading of the gospel's story, which, in Kingsbury's perspective, largely undermines the validity of the reconstruction. "[I]t is difficult, if not impossible, to build a convincing case regarding the social situation of Matthew's community if this case is supported by no more than a fragmentary, piecemeal reading of Matthew's story."[63] This is true of many redaction-critical studies focused on the Matthean disciples. Proof that the disciples understand is usually focused on an analysis of particular words for understanding (e.g., συνιέναι) and therefore on the sections of the gospel in which those words occur with reference to the disciples (for συνιέναι, particularly chapters 13–17).[64] Yet, a sustained reading of the disciples' portrayal throughout the gospel would also take into account the narrative clues that indicate they frequently *misunderstand* Jesus' authority, mission and teaching (in addition to the significance of their abandonment at Jesus' death), making it difficult to speak of the disciples as transparent for the Matthean community.[65]

Given these significant methodological and substantial problems for the viewpoint that the disciples are transparent for the Matthean community, is there a way forward in the pursuit of a connection between Matthew's textual world and his concrete world? While this question is not strictly the task of

---

[61] Verseput, "Faith of the Reader," 12, n. 4. Verseput states that, since the implied reader is required to evaluate the disciples at times, "the modern student must be prepared to surrender the once fashionable conviction that the disciples in Matthew are 'transparent' for the Matthean community."

[62] Howell, *Inclusive,* 234.

[63] Jack Dean Kingsbury, "Conclusion: Analysis of a Conversation," in *Social History of the Matthew Community: Cross Disciplinary Approaches*, ed. David Balch (Minneapolis: Fortress Press, 1991) 269.

[64] Cf. my discussion in ch. 1, pp. 30–31.

[65] E.g., If the disciples are transparent for the gospel's readers, what reality does the disciples' abandonment illuminate within the Matthean community?

narrative criticism[66] and thus this study, some suggestions might be made based on the critique just offered of the concept of transparency.

First, Kingsbury's warning is crucial. If we are to venture a sketch of the Matthean community, it must be based on a comprehensive reading of Matthew's narrative rather than on a "random selection of passages."[67] Syreeni, in his analysis of Peter's characterization, does this kind of sustained reading of the narrative. Although I am not ultimately convinced by his conclusion that Peter embodies "the traditional values of a Jewish-Christian group in Matthew's community,"[68] his analysis of all texts in which Peter appears as well as his sensitivity to Matthew's use of narrative devices moves scholarship in the right direction in pursuit of the evangelist's concrete world.

Second, Johnson helpfully reminds us that the primary meaning of individual literary elements in a gospel is related to their context within the larger literary structure, and not to extra-textual problems of the evangelist's community.[69] This means that, even after we have established the presence of a particular theme in a gospel (e.g., the disciples' "little faith" in Matthew), we cannot simply assume that this theme is present because of the same problem in the Matthean church. Rather, we will need to analyze how this part of the disciples' portrayal fits into the literary purposes of the gospel and then determine, if possible, whether the theme is motivated by theological or polemical concerns.[70]

Finally, if it is possible to reconstruct the Matthean audience from the narrative, then it is crucial that we define the nature and scope of that audience. The widely-agreed upon assumption that each of the Gospels was written from and to a single Christian community is very seldom argued in any sustained and persuasive way. In fact, some New Testament scholars have recently argued that the Gospels were written for a much wider audience than is usually assumed.[71] They contend that the Gospels are "open documents" with an

---

[66] Which "bracket[s] out questions of historicity in order to concentrate on the nature of the text as literature," Powell, *Narrative Criticism*, 8.

[67] Kingsbury, "Analysis," 269.

[68] Syreeni, "Peter as Character," 150.

[69] Johnson, "On Finding the Lukan Community," 92.

[70] Ibid., 92.

[71] Richard Bauckham, ed., *The Gospels for All Christians: Rethinking the Gospel Audiences* (Grand Rapids: Eerdmans, 1998). Cf. also Stanton, who argues for the likelihood of wider circulation of Matthew than typically assumed (*A Gospel for a New People*, 50–51). Carter also calls attention to "the way in which Matthew envisages the lifestyle of the community of disciples in its wider late-first-century societal context;" Warren Carter, "Matthew 4:18–22 and Matthean Discipleship: An Audience-Oriented Perspective," *CBQ* 59 (January, 1997) 58. Cf. also Ogawa, who speaks of inferring the situation of Matthew's

indefinite rather than a specific audience. A number of persuasive arguments ground this minority viewpoint.

(1)   The genre of ancient Greco-Roman *bios*, to which the Gospels belong, would not likely be expected to address a small, quite specific community of people.[72]

(2)   The purpose of a gospel would be to communicate with those unable to be present for oral teaching; i.e., those at a distance from the Evangelist rather than those within his own community.[73]

(3)   Evidence regarding the general character of the early Christian movement does not point to "isolated, self-sufficient communities with little communication between them, but... [to] a network of communities with constant, close communication among themselves."[74]

If there is any merit to this re-conception of the audience of the Gospels and particularly Matthew, then it could be helpful to examine how the sustained themes in the disciples' portrayal point to broad issues facing the early church in the latter part of the first-century. For example, the highlighting of exemplary faith in Jesus' supreme authority against the backdrop of the disciples' "little faith" certainly met a Christian audience whose faith had been tried and possibly shaken not only by increasingly hostile Roman opposition but also by gradual separation from the Jewish community that was the taproot of its identity. In addition, Jesus' warning against preoccupation with status underscored by the disciples' misunderstanding of their role in the kingdom spoke to an audience saturated by strict codes of patronage, status, and honor.[75] Status-consciousness was part and parcel of the first-century world, so that Matthew's message was likely a direct indictment of the entrenched social structure both in the early church and first-century society at large.[76]

---

church from the disciples' portrayal as those of "little faith" not directly but indirectly and more broadly; Akira Ogawa, "Action-Motivating Faith: The Understanding of 'Faith' in the Gospel of Matthew," *AJBI* 19 (1993) 86.

[72] Bauckham, "For Whom Were Gospels Written?" in *The Gospels for All Christians*, 28.

[73] Ibid., 28–30. "The obvious function of writing was its capacity to communicate widely with readers unable to be present at its author's oral teaching" (29).

[74] Ibid., 30. For specific arguments on this last point, cf. Bauckham, "Gospels," 30–44.

[75] For a reading of Matthew that pays attention to these particular social issues, cf. Jerome H. Neyrey, *Honor and Shame in the Gospel of Matthew* (Louisville: Westminster John Knox Press, 1998).

[76] If Matthew is written to a wider audience instead of a single, rather idiosyncratic community, then the sketching of this audience will necessarily be more general than traditional reconstructions have been. So if the observations above seem rather obvious and

THE FUNCTION OF THE DISCIPLES IN MATTHEW'S SYMBOLIC WORLD

In the final analysis, however, it is not the concrete world of Matthew's community that is the primary focus of the meaning of the disciples' portrayal.[77] Instead, the characterization of the disciples primarily functions as part of Matthew's broader configuration of discipleship.[78] Matthean discipleship might broadly be described as "personal attachment to Jesus…and a lifestyle shaped by his commands."[79] The implied author is very interested in setting forth a particular vision of what this discipleship should look like, a vision that will be persuasive for his reader.[80] The disciples' portrayal then functions in Matthew's symbolic world as one aspect of how he communicates his vision of discipleship.[81]

While virtually all scholars—whether they employ narrative-critical or redaction-critical approaches—connect the disciples' portrayal to Matthean discipleship in some fashion, there tends to be a lack of clarity regarding the way the disciples' portrayal contributes to the vision of discipleship in Matthew. Some have used the disciples' portrayal as the major indicator of Matthean discipleship. This has been the tendency in redaction criticism, where,

---

therefore less sophisticated than reconstructions of a more particular Matthean audience, I would argue that this does not render them any less valid. As Stanton points out, if Matthew envisioned that his gospel would circulate widely, "it is no surprise to find that his criticisms of his readers are severe but imprecise" (*A Gospel for a New People,* 51).

[77] "With regard to the Gospels, then, to agree that they emerge from a life-setting does not allow us to conclude that the life-setting is determinative of the document's meaning, either as a whole or in its parts" (Johnson, "On Finding the Lukan Community," 90).

[78] The disciples as character group should not be equated, however, with Matthean discipleship, since the latter ideological category is much broader than the former story element.

[79] Donaldson, "Making Disciples," 44. For discussion of some of the major terms used by Matthew for discipleship, cf. Jack Dean Kingsbury, "The Verb *akolouthein* ("To Follow") as an Index of Matthew's View of His Community," *JBL* 97 (1978) 56–73; for διακονέω, cf. Talvikki Mattila, "Naming the Nameless: Gender and Discipleship in Matthew's Passion Narrative," in *Characterization in the Gospel: Reconceiving Narrative Criticism,* ed. D. Rhoads and K. Syreeni, JSNTSup 184 (Sheffield: Sheffield Academic Press, 1999) 175–77.

[80] "Discipleship…concerns the values that Jesus and the implied author commend to their hearers/readers" (Howell, *Inclusive,* 250).

[81] *How* Matthew communicates his vision of discipleship to his reader is the focus of this discussion (rather than *what* Matthew communicates in that vision), since the disciples' portrayal functions as part of Matthew's *method* of communication. My goal is to provide a model of Matthew's method of imparting discipleship to his reader. This model can then be used to fill in the content of Matthean discipleship. For a brief but helpful description of this content, see Donaldson, "Making Disciples," 44–47. Cf. also Bauer, "Major Characters," 361–62.

for example, the disciples' understanding points to understanding as a feature of Matthean discipleship. According to Wilkins, "…Matthew emphasizes that the essence of true discipleship lies in individuals who understand and obey Jesus' teaching." Wilkins bases this statement on the *portrayal of the disciples* as understanding Jesus' teaching at 16:21; 17:13; and 13:51.[82] Edwards, a narrative critic, draws an even stronger connection between the disciples' portrayal and discipleship, so that there seems to be an exact correspondence between the two. Since his understanding of the disciples' portrayal is more negative than that of redaction studies, his definition of discipleship reflects this ambivalence. "So a disciple…is not an ideal individual who meets Jesus' expectations, but one who recognizes Jesus and who will follow him, in a limited fashion, under most conditions."[83]

This conception of Matthean discipleship, however, is inadequate. While the disciples' portrayal (both negative and positive) is certainly an essential part of Matthew's point of view regarding discipleship, it is not the only or even the primary piece of the puzzle.[84] As most have recognized, *Jesus' teachings* provide a significant amount of the content for Matthean discipleship.[85] Carter helpfully distinguishes the portrayal of the disciples ("the disciples as they are") from the discipleship reflected in Jesus' teaching ("[the disciples] as they should be")[86] and analyzes both of these in his chapter on the disciples as character group. Nevertheless, in the final pages of his chapter, Carter does not

---

[82] Wilkins, "Named and Unnamed Disciples," 422. Cf. also Luz, "Disciples," 121–23; Mark Sheridan, "Disciples and Discipleship in Matthew and Luke" *BTB* 3 (1973) 249.

[83] Edwards, *Portrait*, 143. One wonders if this rather half-hearted effort on the part of a disciple is truly Matthew's view of discipleship.

[84] Their positive portrayal contributes to the substance of Matthean discipleship, while their negative characterization provides a foil for the qualities extolled by the author.

[85] Deutsch affirms that Matthew "understands discipleship in reference to a body of teaching, revelation, tradition that is taught by Jesus;" Celia Deutsch, "Torah, Jesus, and Discipleship in the Gospel of Matthew," *Sidic* 24 (1991) 43–52. Narrative critics affirm that the implied reader is encouraged to hear the teachings of Jesus as directed toward herself by means of the frequent "indefinite and inclusive language" (Howell, *Inclusive*, 251) as well as the significant length of the five discourses; cf. Janice Capel Anderson, "Matthew: Gender and Reading," *Semeia* 28 (1983) 25: "The discourses…become addresses to the implied reader as well as the audiences designated in the narrative." The same perspective is argued by Andrew Lincoln, "Matthew—A Story for Teachers?" in *The Bible in Three Dimensions*, ed. D. Clines, et al. (Sheffield: JSOT Press, 1990) 116.

[86] Warren Carter, *Matthew: Storyteller, Interpreter, Evangelist* (Peabody, MA: Hendrickson, 1996) 243. These two concepts are essentially identical to Patte's "actual disciples" (as they behave in the narrative) and "ideal disciples" (described in Jesus' teaching). See n. 45 above.

clearly delineate *how* these two dimensions intersect to form a coherent picture of Matthean discipleship.[87]

The intersection of the disciples' portrayal and Jesus' teaching regarding discipleship still does not communicate the whole of discipleship for Matthew. Also important are the numerous minor characters who illustrate true discipleship in one way or another. Many of these are women or Gentiles (e.g., the Roman centurion, the hemorrhaging woman, the Canaanite woman, and the women at the cross and the tomb). Although not a part of the character group of the disciples, these minor characters embody aspects of discipleship.[88] In fact, Wilkins includes these characters in "the circle of disciples," which he draws more widely than the character group of the disciples.[89] In most cases, these characters demonstrate a single quality of discipleship (e.g., the Canaanite woman's great faith) which the reader is meant to embrace as a goal of discipleship and thus to emulate.

In addition, Matthew provides the counterpoint to discipleship in characters antagonistic to Jesus, such as the Jewish leaders, Jesus' hometown, and Herod.[90] The qualities exhibited by these various individuals or groups, such as

---

[87] While indicating that the ambivalent portrayal of the disciples means that "the future of the community of disciples...includes insight and confusion, faithlessness and faithfulness, fear and courage," Carter immediately adds, "[s]o in this way disciples must live..." (Carter, *Matthew,* 254). This seems to imply that the *disciples' portrayal* is paradigmatic for discipleship. Yet in his conclusion, he clearly draws upon *Jesus' teachings* as the basis for the traits of the "audience's discipleship" (*Matthew*, 254–55).

[88] Anderson, "Gender and Reading," 24; Wilkins, "Named and Unnamed Disciples," 434; Howell, *Inclusive*, 231–32. According to Wainwright, Matthew's "women characters demonstrate much greater fidelity to this following of Jesus and adherence to him and his way than do many male characters, especially the twelve called disciples;" Elaine Mary Wainwright, *Towards a Feminist Critical Reading of the Gospel according to Matthew* (New York: Walter de Gruyter, 1991) 335. Cf. also Mattila, "Naming the Nameless," 169. Senior speaks of these "outsiders" (minor characters) as exemplifying authentic discipleship; Donald Senior, *The Passion of Jesus in the Gospel of Matthew* (Wilmington, DE: Michael Glazier, 1985) 149. According to Carter, the "audience recognizes in these characters...the traits of disciples even though they are not identified as such...The appearance of these characters assists the audience to recognize the identity and lifestyle that mark discipleship" (Carter, *Matthew*, 243).

[89] Wilkins, "Named and Unnamed Disciples," 439. Wainwright also seems to include these minor characters within that circle, referring to "the discipleship qualities exhibited by the women as well as the men who have come to Jesus as supplicants, who have listened to his teaching and who have followed him;" Elaine Mary Wainwright, "The Gospel of Matthew" in *Searching the Scriptures: A Feminist Commentary*, ed. Elisabeth Schüssler Fiorenza, vol. 2 (New York: Crossroad, 1994) 654–55.

[90] The crowds may or may not be part of this group at various points in the narrative, since they are portrayed more ambivalently than the Jewish leaders. They exhibit both positive and negative responses to Jesus, with the negative responses becoming more prevalent as the

unbelief or hypocrisy, provide a foil for the discipleship Matthew wants to impress upon his reader. According to Donaldson, the contrast provided by those antagonistic to Jesus is one of the devices used by Matthew "to make disciples of his readers."[91] Their function is thus like that of the disciples in the negative aspects of their portrayal, although Jesus' antagonists certainly provide the antithetical perspective for discipleship rather than the disciples' example of less than ideal discipleship.[92]

Finally, Matthew provides a model of discipleship for his implied reader through Jesus' own words and actions. Not only does Jesus *teach* about the qualities of true discipleship, he also *models* many of these qualities in his own speech and deeds.[93] In his final chapter ("Conclusion: Jesus as Exemplary for Discipleship"), Howell points to Matthew's emphasis on Jesus' doing the will of God as a significant aspect of this modeling.[94] This includes Jesus' example of servanthood (8:17; 12:18–21; cf. with importance for discipleship at 20:28) and his example of love (19:13–15; 9:36; 14:14; 15:32; 9:13; 12:7; cf. importance for discipleship at 22:36–40; 5:43–48).[95] "Jesus is exemplary as a model for discipleship because what he experiences and does is also what the disciples must do."[96]

---

story progresses. Cf. Wilkins' description of the crowds as "basically neutral...who are at times seen negatively and at times positively;" Michael Wilkins, *The Concept of Disciple in Matthew's Gospel*, NovTSup 59 (Leiden: E. J. Brill, 1988) 170–71.

[91] Donaldson, "Making Disciples," 44. He includes these groups in his configuration of discipleship along with the disciples' portrayal and Jesus' teaching (42–43). The only part of the composite I am proposing that Donaldson does not mention is the portrayal of various exemplary characters, including Jesus and the minor characters (or "other disciples") who function to illuminate Matthew's perspective on discipleship. As Howell points out, "The implied reader is...able to learn from all the characters, both negatively and positively, what it means to follow Jesus" (*Inclusive*, 250–51).

[92] For example, while the disciples provide a foil to exemplary faith by means of their little (i.e., less than adequate) faith, Jesus' hometown demonstrates the antithetical contrast to faith, that of complete unbelief.

[93] Cf. my discussion of this aspect of discipleship in ch. 3, pp. 65, 80–81.

[94] Howell, *Inclusive*, 251.

[95] Ibid., 252–54. The reader learns of Jesus' model of servanthood primarily from fulfillment quotations used by Matthew, which evoke the servant songs of Isaiah (Matt 8:17; 12:18–21). These fulfillment quotations are really part of another category by which the author communicates with the reader, that of *direct commentary*. In fact, much of the direct commentary in Matthew consists of these fulfillment quotations. I do not treat this as a separate element in my scheme simply because the vast majority of the fulfillment quotations relate to Jesus, his identity and mission, rather than to discipleship.

[96] Howell, *Inclusive*, 259. Cf. also Kupp, *Matthew's Emmanuel*, 242; Kingsbury, "Figure of Jesus," 77, 78.

From these various elements that illuminate discipleship, a methodological model emerges. Matthean discipleship is communicated through a composite whose elements form two layers within the gospel's narration. The focal layer includes the teaching of Jesus regarding true discipleship; the more positive aspects of the disciples' portrayal; the example of numerous minor characters that model characteristics of ideal discipleship; and the example of Jesus himself. The background layer, which provides a foil or contrast to the focal layer, is composed of the portrayals of those in conflict with Jesus' claims and message.[97] This layer also includes Jesus' disciples in the more negative aspects of their portrayal, since they are thereby shown to be in ideological conflict with Jesus over the nature of discipleship. In order to illustrate the way these elements and layers come together to inform discipleship, I will analyze one Matthean theme related to discipleship: the notion of fear. Again, the goal of the present discussion is not to flesh out all values related to Matthean discipleship but to propose a model for conceptualizing the way in which Matthew communicates discipleship to his reader.

Fear within Matthean Discipleship[98]

Fear in Matthew (frequently involving the word φόβος or its cognate verb) is both positively and adversely related to discipleship. The background layer to Matthean discipleship emphasizes that fear of humans—what they think and what they have power to do—is inappropriate. This is shown through the portrayals of Herod and the Jewish leaders. Herod, although wanting to put John to death, does not do so because he fears the crowds (14:5). Herod's consistently negative portrayal throughout Matthew informs the reader that fear of people is not a part of discipleship. This is confirmed by the characterization of the Jewish leaders at 21:26 and 21:46. The Jewish leaders choose not to respond to Jesus' question (21:26) and not to take action against Jesus (21:46) because they are afraid of the crowds. This is also confirmed by 6:1–18, where the hypocrites are condemned for doing piety for human approval rather than

---

[97] The terms, focal layer and background layer, are not meant to indicate the relative importance of the first over the second but to indicate that the implied reader's attention is *focused* more keenly on the positive aspects of discipleship through the contrast with the negative ones. Thus, Bauer can rightly speak of Matthew's expectations for discipleship as a backdrop for the actual behavior of the disciples, since Bauer is focusing on the disciples as characters in his discussion ("Major Characters," 361–62).

[98] Cf. ch. 4, pp. 101–07 for a thorough analysis of the broader theme of faith (in which fear has a role), albeit from the perspective of defining "little faith" rather than from a focus on the importance of faith for Matthean discipleship. Note that all elements of the background and focal layers are included in that analysis.

God's approval.[99] Fearing human responses and seeking human approval are seen as a negative backdrop to the values of true discipleship.

The focal layer of Matthew's discipleship composite emphasizes the nature of "proper fear" as well as reiterating the kind of fear to avoid. In the missionary discourse, Jesus teaches that his disciples are not to fear those who can kill the body (10:26, 28, 31), highlighting by his words what is communicated by the negative examples of Herod and the Jewish leaders, namely, that his followers are not to fear any human response to them. But Jesus also speaks of a proper fear: a fear/awe of God ("...fear him who can destroy both soul and body in hell;" 10:28).[100] But it is not only Jesus' teaching that emphasizes that the fear of God should replace fear of other people. In his own life, Jesus *exemplifies* this quality at his trial and crucifixion. Although the word itself is not used of Jesus in these scenes, he embodies his earlier words that one should not fear those who can kill the body, when he boldly quotes Daniel 7 in reference to himself before Caiaphas (26:64), resulting in a death sentence (26:66).[101]

Turning to the minor characters of the story (who are often exemplary in some way for discipleship) we find "proper fear" exhibited by a number of these characters in response to God's activity or God's messengers. The crowds respond to the healing of the paralytic (and accompanying claim by Jesus that his sins are forgiven) with fear and by glorifying God (9:8). The coupling of these two responses along with God as object of their fear argues for a positive interpretation of their fear. This proper fear is also exhibited by the centurion and guards who fear the earthquake and other miraculous events surrounding Jesus' death and confess: "Truly this man was God's Son!" (27:54).[102] Finally, the women at the tomb respond with "fear and great joy" upon hearing the news of the resurrection from the angel. After seeing Jesus, they "took hold of his feet, and worshiped him" (28:8–9). By linking fear with the positive qualities of glorifying, confession, worship and joy, Matthew shows that the response of

---

[99] Cf. Matt 23 (e.g., 23:13), where Jewish leaders are identified as hypocrites.

[100] Davies and Allison rightly contend that this refers to God rather than the devil; William D. Davies and Dale C. Allison, *A Critical and Exegetical Commentary on the Gospel according to St. Matthew*, ICC (Edinburgh: T&T Clark, 1988–97) 2:206–07. Cf. also Dorothy Jean Weaver, *Matthew's Missionary Discourse: A Literary Critical Analysis*, JSNTSup 38 (Sheffield: JSOT Press, 1990) 109. Franzmann states it this way: "The one fear that is to dominate the life of the [disciple] is not the paralyzing fear of [humans] but the impelling fear of God;" Martin H. Franzmann, *Follow Me: Discipleship according to Saint Matthew* (St Louis: Concordia, 1961) 95.

[101] Pilate's amazement at Jesus' refusal to defend himself against the charges of his accusers also argues for a similar lack of fear in Jesus' portrayal at 27:11–14.

[102] Senior, *Passion of Jesus*, 148.

fear/awe in the presence of God' activity or God's messenger is a proper discipleship response.

The final element to examine is the portrayal of the disciples. As we have come to expect with other of their attributes, the disciples are portrayed both positively and negatively with regard to the attribute of fear. They are afraid at Jesus' transfiguration (17:6–7), showing a proper fear at the miraculous activity of God. This also seems to be the case at 14:26, where they are afraid of Jesus as he walks to them on the water.[103]

Conversely, at 8:26 the disciples are portrayed, not as having a proper fear, but as having a fear associated with "little faith." The disciples wake up Jesus in the boat, afraid for their lives. Jesus questions them, "Why are you afraid, you of little faith?" The word translated "afraid" (in the NRSV) is δειλός, meaning timidity or fear.[104] Here the disciples are not fearing God but are fearing for their own safety in spite of having Jesus in the boat with them. At 14:30 the same situation seems to apply to Peter. After stepping out of the boat, he notices the wind and begins to fear. Jesus rescues him and says, "You of little faith, why did you doubt?" Peter is not showing a proper fear; rather, he fears for his safety in the presence of the very one who enabled him to walk on the water in the first place. Finally, the flight of the disciples at the arrest of Jesus (and Peter's denial as well) demonstrates that they once again fear for their lives (26:56, 69–75). They are expressly doing what Jesus has warned them to avoid: fearing those who can only harm the body (10:28).[105]

Having looked at the trait of fear in relation to Matthean discipleship, it can be concluded that a disciple of Jesus should fear God and stand in awe of his miraculous activity. This is a proper kind of fear. What Matthew warns against, however, is a fear of human response and approval (exemplified in Herod and the Jewish leaders). In addition, by means of the negative side of the disciple' portrayal, Matthew shows that a fear for one's own life and safety is not

---

[103] The admonition of Jesus, "Take heart, it is I; do not be afraid" (14:27), should not be read as an indictment of the disciples but as an encouragement to those who are presented with divine manifestations. The command to not be afraid is given elsewhere in Matthew to those who have not necessarily been described as fearful but are in the presence of God's activity or messenger (e.g., to Joseph at 1:20; to the women at the tomb before the angel speaks at 28:5; cf. also at 17:7 and 28:10 to calm fears explicitly mentioned). In addition, the encouragement to "take heart" (θαρσέω at 14:27) is only given elsewhere in Matthew to two supplicants who come to Jesus for healing and in both those cases is linked to faith (9:2, 22).

[104] Nida and Louw, in their Greek-English lexicon, group δειλός and φόβος in the same semantic field (316–18).

[105] "There is little question that the reader is to infer fear as a trait not only for the disciples who flee at Jesus' arrest…but also for Peter's denial…" (Burnett, "Characterization," 21).

warranted in the presence of the mighty power of Jesus "to determine the destiny of the disciples."[106]

SUMMARY: THE FUNCTION OF THE MATTHEAN DISCIPLES

In order to clarify the issues related to the function of the disciples' portrayal, I have used Syreeni's three-tiered model of the textual world, the concrete world, and the symbolic world of a gospel. In the textual world of Matthew's story, the disciples' more negative portrayal functions as a foil to highlight Jesus' teaching and authority as well as his effective presence for the continuation of his mission (since the disciples' tendency to misunderstand does not provide a guarantee of his legacy and mission). On the discourse level of the textual world, the disciples function both as a point of identification as well as a point of disassociation for the implied reader. After the initial identification the reader has toward the disciples based on their more positive portrayal, the increasingly negative portrayal causes the reader to distance himself/herself from the disciples' behavior and values, so that their portrayal functions as an incentive toward true and complete discipleship.

In Matthew's concrete world, the disciples are not to be identified as transparent for the Matthean community, in spite of the long-standing (redaction-critical) tendency to do so. Rather, the disciples' characterization functions as part of the way Matthew communicates the complex of values he wants to instill in his reader. These (or at least some of these) values may indeed address the issues facing Matthew's audience, but caution needs to be exercised before assuming a one-to-one correspondence between any one such value or theme and Matthew's concrete world.

Finally, the disciples' portrayal functions in Matthew's symbolic world as one part of the larger methodological composite the author uses to communicate his vision of discipleship with the reader. The negative aspects of their portrayal (along with the negative portrayals of Jesus' antagonists) form part of the backdrop against which the ideal of discipleship shines more brightly. The discipleship ideal is then fleshed out in a focal layer consisting of (1) Jesus' teachings; (2) the disciples' positive characteristics; (3) various exemplary (minor) characters who model some aspect of ideal discipleship; and (4) the model of Jesus himself in his words and actions. Through this composite of positive and negative examples provided by various major and minor

---

[106] Weaver, *Missionary Discourse*, 108. For a brief but helpful discussion of fear as it relates to worship in Matthew, cf. Mark Allan Powell, *God With Us: A Pastoral Theology of Matthew's Gospel* (Minneapolis: Fortress Press, 1995) 49–51.

characters, of which Jesus and his teaching is central, Matthew communicates a holistic vision of discipleship meant to captivate, motivate, and ultimately change his reader.

CHAPTER 6

THE DISCIPLES AND DISCIPLESHIP
IN NARRATIVE PERSPECTIVE

CONCLUDING SUMMARY

The goal of this study has been to examine the way the disciples are portrayed in Matthew and how that portrayal functions in the narrative. The particular focus has been on their characterization in 16:21–20:28, since Matthew highlights the interaction between Jesus and his disciples in this section of the gospel.

The prevailing viewpoint of redaction-critical studies affirms that, although characterized by "little faith," the Matthean disciples essentially understand Jesus' identity and teachings. Redaction studies, however, have typically ignored Matthew 18–20 in their analysis of the disciples' portrayal (focusing on Matthew 13–17 instead). In addition, these studies have tended to focus on the direct characterization provided by Matthew (e.g., 17:13: "the disciples understood..."), while virtually ignoring the indirect means by which Matthew communicates about the disciples (i.e., via their own words and actions and the words and actions of others toward them). This in spite of the fact that indirect characterization is the primary means of characterization in Matthew as well as in ancient biography in general.

Narrative criticism on the disciples' portrayal has generally paid more attention to these issues of characterization. Most narrative studies conclude that the disciples frequently misunderstand Jesus in addition to exhibiting "little faith." Nevertheless, there has been no substantial treatment of 16:21–20:28 by

147

narrative critics, in spite of its clear emphasis on the disciples' portrayal.[1] In addition, an important issue still undecided in narrative approaches is whether the disciples progress in their understanding from the beginning of Matthew's story to its end. (For the survey of both redaction and narrative approaches and conclusions, cf. chapter 1.)

The study presented here employed narrative criticism to examine the portrayal of the disciples. After dealing with the introductory issues of defining "the disciples" within Matthew's narrative, providing a rationale for focusing on 16:21–20:28 as a discreet unit for the disciples' portrayal, and defining the method of character analysis used (cf. chapter 2), a detailed analysis of 16:21–20:28 was made. Each section of 16:21–20:28 was analyzed to determine how the disciples are portrayed and the effect of that portrayal upon the flow of the plot in this part of Matthew (cf. chapter 3). The rest of Matthew was then surveyed in regard to the disciples' characterization (cf. chapter 4). The primary conclusion of the entire analysis was that the disciples, while comprehending the identity of Jesus as Messiah (e.g., 16:13–20), are shown to misunderstand consistently the kind of Messiah Jesus is (i.e., his mission to suffer and die) as well as Jesus' teaching about their own part in the kingdom he brings. In this way, they are shown to be in ideological conflict with Jesus, as Jesus counters their human perspective with God's perspective on Messiahship and discipleship. In addition, they lack an adequate faith in (and so a proper understanding of) the extent of Jesus' authority. Finally, because of their propensity toward misunderstanding and "little faith," the disciples fall short of the role Jesus intends them to fulfill in his earthly ministry. Regarding the issue of their growth as characters, Matthew does not show the disciples to progress substantially in either their understanding or their faith. At the end of the gospel, they continue to be those of "little faith," prone to misunderstand (cf. 28:17).

After extensive analysis of the disciples' portrayal, the function of their portrayal was examined (cf. chapter 5). Syreeni's categories of textual (further divided into story and discourse levels), concrete, and symbolic worlds were used to clarify the various levels of the narrative affected by the disciples' portrayal. On the story level of Matthew's textual world, the portrayal of the disciples functions to highlight Jesus' teaching. Their various misguided questions and responses usually elicit a word of teaching from Jesus. Their frequent misunderstanding, however, does not function to highlight the

---

[1] Warren Carter, *Households and Discipleship: A Study of Matthew 19–20*, JSNTSup 103 (Sheffield: JSOT Press, 1994) is an exception, although his emphasis is upon discipleship more than on the disciples' portrayal.

effective teaching of Jesus.[2] Instead, their misunderstanding functions to highlight Jesus' effective presence. If the disciples are prone to misunderstanding, then the guarantee of the accurate transmission of Jesus' teaching is called into question. The Matthean answer to this question is Jesus' presence with his disciples in the post-resurrection era (cf. 18:20; 28:20).

On the discourse level of Matthew's textual world, the disciples' positive and negative qualities impact the implied reader (i.e., the reader implied by the text itself). Their positive qualities (e.g., leaving all to follow Jesus, worshiping Jesus, confessing Jesus' identity as Messiah) cause the implied reader to identify with the disciples (especially in the earlier parts of the gospel). But the negative characterization of the disciples tends to distance the implied reader from them. This distance, in turn, encourages an evaluation of the disciples in light the author's and Jesus' point of view, drawing the reader to embrace the values idealized by Matthew.

Regarding Matthew's concrete world (the world outside of the text), caution should be exercised before assigning the disciples a particular function in relation to Matthew's community or audience. It has been axiomatic in redaction criticism to view the disciples as transparent for the Matthean community in some fashion. This assumption has been questioned by most narrative critics, who emphasize that stories are not told, first and foremost, to illuminate the world outside of the text in any specific way (text as window) but to draw the reader into the story in order to challenge and change them (text as portrait). If the disciples consistently misunderstand Jesus' mission as well as their own, it is unlikely that they stand for Matthew's community (or some part of it) in any sort of direct correspondence. A more modest proposal would be to suggest that the general contours of the disciples' portrayal could be examined in light of the social-historical situation of the latter half of the first century, in order to discern how Matthew's message provides a challenge to his broader audience.

Finally, on the level of Matthew's symbolic world, the portrayal of the disciples functions to illuminate part of Matthean discipleship. The proposed model for understanding the way in which Matthew communicates his vision of discipleship involves two layers: a background layer that acts as a foil to a focal discipleship layer. The background layer includes the negative qualities attributed to the disciples as well as the negative qualities of other characters including Herod and the Jewish leaders (i.e., the antagonists to Jesus' ministry). The focal layer includes the disciples' positive qualities, as well Jesus'

---

[2] The disciples' understanding, according to redaction critics, highlights Jesus as effective teacher, since after his explanations the disciples come to understand. However, if the disciples' are characterized by misunderstanding more often than not, their portrayal cannot function to demonstrate Jesus' effectiveness as teacher.

teachings on discipleship, his own model of discipleship in words and actions, and the words and actions of various exemplary (usually minor) characters who model some aspect of discipleship. The entire composite illuminates Matthew's perspective on discipleship, so that the disciples' portrayal (in both its negative and positive aspects) forms part of the way Matthew communicates discipleship to his reader.

IMPLICATIONS FOR FURTHER STUDY

A number of implications for further study arise from this work. First, a sustained narrative-critical reading of Matthew does not necessarily contradict a redaction-critical reading with regards to the disciples' portrayal. As Trotter's redactional study proves, redaction criticism that takes seriously what is conserved by Matthew as well as what is modified, does arrive at some similar conclusions to this study (e.g., that the disciples are prone to misunderstanding). This finding argues for more dialogue between redaction and narrative approaches than has previously occurred.[3] Narrative criticism's methodological commitment to bracketing out historical issues should not be used as license to ignore dialogue with methods whose more central aims involve historical inquiry. On the other hand, this study has shown at a number of points the helpfulness of a distinctively narrative analysis of Matthew. One such distinctive result of narrative criticism is the recognition that various points of view are represented in the narrative. Identification of *reliable* points of view will help to avoid the propensity to trust the voice of every character in Matthew's story and so will more clearly define the commended perspective.[4] So not only does narrative criticism benefit from dialogue with redaction approaches; redaction critics can profit from listening to narrative critics.[5]

---

[3] The broadened audience of the five major discourses of Jesus is an area where significant agreement exists between methodologies and where inter-disciplinary dialogue would be profitable. Redaction critics speak of the discourses as directed to the Matthean community, while narrative critics understand the implied reader to be addressed in the discourses in a more direct fashion than elsewhere by means of a number of rhetorical strategies. Both recognize the broadened applicability of the discourses.

[4] Cf. ch. 3, pp. 70–71, 81, 110–11 of this study for examples of the use of this narrative insight. As Kingsbury suggests, "...the most fruitful method of ascertaining the theology of Matthew is...the rigorous, systematic investigation of Matthew's 'point of view;'" Jack Dean Kingsbury, "The Rhetoric of Comprehension in the Gospel of Matthew," *NTS* 41 (1995) 376.

[5] "Instead of talking to or at one another, perhaps we can talk with one another respectfully and critically, recognizing that a multiplicity of approaches can coexist— between scholars and sometimes within a single scholar;" Janice Capel Anderson, "Life on the Mississippi: New Currents in Matthean Scholarship 1983–1993," *CurBS* 3 (1995) 172.

Second, more work seems to be necessary in the area of reading Matthew with an awareness of the conventions of ancient narrative/biography. Some narrative approaches favor reading the Gospels using the categories of modern fiction and therefore tend to ignore ancient conventions. This, it seems to me, is the wrong direction to take. Just as study of ancient characterization practices and parameters has assisted in understanding the Matthean disciples,[6] so analysis of other ancient literary conventions can assist in interpretation of the Gospels. For example, Stanton has examined the Greco-Roman rhetorical strategy of comparison (σύγκρισις), a common stylistic technique, and has helpfully pointed out Matthew's use of this convention.[7] This kind of attention to genre and convention should be a strong emphasis within the narrative-critical guild.

A third area for further study that moves beyond methodological considerations involves a reading of Matthew that seeks to do justice to both the narrative and discourse elements of its broader outline. This study has tried to do just that within 16:21–20:28, by showing both the way chapter 18 fits within its narrative context (via plot flow and narrative structure)[8] as well as the way the surrounding narrative context fleshes out in story form Matthean themes in chapter 18.[9] Since there has been a tendency in Matthean scholarship to set up an either/or distinction between the structural proposals of Kingsbury (based on narrative indicators) and Bacon (based on the five Matthean discourses and their alternation with narrative), attempts to read both narrative and discourse sections in a more unified fashion should be welcomed.[10]

---

[6] Cf. ch. 2, pp. 49–53.

[7] Graham Stanton, *A Gospel for a New People: Studies in Matthew* (Edinburgh: T&T Clark, 1992) 77–84. Although Stanton is not a narrative critic, he challenges narrative criticism to pay attention to these ancient conventions (77).

[8] In terms of plot flow, 18:1–5 prepares for 19:13–15 and shows the disciples' rejection of children at 19:13–15 to be highly ironic. In terms of narrative structure, 18:1 and 18:21 fit the broader narrative context where disciples' questions function to elicit Jesus' corrective teaching.

[9] E.g., the disciples' consistent preoccupation with status and position (e.g., 19:13, 25, 27; 20:20–23) fleshes out (is a foil to) the theme of renunciation of desire for status called for by Jesus in 18:1–5.

[10] Examples of such attempts include the seventh chapter ("The Structure of Matthew: Relationship between Great Discourses and Narrative Framework") of David R. Bauer, *The Structure of Matthew's Gospel: A Study in Literary Design*, JSNTSup (Sheffield: Almond Press, 1988); and Craig L. Blomberg, *Matthew*, NAC 22 (Nashville: Broadman Press, 1992) 24–25. Blomberg's goal is an outline that "combines the strengths of Bacon and Kingsbury but moves beyond them as well" (24). Cf. also Chouinard's outline of Matthew; Larry Chouinard, *Matthew*, The College Press NIV Commentary (Joplin, MO: College Press, 1997) 26.

Finally, in this study I have proposed a model for understanding Matthew's method of communicating discipleship to his reader. It is a model that is not only based on lexical evidence but attends to the broader way in which the narrative shapes discipleship concepts. For example, the analysis of "little faith" (in chapter 4) moved from examination of the term, ὀλιγόπιστος, to the broader concept of faith in Matthew in order to explicate the concepts that contrast with "little faith" (e.g., exemplary faith and unbelief). In addition, this broader analysis moved beyond the analysis of lexical evidence (e.g., where and how words for faith/unbelief are used) to a narrative analysis of these concepts (e.g., where and how certain characters are portrayed as possessing unbelief even though not identified by the word, ἀπιστία). This kind of analysis opens the way toward a more comprehensive understanding of Matthean discipleship.[11]

In addition, the specific model proposed for analyzing Matthean discipleship takes account of the complexity of Matthew's method for communicating discipleship. It is not the disciples' portrayal alone or even the combination of their portrayal and Jesus' teaching on discipleship that comprises his method. Instead it is a composite of both negative and positive qualities (the negative providing the foil for the positive), which illuminates ideal discipleship for Matthew. While I have sketched out a way of understanding Matthean discipleship, I have certainly not provided a complete description of Matthean discipleship. It would be productive to examine a variety of the discipleship emphases in Matthew using the model proposed (as I do for the theme of fear in chapter 5). Specific themes examined might include righteousness, forgiveness, doing God's will, and the practice of piety. In any case, much work remains to be done in explicating Matthean discipleship. The analysis of the portrayal and function of the disciples is just one part of that larger task.

---

[11] Cf. Mark Allen Powell, *God With Us: A Pastoral Theology of Matthew's Gospel* (Minneapolis: Fortress, Press, 1995) for a study of Matthean theology that pays attention to narrative issues as well as lexical ones.

BIBLIOGRAPHY

Aarde, Andries G. van. "The Disciples in Matthew's Story." *Hervormde Teologiese Studies Supplement* 5 (1994) 87–104.

———. "Past and Present in Matthean Research: A Review of the Various Interpretation Models." *Hervormde Teologiese Studies Supplement* 5 (1994) 1–33.

Albright, William F., and Christopher S. Mann. *Matthew.* Anchor Bible. Garden City, NY: Doubleday, 1971.

Allen, W. C. *Gospel according to St. Matthew.* International Critical Commentary. Edinburgh: T&T Clark, 1907.

Anderson, Janice Capel. "Life on the Mississippi: New Currents in Matthean Scholarship 1983–1993." *Currents in Research: Biblical Studies* 3 (1995) 169–218.

———. "Matthew: Gender and Reading." *Semeia* 28 (1983) 3–27.

———. "Matthew: Sermon and Story." In *Treasures New and Old: Contributions to Matthean Studies,* ed. David R. Bauer and Mark Allan Powell, 233–50. Atlanta: Scholars Press, 1996.

———. *Matthew's Narrative Web: Over, and Over, and Over Again.* Journal for the Study of the New Testament: Supplement Series 91. Sheffield: JSOT Press, 1994.

Balch, David L., ed. *Social History of the Matthew Community: Cross Disciplinary Approaches.* Minneapolis: Fortress Press, 1991.

Balz, Horst. "συνίημι." In *Exegetical Dictionary of the New Testament,* ed. by Horst Balz and Gerhard Schneider, 3:307–08. Grand Rapids: Eerdmans, 1993.

Barr, James. *The Semantics of Biblical Language.* London: Oxford University Press, 1961.

Barré, Michael L. "The Workers in the Vineyard." *Bible Today* 24 (1986) 173–80.

Bauckham, Richard, ed. *The Gospels for All Christians: Rethinking the Gospel Audiences.* Grand Rapids: Eerdmans, 1998.

Bauer, David R. "The Interpretation of Matthew's Gospel in the Twentieth-Century." *American Theological Library Association: Summary of Proceedings* 42 (1988) 119–45.

———. "The Major Characters of Matthew's Story: Their Function and Significance." *Interpretation* 46 (1992) 357–67.

———. *The Structure of Matthew's Gospel: A Study in Literary Design.* Journal for the Study of the New Testament: Supplement Series 31. Sheffield: Almond Press, 1988.

Beare, Francis W. *The Gospel according to Matthew: A Commentary.* Oxford: Blackwell, 1981.

Best, Ernest. *Disciples and Discipleship: Studies in the Gospel according to Mark.* Edinburgh: T&T Clark, 1986.

Blomberg, Craig. "Marriage, Divorce, Remarriage, and Celibacy: An Exegesis of Matthew 19:3–12." *Trinity Journal* 11 (1990) 161–96.

———. *Matthew.* The New American Commentary 22. Nashville: Broadman Press, 1992.

153

Bonnard, Pierre. *L'Evangile Selon Saint Matthieu.* Commentaire du Nouveau Testament I. Neuchatel: Delachaux & Niestle, 1963.

Booth, Wayne C. *The Rhetoric of Fiction.* 2d ed. Chicago: University of Chicago Press, 1983.

Bornkamm, Günther, Gerhard Barth, and Heinz Joachim Held. *Überlieferung und Auslegung im Matthäusevangelium.* Wissenschaftliche Monographien zum Alten und Neuen Testament 1. Neukirchen: Neukirchener Verlag, 1960.

———. *Tradition and Interpretation in Matthew.* Translated by Percy Scott. Philadelphia: Westminster Press, 1963.

Boyce, James L. "Transformed for Disciple Community: Matthew in Pentecost." *Word and World* 13 (1993) 308–17.

Briscoe, Peter. "Faith Confirmed Through Conflict: The Matthean Redaction of Mark 2:1– 3:6." In *Back to the Sources*, ed. K. Cathcart and J. Healey, 104–28. Dublin: Glendale, 1989.

Brodie, Thomas. "Fish, Temple, Tithe, and Remission: The God-Based Generosity of Deuteronomy 14–15 as One Component of Matthew 17:22–18:35." *Revue Biblique* 99 (1992) 697–718.

Bruner, Frederick D. *Matthew: A Commentary.* 2 Vols. Dallas: Word, 1990.

Burnett, Fred W. "Characterization and Reader Construction." *Semeia* 63 (1993) 3–28.

Carson, D. A. *Matthew.* The Expositor's Bible Commentary 8. Grand Rapids: Zondervan, 1984.

Carter, Warren. "Community Definition and Matthew's Gospel." In *Society of Biblical Literature Seminar Papers*, ed. E. Lovering, Jr., 637–63. Atlanta: Scholars Press, 1997.

———. *Households and Discipleship: A Study of Matthew 19–20.* Journal for the Study of the New Testament: Supplement Series 103. Sheffield: JSOT Press, 1994.

———. "Kernels and Narrative Blocks: The Structure of Matthew's Gospel." *Catholic Biblical Quarterly* 54 (1992) 463–81.

———. *Matthew and the Margins: A Sociopolitical and Religious Reading.* The Bible and Liberation Series. Maryknoll, NY: Orbis Books, 2000.

———. "Matthew 4:18–22 and Matthean Discipleship: An Audience-Oriented Perspective." *Catholic Biblical Quarterly* 59 (1997) 58–75.

———. *Matthew: Storyteller, Interpreter, Evangelist.* Peabody, MA: Hendrickson, 1996.

———. "Paying the Tax to Rome as Subversive Praxis: Matthew 19:24–27." *Journal for the Study of the New Testament* 76 (1999) 3–31.

Chatman, Seymour. *Story and Discourse: Narrative Structure in Fiction and Film.* Ithaca: Cornell University Press, 1978.

Cheney, Emily. "The Mother of the Sons of Zebedee (Matthew 27:56)." *Journal for the Study of the New Testament* 68 (1997) 13–21.

Chouinard, Larry. *Matthew.* The College Press NIV Commentary. Joplin, MO: College Press, 1997.

Clark, Kenneth W. *The Gentile Bias and Other Essays.* Leiden: Brill, 1980.

Combrink, H. J. Bernard. "The Structure of the Gospel of Matthew as Narrative." *Tyndale Bulletin* 34 (1983) 61–90.

Coninck, Frederic. "Le royaume de Dieu comme critique des royaumes des hommes." *Foi et vie* 85 (1986) 47–72.

Cope, Lamar. *Matthew: A Scribe Trained for the Kingdom of Heaven.* Catholic Biblical Quarterly Monograph Series 5. Washington: Catholic Biblical Association, 1976.

Crosby, Michael H. *House of Disciples: Church, Economics, and Justice in Matthew.* Maryknoll, NY: Orbis Books, 1988.

Crossan, John D. *In Parables: The Challenge of the Historical Jesus.* New York: Harper & Row, 1973.

Culpepper, R. Alan. *Anatomy of the Fourth Gospel: A Study in Literary Design.* Philadelphia: Fortress, 1983.

Davies, William D. and Dale C. Allison. *A Critical and Exegetical Commentary on the Gospel according to St. Matthew.* International Critical Commentary. 3 vols. Edinburgh: T&T Clark, 1988–97.

DeBoer, Martinus C. "Ten Thousand Talents? Matthew's Interpretation and Redaction of the Parable of the Unforgiving Servant (Matt 18:23–35)." *Catholic Biblical Quarterly* 50 (1988) 214–32.

Deutsch, Celia. *Hidden Wisdom and the Easy Yoke: Wisdom, Torah, and Discipleship in Matthew 11:25–30.* Journal for the Study of the New Testament: Supplement Series 18. Sheffield: JSOT Press, 1987.

———. "Torah, Jesus, and Discipleship in the Gospel of Matthew." *Sidic* 24 (1991) 43–52.

Dinter, Paul E. "Disabled for the Kingdom: Celibacy, Scripture and Tradition." *Commonweal* [NY] 117 (1990) 571–77.

Dodd, Charles H. "The Dialogue Form in the Gospels." *Bulletin of the John Rylands Library* 37 (1954–1955) 54–67.

Donaldson, Terence L. "Guiding Readers—Making Disciples: Discipleship in Matthew's Narrative Strategy." In *Patterns of Discipleship in the New Testament*, ed. Richard N. Longenecker, 30–49. Grand Rapids: Eerdmans, 1996.

Doyle, B. Rod. "Disciples as Sages and Scribes in Matthew's Gospel." *Word in Life* [North Sydney, NSW] 32 (1984) 4–9.

———. "Disciples in Matthew: A Challenge for the Church Today." *East Asian Pastoral Review* 29 (1992) 306–29.

———. "Matthew's Intention as Discerned by His Structure." *Revue Biblique* 95 (1988) 34–54.

———. "The Place of the Parable of the Labourers in the Vineyard in Matthew 20:1–16." *Australian Biblical Review* 42 (1994) 39–58.

Duling, Dennis C. "'Egalitarian' Ideology, Leadership, and Factional Conflict within the Matthean Group." *Biblical Theology Bulletin* 27 (1997) 124–37.

———. "Matthew 18:15–17: Conflict, Confrontation, and Conflict Resolution in a 'Fictive Kin' Association." *Biblical Theology Bulletin* 29 (1999) 4–22.

Edwards, Richard A. "Characterization of the Disciples as a Feature of Matthew's Narrative." In *The Four Gospels*, ed. F. Segbroeck, 2:1305–23. Leuvan: University Press, 1992.

———. *Matthew's Narrative Portrait of Disciples.* Valley Forge: Trinity Press International, 1997.

———. "Reading Matthew: The Gospel as Narrative." *Listening: Journal of Religion and Culture* 24 (1989) 251–61.

———. "Uncertain Faith: Matthew's Portrait of the Disciples." In *Discipleship in the New Testament*, ed. Fernando F. Segovia, 47–61. Philadelphia: Fortress, 1985.

Efird, James M. "Matthew 16:21–27." *Interpretation* 35 (1981) 284–89.

Elliott, John H. "Matthew 20:1–15: A Parable of Invidious Comparison and Evil Eye Accusation." *Biblical Theology Bulletin* 22 (1992) 52–65.

Ellis, Peter F. "But Some Doubted." *New Testament Studies* 14 (1968) 574–80.

Engelbrecht, J. "Are All the Commentaries on Matthew Really Necessary?" *Religion and Theologie* 2 (1995) 206–15.

Fortna, Robert T. "You Have Made Them Equal to Us! (Matthew 20:1–16)." *Journal of Theology for Southern Africa* 72 (1990) 66–72.

Fowl, Stephen E. "The Role of Authorial Intention in the Theological Interpretation of Scripture." In *Between Two Horizons: Spanning New Testament Studies and Systematic Theology*, ed. by Joel B. Green and Max Turner, 71–87. Grand Rapids: Eerdmans, 2000.

Fowler, Robert M. "Who is 'the Reader' in Reader Response Criticism?" *Semeia* 31 (1985) 5–23.

France, Richard T. *Matthew: Evangelist and Teacher*. Grand Rapids: Zondervan, 1989.

———. "Matthew's Gospel in Recent Study." *Themelios* 14 (1988) 41–46.

Frankemölle, Hubert. *Jahwebund und Kirche Christi*. Münster: Aschendorff, 1974.

Franzmann, Martin H. *Follow Me: Discipleship according to Saint Matthew*. St. Louis: Concordia, 1961.

Freyne, Sean. *The Twelve: Disciples and Apostles: A Study in the Theology of the First Three Gospels*. London: Sheed and Ward, 1968.

Garland, David. "Matthew's Understanding of the Temple Tax." In *Society of Biblical Literature Seminar Papers* 26:190–209. Atlanta: Scholars Press, 1987.

———. *Reading Matthew: A Literary and Theological Commentary on the First Gospel*. New York: Crossroad, 1993.

Ginsberg, Warren. *The Cast of Character: The Representation of Personality in Ancient and Medieval Literature*. Toronto: University of Toronto Press, 1983.

Gnilka, Joachim. *Das Matthäusevangelium*. Herders theologischer Kommentar zum Neuen Testament. Freiburg: Herder, 1986.

Goulder, Michael D. *Midrash and Lection in Matthew*. London: SPCK, 1974.

Grayston, K. "The Translation of Matthew 28:17." *Journal for the Study of the New Testament* 21 (1984) 105–09.

Grundmann, Walter. *Das Evangelium nach Matthaus*. Theologischer Handkommentar zum Neuen Testament I. Berlin: Evangelische Verlagsanstalt, 1968.

Gundry, Robert H. *Matthew: A Commentary on His Handbook for a Mixed Church under Persecution*. 2d ed. Grand Rapids: Eerdmans, 1994.

———. "On Interpreting Matthew's Editorial Comments." *Westminster Theological Journal* 47 (1985) 319–28.

———. "On True and False Disciples in Matthew 8:18–22." *New Testament Studies* 40 (1994) 433–41.

———. *The Use of the Old Testament in Matthew's Gospel with Special Reference to the Messianic Hope*. Leiden: E. J. Brill, 1967.

Hagner, Donald A. *Matthew*. 2 vols. Word Biblical Commentary. Dallas: Word Books, 1993.

Hare, Douglas. *Matthew*. Interpretation. Louisville: John Knox Press, 1993.

Harrington, Daniel J. *The Gospel of Matthew*. Sacra pagina. Collegeville, MN: Liturgical Press, 1991.

Hartin, Patrick J. "Disciples as Authorities within Matthew's Christian–Jewish Community." *Neotestamentica* 32 (1998) 389–404.

Hendriksen, William. *Exposition of the Gospel according to Matthew*. New Testament Commentary. Grand Rapids: Baker, 1973.

Hill, David. "Some Recent Trends in Matthean Studies." *Irish Biblical Studies* 1 (1979) 139–49.

———. *The Gospel of Matthew*. New Century Bible. London: Marshall, Morgan, and Scott, 1972.

Hobbs, T. Raymond. "Crossing Cultural Bridges: The Biblical World." *McMaster Journal of Theology* 1 (1990) 1–21.

Horst, P. W. van der. "Once More: The Translation of οἱ δέ in Matthew 28:17." *Journal for the Study of the New Testament* 27 (1986) 27–30.

Howell, David B. *Matthew's Inclusive Story: A Study in the Narrative Rhetoric of the First Gospel.* Journal for the Study of the New Testament: Supplement Series 42. Sheffield: JSOT Press, 1990.

Hultgren, Arland J. *The Parables of Jesus: A Commentary.* The Bible in its World. Grand Rapids: Eerdmans, 2000.

Iser, Wolfgang. *The Implied Reader.* Baltimore: The Johns Hopkins University Press, 1974.

Johnson, Luke Timothy. "On Finding the Lukan Community: A Cautious Cautionary Essay." In *Society of Biblical Literature 1979 Seminar Papers*, ed. Paul J. Achtemeier, 1:87–100. Missoula, MT: Scholars Press, 1979.

Juel, Donald H. "Making Disciples: The Mission of the Church in the Gospel according to Matthew." In *Bible and Mission*, ed. Wayne Stumme, 75–86. Minneapolis: Augsburg, 1986.

Keegan, Terence J. *Interpreting the Bible: A Popular Introduction to Biblical Hermeneutics.* New York: Paulist Press, 1985.

Keener, Craig S. *A Commentary on the Gospel of Matthew.* Grand Rapids: Eerdmans, 1999.

Kennedy, George A. *New Testament Interpretation through Rhetorical Criticism.* Chapel Hill, NC: The University of North Carolina Press, 1984.

Kingsbury, Jack D. "The Figure of Jesus in Matthew's Story: A Literary-Critical Probe." *Journal for the Study of the New Testament* 21 (1984) 3–36.

———. "The Figure of Peter in Matthew's Gospel as a Theological Problem." *Journal of Biblical Literature* 98 (1979) 67–83.

———. *Matthew as Story.* 2d ed. Philadelphia: Fortress Press, 1988.

———. *Matthew: Structure, Christology, Kingdom.* Philadelphia: Fortress Press, 1975.

———. "On Following Jesus: The 'Eager' Scribe and the 'Reluctant' Disciple (Matthew 8:18–22)." *New Testament Studies* 34 (1988) 45–59.

———. "The Plot of Matthew's Story." *Interpretation* 46 (1992) 347–56.

———. "Reflections on 'The Reader' of Matthew's Gospel." *New Testament Studies* 34 (1988) 443–60.

———. "The Rhetoric of Comprehension in the Gospel of Matthew." *New Testament Studies* 41 (1995) 358–77.

———. "The Verb *akolouthein* ("To Follow") as an Index of Matthew's View of His Community." *Journal of Biblical Literature* 97 (1978) 56–73.

Kodell, Jerome. "Celibacy Logion in Mt 19:12," *Biblical Theology Bulletin* 8 (1978) 19–23.

Kopas, Jane. "Jesus and Women in Matthew." *Theology Today* 47 (1990) 13–21.

Kupp, David D. *Matthew's Emmanuel: Divine Presence and God's People in the First Gospel.* Society for New Testament Studies Monograph Series 90, ed. Margaret E. Thrall. Cambridge: Cambridge University Press, 1996.

Kvalbein, Hans. "Go Therefore and Make Disciples: The Concept of Discipleship in the New Testament." *Themelios* 13 (1988) 48–53.

Ladd, George E. *A Theology of the New Testament.* Grand Rapids: Eerdmans, 1974.

Lincoln, Andrew. "Matthew—A Story for Teachers?" In *The Bible in Three Dimensions*, ed. D. Clines, et al., 103–25. Sheffield: JSOT Press, 1990.

Luomanen, Petri. *Entering the Kingdom of Heaven: A Study on the Structure of Matthew's View of Salvation.* Tübingen: Mohr Siebeck, 1998.

Luz, Ulrich. *Das Evangelium nach Matthäus.* Evangelisch-Katholischer Kommentar zum Neuen Testament. 3 vols. Zurich: Benziger/ Neukirchener, 1985–1997.

———. *Matthew 1–7: A Commentary.* Translated by Wilhelm C. Linss. Minneapolis: Augsburg, 1989.

———. *Matthew 8–20.* Translated by James E. Crouch. Hermeneia. Minneapolis: Fortress Press, 2001.

———. *Matthew in History: Interpretation, Influence, and Effects.* Minneapolis: Fortress Press, 1994.

———. *The Theology of the Gospel of Matthew.* New Testament Theology. Cambridge: Cambridge University Press, 1995.

Mailloux, Steven. "Learning to Read: Interpretation and Reader-Response Criticism." *Studies in Literary Imagination* 12 (1979) 93–108.

Malbon, Elizabeth Struthers. "Disciples/Crowds/Whoever: Marcan Characters and Readers." *Novum Testamentum* 28 (1986) 104–30.

Malina, Bruce J., and Jerome H. Neyrey. *Calling Jesus Names: The Social Value of Labels in Matthew.* Sonoma, CA: Polebridge Press, 1988.

Matera, Frank J. "The Plot of Matthew's Gospel." *Catholic Biblical Quarterly* 49 (1987) 233–53.

McKay, K. L. "The Use of *hoi de* in Matthew 28:17: A Response to K. Grayson." *Journal for the Study of the New Testament* 24 (1985) 71–72.

Meier, John P. *Matthew.* New Testament Message 3. Wilmington: Glazier, 1980.

———. *The Vision of Matthew, Christ, Church, and Morality in the First Gospel.* New York: Paulist Press, 1979.

Melbourne, Bertram L. *Slow to Understand: The Disciples in Synoptic Perspective.* Lanham, MD: University Press of America, 1988.

Minear, Paul S. "The Disciples and the Crowds in the Gospel of Matthew." *Anglican Theological Review Supplement* 3 (1974) 28–44.

———. *Matthew: The Teacher's Gospel.* New York: Pilgrim, 1982.

Moore, Stephen. *Literary Criticism and the Gospels: The Theoretical Challenge.* New Haven: Yale University Press, 1989.

Mounce, Robert H. *Matthew.* New International Biblical Commentary on the New Testament. Peabody, MA: Hendrickson, 1991.

Neyrey, Jerome H. *Honor and Shame in the Gospel of Matthew.* Louisville: Westminster John Knox Press, 1998.

Ogawa, Akira. "Action-Motivating Faith. The Understanding of 'Faith' in the Gospel of Matthew." *Annual of the Japanese Biblical Institute* 19 (1993) 53–86.

Orton, David E. *The Understanding Scribe: Matthew and the Apocalyptic Ideal.* Journal for the Study of the New Testament: Supplement Series 25. Sheffield: Sheffield Academic Press, 1989.

Overman, J. Andrew. *Matthew's Gospel and Formative Judaism: The Social World of the Matthean Community.* Minneapolis: Fortress, 1990.

Patte, Daniel. "Bringing Out of the Gospel-Treasure What is New and What is Old: Two Parables in Matthew 18–23." *Quarterly Review* 10 (1990) 79–108.

———. *Discipleship according to the Sermon on the Mount: Four Legitimate Readings, Four Plausible Views of Discipleship and Their Relative Values.* Valley Forge, PA: Trinity Press International, 1996.

———. *The Gospel according to Matthew: A Structural Commentary on Matthew's Faith.* Philadelphia: Fortress Press, 1987.

Pelling, C., ed. *Characterization and Individuality in Greek Literature.* Oxford: Clarendon Press, 1990.

Penner, James A. "Revelation and Discipleship in Matthew's Transfiguration Account." *Bibliotheca sacra* 152 (1995) 201–10.

Powell, Mark Allan. "Characterization on the Phraseological Plane in the Gospel of Matthew." In *Treasures New and Old: Recent Contributions to Matthean Studies.* Society of Biblical Literature Symposium Series, ed. David R. Bauer and Mark Allan Powell, 1:161–77. Atlanta: Scholars Press, 1996.

————. "Expected and Unexpected Readings of Matthew: What the Reader Knows." *Asbury Theological Journal* 48 (1993) 31–51.

————. *God With Us: A Pastoral Theology of Matthew's Gospel.* Minneapolis: Fortress Press, 1995.

————. "The Mission of Jesus and the Mission of the Church in the Gospel of Matthew." *Trinity Seminary Review* 16 (1994) 77–89.

————. "The Plot and Subplots of Matthew's Gospel." *New Testament Studies* 32 (1992) 187–204.

————. "Toward a Narrative-Critical Understanding of Matthew." *Interpretation* 46 (1992) 341–46.

————. *What is Narrative Criticism?* Guides to Biblical Scholarship. Minneapolis: Fortress, 1990.

Ramshaw, Elaine J. "Power and Forgiveness in Matthew 18." *Word and World* 18 (1998) 397–404.

Rhoads, David, and Kari Syreeni, ed. *Characterization in the Gospel: Reconceiving Narrative Criticism.* Journal for the Study of the New Testament: Supplement Series 184. Sheffield: Sheffield Academic Press, 1999.

————, and Donald Michie. *Mark as Story: An Introduction to the Narrative of a Gospel.* Philadelphia: Fortress, 1982.

————, Joanna Dewey, and Donald Michie. *Mark as Story: An Introduction to the Narrative of a Gospel.* 2d ed. Minneapolis: Fortress, 1999.

Ringe, Sharon H. "Solidarity and Contextuality Readings of Matthew 18:21–35." In *Reading from this Place*, ed. Fernando F. Segovia and Mary Ann Tolbert, 1:199–212. Minneapolis: Fortress Press, 1995.

Russell, D. A. "On Reading Plutarch's *Lives*." *Greece and Rome* 13 (1976) 139–54.

Sand, Alexander. *Das Evangelium nach Matthäus.* Regensburger Neues Testament. Regensburg: Pustet, 1986.

Scholes, Robert, and Robert Kellogg. *The Nature of Narrative.* New York: Oxford University Press, 1966.

Schottroff, Luise. "Human Solidarity and the Goodness of God: The Parable of the Workers in the Vineyard." In *God of the Lowly: Socio-Historical Interpretations of the Bible*, ed. Willy Schottroff and Wolfgang Stegemann, 129–47. Maryknoll, NY: Orbis Books, 1984.

Schweizer, Eduard. *The Good News according to Matthew.* Translated by David E. Green. Atlanta: John Knox, 1975.

————. *Lordship and Discipleship.* London: SCM, 1960.

————. *Matthäus und seine Gemeinde.* Stuttgarter Bibelstudien 71. Stuttgart: Verlag Katholisches Bibelwerk, 1974.

Scott, Bernard B. *Hear Then the Parable.* Minneapolis: Fortress Press, 1989.

————. "The King's Accounting: Matthew 18:23–34." *Journal of Biblical Literature* 104 (1985) 429–42.

Senior, Donald. *Matthew.* Abingdon New Testament Commentaries. Nashville: Abingdon Press, 1998.

————. "Matthew 18:21–35." *Interpretation* 41 (1987) 403–07.

————. *The Passion of Jesus in the Gospel of Matthew*. Wilmington, DE: Michael Glazier, 1985.

————. *What are They Saying About Matthew?* 2d ed. New York: Paulist Press, 1996.

Sheridan, Mark. "Disciples and Discipleship in Matthew and Luke." *Biblical Theology Bulletin* 3 (1973) 235–55.

Shiner, Whitney T. *Follow Me! Disciples in Markan Rhetoric*. Society of Biblical Literature Dissertation Series 145. Atlanta: Scholars Press, 1995.

Staley, Jeffrey Lloyd. *The Print's First Kiss: A Rhetorical Investigation of the Implied Reader in the Fourth Gospel*. Society of Biblical Literature Dissertation Series 82. Atlanta: Scholars Press, 1988.

Stanton, Graham. *A Gospel for a New People: Studies in Matthew*. Edinburgh: T&T Clark, 1992.

————, ed. *The Interpretation of Matthew*. 2d ed. Edinburgh: T&T Clark, 1995.

————. *Jesus of Nazareth in New Testament Preaching*. Society for New Testament Studies Monograph Series 27. Cambridge: Cambridge University Press, 1974.

————. "Matthew's Gospel: A Survey of Some Recent Commentaries." *Bible Translator* 46 (1995) 131–40.

————. "The Origin and Purpose of Matthew's Gospel: Matthean Scholarship from 1945–1980." *Aufstieg und Niedergang der römischen Welt* 2.25.3, 1891–1951. Berlin: Walter de Gruyter, 1985.

Stendahl, Krister. *The School of St. Matthew*. 2d ed. Philadelphia: Fortress, 1968.

Stock, Augustine. *The Method and Message of Matthew*. Collegeville, MN: Liturgical Press, 1994.

Strecker, Georg. *Der Weg der Gerechtigkeit*. Göttingen: Vandenhoeck & Ruprecht, 1962.

Syreeni, Kari. "Separation and Identity: Aspects of the Symbolic World of Matt 6:1–18," *New Testament Studies* 40 (1994) 522–41.

Tannehill, Robert C. "The Disciples in Mark: The Function of a Narrative Role." *Journal of Religion* 57 (1977) 386–405.

————. *The Narrative Unity of Luke-Acts: A Literary Interpretation*. Vol. 1. Philadelphia: Fortress, 1986.

Thiemann, Ronald F. "The Unnamed Woman at Bethany." *Theology Today* 44 (1987) 179–88.

Thompson, William G. *Matthew's Advice to a Divided Community: Matthew 17:22–18:35*. Rome: Biblical Institute Press, 1970.

Tolbert, Mary Ann. "How the Gospel of Mark Builds Character." *Interpretation* 47 (1993) 347–57.

Trilling, Wolfgang. *The Gospel according to St. Matthew*. New York: Herder & Herder, 1969.

————. *Das wahre Israel*. München: Kösel, 1964.

Trotter, Andrew H. "Understanding and Stumbling: A Study of the Disciples' Understanding of Jesus and His Teaching in the Gospel of Matthew." Ph.D. diss., Cambridge University, 1986.

Verseput, Donald J. "The Davidic Messiah and Matthew's Jewish Christianity." In *Society of Biblical Literature Seminar Papers*, 102–16. Atlanta: Scholars Press, 1995.

————. "The Faith of the Reader and the Narrative of Matthew 13:53–16:20." *Journal for the Study of the New Testament* 46 (1992) 3–24.

————. "Jesus' Pilgrimage to Jerusalem and Encounter in the Temple: A Geographical Motif in Matthew's Gospel." *Novum Testamentum* 36 (1994) 105–21.

————. "The Role and Meaning of the 'Son of God' Title in Matthew's Gospel." *New Testament Studies* 33 (1987) 532–56.

Vigen, Larry A. "To Think the Things of God: A Discoursive Reading of Matthew 16:13–18:35." Ph.D. diss., Vanderbilt University, 1985.

Wainwright, Elaine Mary. "The Gospel of Matthew." In *Searching the Scriptures: A Feminist Commentary*, ed. Elisabeth Schüssler Fiorenza, 2:635–77. New York: Crossroad, 1994.

———. *Shall We Look for Another? A Feminist Rereading of the Matthean Jesus.* The Bible and Liberation Series. Maryknoll, NY: Orbis Books, 1998.

———. "Tradition Makers/Tradition Shapers: Women of the Matthean Tradition." *Word and World* 18 (1998) 380–88.

———. *Towards a Feminist Critical Reading of the Gospel according to Matthew.* New York: Walter de Gruyter, 1991.

Wallace, Daniel B. *Greek Grammar Beyond the Basics: An Exegetical Syntax of the New Testament.* Grand Rapids: Zondervan, 1996.

Weaver, Dorothy Jean. *Matthew's Missionary Discourse: A Literary Critical Analysis.* Journal for the Study of the New Testament: Supplement Series 38. Sheffield: JSOT Press, 1990.

Weber, Kathleen. "Plot and Matthew." In *Society of Biblical Literature 1996 Seminar Papers*, 400–31. Atlanta: Scholars Press, 1996.

Wiedemann, Thomas. *Adults and Children in the Roman Empire.* New Haven: Yale University Press, 1989.

Wilkins, Michael James. *The Concept of Disciple in Matthew's Gospel.* Novum Testamentum Supplements 59. Leiden: E. J. Brill, 1988.

———. "Named and Unnamed Disciples in Matthew: A Literary/Theological Study." In *1991 Society of Biblical Literature Seminar Papers*, 418–39. Atlanta: Scholars Press, 1991.

Wink, Walter. *John the Baptist in the Gospel Tradition.* Cambridge: Cambridge University Press, 1968.

Wrede, William. *The Messianic Secret.* Translated by J. C. G. Greig. Cambridge: James Clarke, 1971.

Wright, N. T. *The New Testament and the People of God.* Minneapolis: Fortress, 1992.

Zumstein, Jean. *La condition du croyant dans l'Evangile selon Matthieu.* Orbis biblicus et orientalis 16. Göttingen: Vandenhoeck & Ruprecht, 1977.

INDEX OF BIBLICAL AND OTHER ANCIENT TEXTS

MODERN AUTHOR INDEX